PRIDE OF OUR PEOPLE

*The Stories of One Hundred Outstanding
Jewish Men and Women*

BY DAVID C. GROSS

PRIDE OF OUR PEOPLE

1,001 QUESTIONS AND ANSWERS ABOUT JUDAISM

A DICTIONARY OF THE JEWISH RELIGION (ED.),
with Ben Isaacson

LOVE POEMS FROM THE HEBREW (ED.)

SHALOM CALENDAR FOR YOUNG PEOPLE

Edited and Translated by David C. Gross

ONE HUNDRED CHILDREN
by Lena Kuchler-Silberman

THE HUNTER
by Tuviah Friedman

PRIDE OF OUR PEOPLE

The Stories of One Hundred Outstanding Jewish Men and Women

DAVID C. GROSS

Portraits by William D. Bramhall, Jr.

DOUBLEDAY & COMPANY, INC.
GARDEN CITY, NEW YORK
1979

Grateful acknowledgment is made for permission to reprint lines of poetry from "Ode to Zion" and "My Heart Is in the East" in *Jehuda Halevi: Selected Poems*, edited by Nina Salaman, copyrighted 1924 by and used through the courtesy of The Jewish Publication Society of America.

BOOK DESIGN BY BENTE HAMANN

LIBRARY OF CONGRESS CATALOGING IN PUBLICATION DATA

Gross, David C.   1923–
    Pride of Our People.

    Includes index.
    SUMMARY: Includes biographies and portraits
    of notable Jewish men and women,
        some famous, others unknown,
        in both ancient and modern times.
    1. Jews—Biography—Juvenile literature.
    [1. Jews—Biography]   I. Title.
    DS115.G7   920'.0092'924   [920]
            ISBN: 0-385-13573-4
Library of Congress Catalog Card Number 77–25592

First Edition

For my children, and their children

PREFACE

———————————

We live in an age with few heroic personalities—men and women whose lives are proof positive of the great heights to which a mortal person can reach. On all sides we see the overwhelming materialist philosophy that has engulfed the world, leading many people to become cynical and deeply suspicious of the eternal truths taught by all great religious movements.

The Jewish people in particular are wary of "great figures." Comparisons inevitably arise between someone who is said to be a "great personality" and those revered figures who have become part and parcel of Jewish tradition, whose lives and works have been taught and expounded on—the incomparable biblical personalities, and the handful of outstanding people who made their mark on Jewish history in postbiblical days. These were selfless, dedicated men and women, and comparisons with modern newcomers invariably lead to a feeling of dubiousness.

Today, most Jews approach the rabbis in the community with an innate sense of respect and honor, sometimes even awe, and when it turns out that a spiritual leader is after all a human being like everyone else, heads are shaken, and one hears, "Of course, I could have told you so."

And yet there are truly heroic Jewish figures in our time, and if we do not know about them, it is precisely because part of their greatness lies in the fact that they eschew personal publicity. To perform the *mitzvah*, the good deed prescribed in Jewish teaching, that is the crux of the matter. To seek out recognition and honor is to negate the good deed itself.

In almost every generation of Jewish history—stretching back to the days of Abraham and right up to our own day—there have been many thousands of exemplary Jewish men and women whose lives served to inspire young and old.

In attempting to offer a cross section of one hundred such biographical sketches, I have had to winnow down the list to a select number, whose lives and achievements would form a cohesive pattern of people who attained prominence in their respective fields of endeavor and who simultaneously remained dedicated, committed members, and often leaders, of the Jewish community.

The areas of endeavor encompassed include science and government, education and politics, art and entertainment, industry and scholarship, literature and religion, social service and medicine.

One additional category is included, one that is difficult to define. And that is the self-sacrificial heroism of men and women who gave their all to help rescue or at least bring succor to their fellow Jews who in the course of the past half century faced death and destruction at the hands of the Nazis.

The lives of great men and women often serve to help mold the still malleable minds and hearts of young people. It is my earnest hope that the exemplary lives of the one hundred men and women portrayed in this volume will help fashion the future of a new generation of Jewish young people.

D.C.G.

CONTENTS

Contents

Contents

xiii

Contents

Contents

xv

Contents

Contents

xvii

Contents

PRIDE OF OUR PEOPLE

The Stories of One Hundred Outstanding
Jewish Men and Women

JONAS SALK

The Man Who Conquered Polio

NOWADAYS NEARLY EVERY CHILD is inoculated with the Salk antipolio vaccine as a routine measure. But prior to 1955 there was no such vaccine, and tens of thousands of children and many adults were afflicted with this dread killer that crippled limbs and seemed to have no cure. The world still remembers the appearance of President Franklin D. Roosevelt, who contracted polio as an adult and spent the rest of his life in a chair, unable to walk without steel braces and the help of others.

Jonas Salk was born in New York in 1914 and, like most boys, concentrated on baseball, although he was early acknowledged to be an exceptional student. He was admitted to the City College of New York at the age of fifteen, planning to become a lawyer. To broaden his background, he also enrolled in a science course, and quickly realized that this was where his real interests lay.

He was accepted at the medical school of New York University and decided that he would devote himself to medical research, and within a matter of years he was instrumental in developing vaccines against the flu. The great scourge of polio remained a challenge to every research-minded scientist, and Dr. Salk wanted to see if he could find a preventative.

When the University of Pittsburgh asked him to set up a special virus laboratory, he accepted, and for the next eight years he devoted nearly every hour to seeking a vaccine against the dread disease. Colleagues said he worked twenty hours a day, every day of the week, as he tried one formulation after another to discover the vaccine that would work. After discovering what he felt was the suitable vaccine, he knew it still had to be tested on human beings, and used both himself and his own children for the experimental injections. The first results were encouraging, and he then proceeded to test more vaccinations with additional numbers of people. In 1955 he announced to a startled and grateful world that he had found the vaccine that would prevent polio. It was a milestone in medical annals, and a day thankful parents would always remember.

The vaccine was named for him, and has become a potent preventative against the feared disease among tens of millions of people. He received honors and awards from many governments and institutions, including the Presidential Citation and the Congressional Medal for Distinguished Achievement.

After serving for a number of years as a consultant on viruses to the United Nations World Health Organization, he established the Salk Institute for Biological Studies at La Jolla, California, of which he is the director. One of the targets of the research specialists gathered at that center is the conquest of at least some forms of cancer.

Salk has visited Israel frequently, lecturing to university and medical groups and expressing his admiration for the high quality of medical research that is being carried out there.

STEPHEN S. WISE

The Progressive, Fighting Rabbi

ONE OF THE BEST-KNOWN RABBIS IN THE UNITED STATES was Stephen S. Wise. When he spoke from the pulpit, members of the congregation had the feeling that they were listening to a modern prophet who had just stepped out of the pages of the Bible.

He was born in 1874 in Hungary, and was brought to the United States as an infant. From his early youth he decided to become a rabbi, following in his father's footsteps. He graduated from Columbia University at the age of eighteen, and a year later he was ordained, serving at first as assistant rabbi of New York's Congregation B'nai Jeshurun.

A few years later he accepted a call to become the rabbi of a congregation in Portland, Oregon, where he served for about six years before returning to New York. In Oregon he revolutionized the traditional rabbinical role by calling for interfaith activities, urging improved civic and social service programs, and in general working to make Judaism a living, contemporary part of society. To demonstrate where his interests lay, he became a volunteer commissioner of child labor in Oregon, striving to improve the terrible conditions that then existed for young boys and girls who were forced to work at an early age for long hours and meager pay.

The leaders of Temple Emanu-El on New York's Fifth Avenue invited him to come to New York to become their rabbi, for news of his dynamic leadership had traveled east and they felt that

the tall, deep-voiced rabbi would do much to invigorate the congregation. However, when Rabbi Wise made it clear that he would accept the position only on condition that he would be completely free to preach on what he wanted and to say specifically what he felt to be the truth, the offer was withdrawn.

Rabbi Wise went on to establish a new congregation, the Free Synagogue, in which he was free to preach as he saw fit. There were no formal membership dues, and instead members were asked to contribute whatever they could. For a number of years the Free Synagogue services were held in theaters and concert halls, but eventually funds were raised to establish a formal synagogue.

Rabbi Wise was one of the earliest leaders of the Zionist movement in the United States and became head of the American branch of the world movement shortly after he met Theodor Herzl at a World Zionist Congress in Basel. After the end of World War I he was one of the representatives of the world Zionist movement at the Versailles Peace Conference, pleading for a homeland for European Jews who, he explained, had to leave their homes for a new life. He was an indefatigable man and helped organize various Zionist groups in the United States as well as the American Jewish Congress, the World Jewish Congress, the Jewish Institute of Religion, and other groups. He was also a tireless writer and for many years edited a Jewish magazine, *Opinion*, that he had established. He also translated and edited Ibn Gabirol's *Improvement of the Moral Qualities*, and produced the first contemporary translation of the Book of Judges, for inclusion in the authorized Jewish translation of the Holy Scriptures.

More than anything else, however, Wise was a fighter for justice. He fought for the establishment of the National Association for the Advancement of Colored People and the American Civil Liberties Union, and participated in various efforts to improve the conditions of child laborers, the aged, and unorganized factory workers. One of his most famous battles was in behalf of the workers at the U. S. Steel Corporation who demanded the right to have a union.

He became active in political affairs, supported President Woodrow Wilson, and later became closely identified with President Franklin D. Roosevelt. He joined forces with a number of New York Christian clergymen and political leaders and forced the mayor of New York, James J. Walker, whose regime was generally acknowledged to be filled with corruption, to resign.

When the Nazi regime came to power in Germany in 1933, Rabbi Wise was one of the first to speak out openly against it and led in drives to help the early victims of Nazism. Throughout the years of World War II, as news of the massacres of European Jews continued to mount, he endeavored to influence the White House and the State Department to take extraordinary measures to rescue endangered Jewish communities. One of the deepest disappointments of his life was the realization that despite his best efforts, little was done by the United States to help save the Jews of Europe.

Although he could look back with pride on a life of great achievement—laws that virtually abolished child labor in the United States, freedom of speech for rabbis in the pulpit, a progressive attitude toward labor unions, expanding opportunities for minorities, and even the proclamation of Israel's independence in 1948—Rabbi Wise died at the age of seventy-five, deeply grieved at the realization that he had failed to persuade the U.S. government to undertake a meaningful rescue effort for his people in Europe.

SIMON WIESENTHAL

The Nazi-hunter

IN 1933 ADOLF HITLER TOOK POWER IN GERMANY and launched the Nazi era, which ended only in 1945, after the defeat of Germany and its allies in one of history's worst wars, World War II. During that period of a dozen years, which saw hundreds of thousands of soldiers from practically all European countries, the United States, and Japan killed and wounded, a horrible event took place that to this day people find difficult to understand: the deliberate extermination of six million Jews in Europe, who represented fully one third of the world's Jewish community. The disaster has come to be known as the Holocaust.

One of the pitifully small number of Jews who survived the Nazi concentration camps is a man named Simon Wiesenthal. Like so many other survivors of the Nazi era, he lost his family as well as his interest in resuming his profession as an architect after the war ended. A man of indomitable will, he established a small office in Vienna for the sole purpose of tracking down every man and woman who had been a Nazi war criminal and bringing them to justice.

There were those who said it was a hopeless task and that finding the Nazis would be impossible. Others urged him to concentrate on the future and try to rebuild his life. But Wiesenthal reasoned otherwise: He said that the Nazis had to be punished so that no such system of pure evil could ever be allowed to develop again. He said also that allowing them to live without punishment,

7

without justice taking its course, would hand them a victory over the Jews and the other people they had massacred, and that must not be allowed to happen.

In the course of thirty years, with the support of volunteers from all parts of the world who share his feelings about letting unrepentant Nazis get off scot free, he has tracked down more than three thousand Nazi criminals, of whom more than a third have been brought to trial, the vast majority of whom have been convicted and punished. One of the most notorious of these was Adolf Eichmann, who was kidnapped by Israeli agents and brought to Jerusalem where he was put on trial, with millions of people able to view the proceedings via television.

New Nazi groups have offered to pay one million marks to anyone who would assassinate Wiesenthal. His Documentation Center in Vienna and the invaluable files it contains are carefully guarded around the clock, and Wiesenthal himself always travels with an armed guard. He does not lightly dismiss any of the modern versions of Nazi organizations that have sprung up in various countries, including the United States.

His office in Vienna is now collecting samples of Nazi-type hate publications that call for assaults against Jews and other minority groups, and, wherever and whenever he can, he urges government authorities to quash these groups at once. They are based, he explains, on expressions of racial and religious hatred, on sentiments that proclaim the superiority of one group over another, and on the ambitions of evil men who are willing to exploit unrest, discontent, and disturbed people's frustrations for their own benefit.

Wiesenthal is especially sensitive about the United States, which he admires and looks up to as the model of all free nations. He remembers that although he now weighs two hundred pounds, he was a skeletal ninety pounds when American forces liberated him toward the end of the Second World War. The United States must outlaw all hate groups, he insists, because it is "the only way to protect innocent people from indoctrinated crazies."

Wiesenthal has been lecturing to college organizations and many other Jewish and non-Jewish groups, but he realizes that he is approaching seventy and he does not have much time left to press his hunt for Nazis. He has said that the "Nazis I hunt down are not the problem anymore—they want to live out the rest of

9

their lives in peace, and I hunt them down only because they committed crimes and must be punished.

"The real problem of today are the Nazis who have been indoctrinated by Nazi philosophy. We must find a method of undoing their indoctrination."

There is no doubt that so long as he is able to, Simon Wiesenthal will continue his virtually one-man battle against Nazis, both those of the past and those of today and tomorrow.

NATHAN STRAUS

Milk for All the People

MILK, THAT WONDERFUL, ALL-PURPOSE FOOD that helps infants and small children grow into healthy adults, is something taken for granted by most people—but it was not too long ago that it was spreading disease rather than encouraging health, and therein lies the story of a modest, determined Jew who had come to the United States as a small child, attained great wealth, and used almost all of it for the performance of good deeds, among them the transformation of milk into the vital food it has become for millions upon millions of people throughout the world.

Nathan Straus was born in 1848 in Germany and was brought to the United States as a small boy. After living at first in the South, he and his family moved to New York, where he soon found work in a store. Ambitious and studious, young Nathan studied bookkeeping after working hours, and eventually became the store's chief bookkeeper. In the course of time he became a partner in the great Macy's department stores, and began to build his fortune.

In the latter part of the nineteenth century, the Lower East Side area of New York City was a major center for immigrants, many of them Jews, all of them poor, many just managing to keep body and soul together, living in firetrap slums. Straus had heard about conditions in the area, but it was only after he paid a personal visit there that he realized how awful were the lives of the people who were forced to live in that neighborhood. He was a

man of great compassion for the poor and he made up his mind to try to help. When he learned that one of the greatest problems besetting the immigrants was the death of small infants, apparently because they were being fed contaminated milk, he knew that he had to do something about it.

Across the ocean, in France, the brilliant scientist Louis Pasteur had announced that he knew what it was in milk that caused small children to become ill and die, and he had devised a method of preventing this terrible scourge. What must seem perfectly simple and logical to people nowadays was scoffed at when Pasteur first proposed it—heating the milk and maintaining it at high enough temperature for a given period to kill the germs in it, then letting it cool, and packing the precious fluid in sterilized containers. Strange as it may seem, people laughed at Pasteur, including many physicians, some of whom claimed that since the French scientist was not even a medical doctor, he could not know anything of disease.

But in New York the department store owner Nathan Straus was convinced that Pasteur was right and everyone who mocked him was wrong. He took leave of his business, sailed for France, and, after studying at first hand the Pasteur method of sterilization, hurried back to the United States to introduce the new method to American milk producers.

The processors of milk were outraged by Straus, and attacked him for meddling in their business. His pleas that impure milk was killing thousands of babies were ignored. Straus thereupon established a network of health stations, where he sold pasteurized milk to the people who lived in New York's poor section at less than the cost of producing it, making up the difference from his own funds.

The "milk battle" between Straus and the milk-industry leaders continued for a number of years, but after a while it became clear to everyone that the children who were being raised on pasteurized milk were not falling sick, while those who were drinking the untreated milk continued to grow sick and die.

Gradually various government agencies became involved in the dispute, and soon one city after another, and eventually most of the world, ordered all milk to be pasteurized before it was sold to the public. Straus had won his battle, in the course of which he saved the lives of countless numbers of babies. New York was so grateful to him that in 1898 he was named president of the Board of Health.

The profound satisfaction that he had received from his work in the milk situation encouraged him to expand his nonprofit chain of stores for the poor, and now he added coal and regular food staples for the needy at prices below what they cost him.

A few years later he established the first tuberculosis-prevention center for children. When a worldwide conference dedicated to the protection of infants took place in Berlin in 1909, the President of the United States sent Straus to lead the American delegation. In the course of World War I, when news reports of the terrible suffering of hundreds of thousands of Jews in eastern Europe reached the United States, he personally donated one hundred thousand dollars for relief work—a sum comparable to at least a million dollars today.

After the end of the war, as tens of thousands of Jews began to arrive in Palestine to lay the groundwork for what is today the State of Israel, Nathan Straus became vitally interested in the pioneering work going on there. He announced his support for the Zionist goal and, after visiting Palestine, set up health stations, milk depots, and schools there. Before he died in 1931, at the age of eighty-three, he had given away more than two thirds of his vast fortune to many projects in Palestine. In his honor and memory the coastal city of Nathanya, north of Tel Aviv, bears his name.

Straus believed firmly each person had a responsibility to leave the world a better place than when he arrived on the scene. By his persuading people to use sterilized milk and by his large gifts for health and education in Palestine and the example he set for all people of means, he left a name that is always recalled with respect, admiration, and love.

ARYEH L. ELIAV

He Led Eight Hundred Young Women to Safety

A GREAT POET ONCE WROTE, "The child is father of the man." Our interest early in life often influences our later actions. One of the best examples of this is Aryeh Lyova Eliav, for many years a member of the Knesset (parliament) in Israel, who has been known for a number of years as a "dove" in Israeli politics—one of those ready to give back all of the territories captured by Israel in the Six Day War of 1967 in exchange for a promise of peace from the Arab nations.

Eliav—his middle name, by which most people actually call him, is a Russian word meaning lion cub—was born in Moscow in 1921 and came to Palestine while still an infant. Like every able-bodied member of the Jewish community in pre-Israel Palestine, he joined the underground Haganah defense organization while still in his teens, and later, during World War II, he served with the British Eighth Army, both in the Middle East and in Europe. He holds a reserve position as a high-ranking officer in the Israel defense establishment.

Despite the many years he spent in the armed services, Eliav has always been drawn away from violence and toward positive pacific deeds. His entire lifetime has been one of constructive action; he relied on his deeds rather than on words.

Long before the worldwide movement began to help press for the emigration of Jews who wished to leave the Soviet Union and rejoin their coreligionists in Israel and elsewhere, he made a secret, countrywide tour of Russia to see for himself the situation of the Jews there. He wished to assess their interest in Judaism and in the

15

Jewish people more than a half century after the rise of the Soviet government, which discouraged any religious life and which persisted in stamping out any Jewish religious or cultural vestiges. He wished to see for himself if the *pintele Yid*—that tiny spark of Jewish identity—still burned, no matter how weakly, in the soul of Soviet Jewry.

What he saw led him to believe that there were huge masses of Russian Jews who still yearned for identification with the rest of the Jewish people. He wrote a book, under the pseudonym "Ben Ami," or "Son of My People," titled *Between Hammer and Sickle*, portraying graphically the strong feelings of Russian Jewry for an opportunity to be reunited with the Jewish people outside the U.S.S.R.

Eliav's book appeared in English, Hebrew, Spanish, and a number of other languages, and helped lay the groundwork for what has become a continuing movement of Soviet Jewish emigration—which in less than a decade saw some 150,000 Russian Jews receive permission to leave the Soviet Union and begin a new existence, as Jews unafraid to lead Jewish lives. The vast majority of them have been resettled in Israel.

In 1948, soon after Israel proclaimed its independence, Eliav, who had had some experience as a sea captain, was named a high officer in the fledgling Israeli navy. During the Sinai War of 1956, while the bulk of Israeli armed forces struck out across the Sinai wilderness toward Egypt, determined to crush the bases from which terrorists had been carrying out incursions into Israel, Eliav led a secret rescue operation: He commanded a small vessel that slipped into Port Said, in Egypt, took on several hundred Egyptian Jews, and brought them back safely to Israel.

A few years later Israel was looking for someone who had the determination and skill to supervise the establishment of a strategic region where tens of thousands of new immigrants were slated to be settled, and where there was no shortage of anticipated problems—economic, social, educational, security. Eliav took on the assignment and succeeded admirably in laying the groundwork for what is now the prosperous Lachish region. Jews from a wide variety of backgrounds, from many parts of the world, have established themselves in the area, working productively in agriculture and industry and living peacefully side by side.

But perhaps his most remarkable exploit is the least known

one—the rescue of a shipload of eight hundred young Jewish women from post-Nazi Europe and their safe delivery to the shores of pre-Israel Palestine.

We have to go back a little in recent history: Toward the end of World War II, early in 1945, several hundred young Jewish women who had been interned in Nazi concentration camps were permitted by the German authorities to leave for neutral Sweden, in the hope by some top Nazi officials, notably Heinrich Himmler, that this humane action would help offset the record of war crimes they had committed.

The small Jewish community in Sweden, the Swedish Red Cross, and the American Jewish Joint Distribution Committee took these survivors of Hitler barbarism under their wing and made every effort to help them rebuild their shattered lives. Most of the girls knew that their families had been destroyed by the Nazis.

When the war in Europe ended in April 1945, the Jews of the world thought that the doors of Palestine, then a British Mandate, would be flung open and the survivors of Nazism would finally be allowed to enter the Promised Land. But this was not to be: The British, despite the Holocaust in which six million Jews perished in Europe, and in the face of appeals from practically every decent world leader, including President Truman, clamped a freeze on any further Jewish immigration to Palestine.

The Jews were stunned and outraged, but they did not bide their time. Between mid-1945 and the establishment of Israel in May 1948 there developed a makeshift, clandestine Jewish passenger service: Old, unseaworthy, battered ships of every description and from many parts of the world were purchased, refitted, and transformed into vessels that would ferry Jewish survivors from European ports to the shores of Palestine under the noses of the British warships that sought to stop them.

Eliav became heavily involved in this operation and carried out a number of such rescue sailings, at first as a Haganah officer attached to a particular vessel and later as captain of a rescue ship. One of these voyages took place on the S.S. *Ulua*, a small old American vessel that had been used to transport bananas from Central America to New Orleans.

With Eliav in charge, the *Ulua* was ordered to proceed to Sweden to take on the eight hundred young Jewish women, rang-ing in age from sixteen to thirty who had expressed a desire to go to Palestine notwithstanding the British ban on immigration. Some of the women were ardent Socialists, and others had remained ultra-Orthodox in their beliefs. They were united by a desire to begin life anew in the Holy Land.

The story of that voyage is one of the extraordinary sagas of our time. Government officials in Sweden, Denmark, France, Italy, and North Africa had to be persuaded to allow the ship through their areas. In some cases deception was used rather than waste time on efforts to persuade local officials. The ship sailed through the North Sea, into the English Channel, down the coast of France, and then entered the Mediterranean, her goal the shores of Palestine at the eastern end.

In the turbulent, treacherous waters of the Bay of Biscay a catastrophic storm broke out that threatened to sink all hands on board, passengers and crew alike. Always looming in the background were British vessels, shadowing the *Ulua*'s journey, ready to strike when she reached the territorial waters of Palestine.

When the *Ulua* stopped in Italy to take on supplies, another Haganah officer approached Eliav and pleaded with him to take on several hundred additional survivors—men and boys who were waiting for a vessel that would take them to Palestine. The *Ulua* was already dangerously overcrowded, but the eight hundred women insisted that the new passengers be brought on board and join in the journey to Palestine. To help make room for the newcomers, the young women threw their meager belongings overboard, and welcomed their fellow survivors onto their vessel of hope.

Not far from the Palestinian coastline the British vessels struck, seizing the ship and detaining all the passengers and crew members. The Jews were shipped to detention camps on the island of Cyprus, from where they later were all brought, undaunted, to Israel.

One of the eight hundred women later accepted Eliav's proposal of marriage. They are today the parents of three children, all born in Israel.

Although many Israelis do not agree with Eliav's political views today, there is no one in the country who does not regard him as a selfless, dedicated man, intent on aiding his fellow human beings.

SOLOMON SCHECHTER

Treasures in a Cairo Synagogue

MOST PEOPLE THINK OF RABBIS as people who lead synagogue services, or who deliver sermons or perform weddings or deliver speeches at various gatherings. Rabbis do all these things, true, but they do a great many other things as well. One of the great rabbinical personalities of recent years was a discoverer, and his discovery has enriched Jewish knowledge and scholarship and continues to do so.

Solomon Schechter was born in 1847 in Rumania, the son of a *shohet*, a ritual slaughterer. He was an outstanding student, and, after studying in his home community and then in Berlin, he proceeded to London, where his great reputation as a scholar had preceded him. He became a member of the faculty of Cambridge University, where he taught rabbinics and Talmud, and also taught Hebrew at University College in London.

One day two English ladies who had just returned from a trip to Egypt came to the eminent scholar. They told him they had bought a souvenir in a small Cairo shop and wondered if Professor Schechter could tell them what it said. Whereupon one of the women withdrew from her purse an ancient-looking sheet of paper with indecipherable Hebrew markings. Schechter examined the paper, and his heart leaped. He was certain this was a fragment of a very old, very precious Hebrew text that could help shed light on a number of shadowy chapters in Jewish history. He soon decided that he would have to trace the origin of this small sample and see if he could find anything else of value.

That summer, with his children safely sent off to summer camp, he and his wife sailed for Cairo. Schechter called on the leading rabbi, identified himself, and explained what he was looking for. The rabbi smiled. He explained that, unlike other Jewish communities, the Cairo community did not like to bury worn-out documents and books but instead stored them in a *genizah*, a secret hiding place, usually found in a synagogue. He suggested that Schechter go to a particular synagogue and tell the *shamash*, the sexton, that he had been given permission to take away from the genizah any and all old papers and books that were stored there.

The shamash led Schechter up a rickety flight of stairs which led to a dark, dusty room where no one had set foot for as long as could be remembered. Schechter lit a lantern in the tiny enclosure, held it aloft, and could not believe his eyes. He had discovered a great treasure of Jewish scholarship! The dry air of Egypt had helped to keep most of the papers in excellent condition. There were stacks of ancient books centuries old, parchment rolls, loose sheets containing texts, commentaries, histories. When Schechter brought the materials from the Cairo genizah back to England, he created a sensation. This was one of the greatest scholarly discoveries, and it helped make him famous worldwide. Although other scholars had known of the treasure in the genizah, Schechter made the contents available to the world.

One of the results of his new reputation turned out to be an invitation to come to New York to head up the new Jewish Theological Seminary, which had been established to train rabbis and educators in the newly emerging Conservative movement. From 1902 until his death in 1915 he headed the seminary, bringing to it distinguished scholars and teachers and infusing the Conservative wing of Judaism with a new, dynamic approach. For many years the institution was unofficially called "Schechter's Seminary."

Schechter strengthened and broadened the newly developing Conservative movement, and the new network of Jewish day schools sponsored by the movement are now called Solomon Schechter Schools in his memory. He explained his interpretation of Conservative Judaism as follows:

"It is not the revealed Bible that is of first importance to the Jew, but the Bible as it repeats itself in history, as it is interpreted by tradition. . . . the interpretation of Scripture is a product of changing historical influences. . . . the center of authority is actually removed from the Bible and placed in some living body, which, by reason of its being in touch with the ideal aspirations and the religious needs of the age, is best able to determine the nature of the Secondary Meaning. . . . this living body is the collective conscience of [all the people of] Israel."

Two years before his death, Schechter launched the nationwide organization of Conservative Jews known as the United Synagogue of America. The Conservative movement, which stresses its aim of conserving the best of traditional Judaism while adapting to the changing needs of modern society, is the largest wing of the American Jewish religious community, encompassing nearly nine hundred synagogues with a membership of more than a quarter of a million families.

Schechter said his movement sought to "teach the truth of Torah, the need to keep the Sabbath, and the rules about kosher food. We can be Zionists, we must teach our children Hebrew, and make Hebrew the language of Jewish prayer in America," he said.

Schechter was an imposing-looking man who sported a full beard that turned from red to snow white over the years. When he died, he left behind him not only the rich treasure that he had unearthed at the Cairo genizah but also the foundations for a vibrant, new Jewish religious life in the New World.

YITZHAK BEN-ZVI

President of All the People

WHEN YITZHAK BEN-ZVI DIED in 1963, he had lived a full life, beginning with his early youth in Russia, when he was in charge of a secret arms depot for use against Russian pogromists during the days of the czarist regime, and ending with his having served for two terms as President of Israel.

He was a tall, gentle, assured person who could, when necessary, be tough. Deep down, he was a scholar who enjoyed uncovering knowledge about the Jewish people that had remained hidden and presenting this data to the world as an additional brick of what he considered to be the structure of Israel. He always managed to convey an impression of dignity, dedication, and cheerfulness, and cared little for personal glory or honor.

Yitzhak Ben-Zvi was born in 1884 in the Ukraine, in southern Russia, and at an early age became identified with the labor Zionist movement. As a teen-ager he was arrested with members of his family after the czarist Russian police found caches of arms in their home—guns and ammunition that had been stored there in the event of still another outbreak of violence against the local Jewish community.

Ben-Zvi managed to escape from prison, and the next year, at the age of twenty-three, he arrived in Palestine, then a desolate part of the old Turkish empire, determined to participate with other young, idealistic Jews in the establishment of a new Jewish society that would lead to the re-establishment of the ancient Jewish homeland.

Two years later he organized one of the first Jewish self-defense organizations in the country, Hashomer, and led it, and also became an editor of a new labor Zionist magazine. But when the Turks joined forces with the Germans in World War I, Ben-Zvi and a number of other young leaders of the small Jewish community were arrested and later deported.

A lifelong friend, David Ben-Gurion, and Ben-Zvi together made their way to the United States, where they organized a branch of the labor Zionist movement and also urged the creation of a separate Jewish military force that would fight alongside the Allies and help free Palestine from the Turks. When the Jewish Legion was established, both Ben-Zvi and Ben-Gurion were among the first recruits to be sent to the Middle East, where they fought as a unit of the British army. After the war ended, they returned to Palestine and secretly organized the Haganah, the self-defense Jewish organization that was the forerunner of the modern Israeli army.

For the next quarter of a century, Ben-Zvi was a major part of the leadership of the small but growing Jewish community of Palestine. He accepted whatever assignments the other leaders of the movement felt he could do best, and carried out every task with great skill and devotion. Throughout this period he wrote hundreds of articles for newspapers and magazines, preaching the message of the labor Zionist cause, and taking a scholar's interest in a subject that had fascinated him from the time he was a young man—the fate and history of tiny, isolated, and practically forgotten Jewish communities cut off from the mainstream of the Jewish people for many centuries.

Ben-Zvi investigated and found that there were Jewish communities, some of them unbelievably primitive, living as cave-dwellers in the remote Atlas Mountains of northern Africa; in an almost completely inaccessible sector of the Arabian Peninsula there was a tribe of Habani Jews, tall, fierce, horse-riding, desert people; in Ethiopia there was a group of Falasha Jews, dark of skin, who practiced what could almost be described as an ancient biblical form of Judaism. And there were still more, some communities that were relatively large in number—such as the Jews of Yemen, Iraq, Afghanistan, and Iran, as well as groups of Jews who lived in far-off corners of the Soviet Union—all of whom held their own individual forms of worship, dress, and customs and all of whom felt themselves to be part and parcel of the Jewish people.

Soon after the establishment of Israel in 1948, Ben-Zvi organized a special institute for the study of these Jewish communities and sects, including the Samaritans and Karaites, who were not usually accepted by most authorities as full-fledged Jews. Ben-Zvi's original research was helpful in bringing about a broader understanding of these Jews' background, and his sympathetic attitude toward them helped to bring them in many cases back to Israel and to a full-scale observance of Jewish traditions and laws as they are generally known in the twentieth century.

After the death of Israel's first President, Chaim Weizmann, in 1952, Yitzhak Ben-Zvi was elected President. He served two five-year terms and was in his third term of office when he died at the age of seventy-nine. The Institute for the Study of Oriental Jewish Communities in the Middle East, which he launched in 1948, was renamed for him, and today this unique scholarly center carries on serious study of fascinating, little-known groups of Jews.

Ben-Zvi had a lifelong love affair with the Jewish people, and in pursuing scientific data about isolated Jewish tribes and sects, he was carrying on an old tradition of Jewish historians who continued to try to learn the truth about the ancient lost Ten Tribes of Israel.

ISAAC BASHEVIS SINGER

Storyteller to the World

HIS NOVELS AND STORIES have been translated into many languages, and even though Isaac Bashevis Singer writes in Yiddish and concentrates on the life of the Jewish *shtetl* that no longer exists, he has succeeded in creating a vast audience of readers eager for every word he puts to paper. In 1978 he received the Nobel Prize in literature, for which he had been nominated by the famed critic Edmund Wilson; and Rebecca West, herself one of the leading authors of the day, has said that he is the greatest living contemporary writer.

Sophisticated readers of *The New Yorker* magazine, lovers of literature in Japan, Germany, Israel, Brazil, and many other countries, Jews and non-Jews alike have found that reading a Singer story or novel is an experience unlike any other. With great skill, almost magically, he succeeds in a few swift strokes of his pen in portraying the character and personality of a man, a woman, a child, in circumstances that are often quite foreign to most of his readers, and manages to keep his readers' interest at almost fever pitch. Many critics have explained his worldwide following as his uncanny ability to tell a story about an individual in terms that are immediately universal. A small, frail man in his seventies with a rosy complexion and an almost entirely bald head, he is a gentle, highly sensitive, and skeptical chronicler of an era and a society that no longer exist but that still contain a vibrant message for modern readers.

Singer was born in a small town near Warsaw, Poland, the son and grandson of rabbis, and for a while was himself a rabbinical student. He worked in his youth as a newspaper translator, proofreader, and reporter, all the time reading, observing, listening to people, and preparing himself for a career as a storyteller.

To Singer, literature must be first and foremost a good story, and although he insists that he has no great social or political messages to convey through his work, readers have written him to say that he has helped them to see life anew after they had become deeply discouraged. His narratives blend a sometimes pessimistic view of life with a lyrical belief that "that's the way life is—and you might as well get used to it."

Singer left Poland in the mid-1930s and came to the United States, explaining that he could see the threat of war and destruction years before the Nazis launched World War II. For many years he labored at his Yiddish writing to earn a modest living, supported by his second wife, who held down a sales job in a New York store. (Singer's first wife, an avowed Communist, took their son to Russia, and eventually settled in Israel. At least once a year Singer travels to Israel to visit his son and grandchildren, who live on a kibbutz.)

Singer has always had profound interest in the supernatural, and he believes that in decades to come science will unearth concrete information about extrasensory perception and what is today called the occult, making these areas respectable subjects for serious study. He considers himself a religious man; although he is not observant of Jewish ritual, he says, "Whenever I am in trouble, I pray. And since I'm always in trouble, I pray a lot."

Over the years his work has been translated into English, and as his knowledge of his adopted language has expanded, he has worked more closely than ever with his translators to ensure just the right word and phrase. He has also become a popular lecturer and frankly enjoys the lecture circuit, since it gives him an opportunity to meet people, and this, he says, is his greatest hobby and nourishment—getting to know people, imagining what they are really like, and sooner or later incorporating this information into his writing. About half of the material in his stories, he admits, is more or less autobiographical.

Singer says that, when he writes a story, he does so to satisfy himself and does not think of his readers—explaining that his first readers in Yiddish are older, East European Jews who read the *Jewish Daily Forward*, a Yiddish newspaper, while subsequent readers in translation could be American college professors or Japanese housewives. "A book," he maintains, "is not [the author's] private property. Everybody can find in it what he finds; [it] has an independent kind of life."

The author lives on New York's teeming West Side, and despite the absence of many fellow Yiddish writers in the area, he finds the ambience of the city a constant challenge and source of wonder. He has become deeply attached to America, where he has lived for more than forty years. "My Jewishness is of great importance to me, but I really feel that I am a longtime American and this is my country. I belong to those writers who are grateful to their adopted country."

He maintains an intense interest in Israel and is hopeful for that country's future. "The hatred of Israel is a neurosis," he says. "Things may look bad [for Israel], but in our history things look bad all the time, and we have outlived scores of nations. We Jews have been living in an eternal, permanent crisis."

In recent years Singer has become a vegetarian and only regrets that he did not give up eating meat and fish at an earlier date. He explains that the idea of killing another creature in order to eat it is diametrically opposite to the inner, humane spirit that rests in each person.

Singer loves to spend his mornings in bed, writing for hours in a notebook, and in the afternoons he edits some of his earlier work or transcribes on a battered Yiddish typewriter. Watching him set down word after word on paper, his blue eyes shining with genuine pleasure as he does so, one remembers that he often writes about a *dybbuk*, a foreign spirit that has entered a person's body, for he too seems at the moment possessed and obsessed by a power stronger than himself.

GOLDA MEIR

The Lady Prime Minister

CONSIDERED ONE OF THE OUTSTANDING JEWISH WOMEN of the century and admired by Jews and non-Jews alike for her sincerity, forthrightness, and courage, Golda Meir became a legend in her own lifetime.

She was best known as one of the few women in the world who have directed the destiny of a sovereign country, in her case, as Prime Minister of Israel. In Israel and among Jews in all parts of the world she was known affectionately simply by her first name—she has had such a strong impact on her people that there is really only one Golda in the twentieth century.

She was born Golda Mabovich in Kiev, Russia, in 1898, the daughter of a carpenter. The Jewish communities of czarist Russia were still being subjected to pogroms. Golda Meir has often recalled the impression made on her, when she saw her father boarding up the modest house they occupied in order to keep out bands of hooligans who preyed on defenseless Jewish families.

At the age of eight she came to Milwaukee with her family, where she grew up and graduated from a local teachers' training school. As a teen-ager, hearing of the anti-Jewish massacres that accompanied the Bolshevik Revolution in 1917, she made up her mind that the answer to the "Jewish problem" was Zionism, especially the Socialist version that she felt would guarantee a decent life for all classes of people.

Life in Milwaukee was incomparably better than what the family had known in Russia. Golda's father was employed in the city's railroad yard, and her mother augmented the family income by operating a dairy store. Through her formative years Golda helped her mother and also found time to develop friendships with some of the neighborhood girls, with whom she was to maintain lifetime ties.

She always excelled in her studies, although years later she admitted that helping her mother run the family store put an extra burden on her which she resented since it often made her late for class. Her older sister, a confirmed Socialist, refused to help out on principle; she wanted to have nothing to do with a capitalist enterprise.

Her early interest in her fellow men and women was evident even she was still a young student. When she learned that some of the poorer students could not afford to buy the required textbooks, she organized a fund-raising event, inviting the wealthier students and their parents, as well as other people in the neighborhood—and solicited those present for funds to aid the needy students. People opened their pocketbooks and contributed, an event that made Golda's parents beam with pride. At the time, she was all of twelve.

A family crisis ensued when Golda, at the age of fourteen, refused to terminate her studies, as her parents expected her to do. She was determined to get much more education, a demand that her parents could not understand, having come from a society where most girls received even less education than Golda had already obtained. Determined to have her way, Golda fled home and went to live with her sister's family in Denver for a year and a half, until her parents finally relented and agreed to let her go on with her education.

She continued her schooling in Milwaukee, including attending an afternoon Jewish school which was supposed to teach Hebrew but where she wound up learning more Yiddish than the biblical language. Life in the Mabovich household was always exciting, since Golda's mother kept an "open sofa" in the living room for itinerant visitors; these were likely to be visiting lecturers who disdained the Milwaukee hotels, or early Socialist preachers, or distant relatives on their way to new homes in various parts of the United States.

During World War I Golda helped her father, who was involved in an organization seeking to provide aid to Jews in Europe who were caught in the war zones. Around this time, she began to deliver public lectures, often in Yiddish, usually at literary gatherings.

Soon after the war ended in 1918, Golda made up her mind that as a Zionist she belonged in Palestine, helping to fashion a new homeland. "I loved America," she has said, "but I couldn't understand how one could be a Zionist without going to Palestine."

At the age of nineteen she married Morris Myerson, a fellow Socialist, but only on condition that he would agree to go with her to Palestine. Myerson was not a Zionist, but he agreed to her condition. In May 1921 Golda, her husband, and her sister Sheine and two children sailed for Palestine on a barely seaworthy vessel that took fifty-four days to cross the seas. The group arrived in Jaffa in July, by train from Alexandria, Egypt, because Arabs were then rioting in Palestine and refused to allow Jewish passengers arriving by sea to disembark.

The first years in Palestine were incredibly hard for the small party of newcomers, although Golda has written that life on the kibbutz for her at least was one of the finest periods in her life. In the course of time, she became known in the fledgling labor movement in Palestine as a potentially effective woman leader and was persuaded to give up the kibbutz life and devote her energies to the Histadrut, the small but growing national labor confederation.

The confidence that the early Zionist leaders had in her was soon justified, and by 1928 she had become head of the Working Women's Council, and six years later, after a two-year stint raising funds in the United States, she was invited to become a member of the executive of the Histadrut. She began to play an increasingly important role in the political activities of the Histadrut right through the 1940s. In 1946, when the British Mandatory authorities arrested practically all the leaders of the Jewish community in Palestine, she became the acting head of the Jewish Agency's political department, in effect the community's official representative to the British.

35

There have been many dramatic moments in Golda's life and two that stand out are the fund-raising trip she made to the United States early in 1948, four months before the proclamation of Israeli statehood, and a trip she made in disguise to the king of Jordan four days before Israel's independence was announced.

On her trip to the United States, Golda visited a number of Jewish communities, telling them that the Holocaust in which six million Jews had perished would have been in vain if Israel were not established to make a haven for the survivors and for any other Jews who would require a refuge in the future. By her eloquence and candor she helped raise tens of millions of dollars that were desperately needed at the time, since the thousands of Jewish refugees were streaming into Palestine despite the official ban on immigration imposed by the British Mandatory authorities.

Her trip to Amman to see King Abdullah and plead with him to stay out of any war that might follow on the heels of an Israeli announcement of independence was filled with great personal risk. She managed to talk with the king, who in effect told her that he would like to abide by her wishes and stay out of any fighting that might take place, but it was a matter of "honor" or "fate" and he could not do so. Nevertheless, he saw to it that she returned safely to the Israeli side of the border.

She was named the Israeli ambassador to Moscow in 1948, and her arrival in the Soviet capital is credited with the early demonstrations by Russian Jews demanding to be allowed to join their coreligionists abroad. Later she served as Minister of Labor and as Foreign Minister, and in the latter role she became known for her tough, yet sincere addresses at the United Nations, where she offered to establish peaceful relations with any Arab nation willing to sit down with Israel and negotiate a treaty.

As Foreign Minister, she toured many African countries and helped to forge strong bonds of friendship with several developing nations. Photographs of her teaching black women in remote villages how to dance the Israeli *hora* were printed in newspapers around the world. In 1969, following the death of Levi Eshkol, Golda Meir became the fourth Prime Minister of Israel, a post she held until 1974.

One of the most painful moments for her was the decision she reached to step down as Prime Minister in the aftermath of the

Yom Kippur War of 1973. Although the war began with an attack by Egypt and Syria, many Israeli leaders blamed themselves for having been unprepared for such an event. The high loss of life in that war and the subsequent drop in morale among most Israelis led her to decide to resign, although she personally has never been accused of having made any wrong decisions with regard to the outbreak or conduct of the war.

She has been regarded in Israel as an elder stateswoman to whom young and aspiring politicians came with their problems. A Broadway play featuring the noted actress Anne Bancroft opened in New York in 1977, depicting her remarkable life story. Aptly, it was titled simply *Golda*.

Toward the end of 1978, at the age of eighty, she died in a Jerusalem hospital. Leading world figures voiced their admiration for her lifetime of achievement. Perhaps one of the most poignant messages of condolence came from the President of Egypt, Anwar Sadat, who said, "I received with sorrow the news of Mrs. Meir's death. I must, for the sake of history, praise her as an honest foe during the situation of confrontation between us, which we all hope is over forever."

FRANCIS SALVADOR

For the Sake of Liberty

HE WAS THE FIRST JEW TO DIE in the cause of American liberty. Some people called him the "Jewish Paul Revere." There is no doubt that the devotion that he showed to the United States has shone as an example to be emulated by thousands of his fellow Jews who came to the shores of America in succeeding generations.

Francis Salvador was born in England, the son of a wealthy family. A few generations earlier his family had fled from the Inquisition in Spain and Portugal, posing for a while as Christians and then later, when they found haven in Holland and later in England, re-emerging as Jews.

Francis's uncle, Joseph Salvador, was a highly respected member of the community, having served as president of a synagogue in London and at one time having been asked for a loan by the royal family. Like many wealthy Englishmen at the time, he had purchased large tracts of land in the colony of South Carolina.

The family fortune was invested heavily in the Dutch East India Company and in a number of enterprises in Portugal. Quite suddenly the fortune was wiped out—the Dutch company failed, and a series of devastating earthquakes destroyed the Salvador investments in Portugal.

Francis decided to go to America to see if he could rebuild the family's wealth on the strength of the South Carolina holdings. When he arrived in South Carolina, he underwent a marked change. He had been brought up to respect wealth and position, but here in the American colonies there was talk of a new system of government in which all men would be free and equal. The colonists found that they had a new supporter in Salvador, not withstanding his wealthy, aristocratic background.

He became an active leader of the colonists in South Carolina, and watched his lands prospering at the same time. Friends suggested that he become a delegate to the provincial congress that was scheduled to assemble in Charleston, but he declined—until he heard that some people objected to him because he was Jewish. That made him change his mind.

At a large meeting before the election to the congress was scheduled to be held, Francis Salvador rose and declared to the colonists: "My fellow Americans: I have cast my lot with the Revolution. It was my intention to do my modest share without holding any public office, but I heard there were objections to my religion. The soil of America shall not know the poisonous weed of religious intolerance! My people left Portugal because of religious hatreds and persecutions. Here we are building a world where men shall be free to worship in accordance with their conscience.

"Is there one here who has known me to cheat? Have I been false to the ideals of the Revolution? If I have not done these things, I feel I deserve the votes of my neighbors. I crave the opportunity to serve the Revolution. My Jewish antecedence will spur me to fulfill my duty more fully. On that I give you my word. May God prosper our cause."

He was elected by a large majority and helped transform the South Carolina colony into one of the original thirteen states of the Union.

When war broke out between England and the colonists, Salvador tried to win over the Cherokee Indians to the cause of the Americans. Although he made many friends among the Indians, Salvador failed to convince them that the young American nation could withstand the armed might of the British Empire. The Indians chose to take up arms on the side of the British, convinced that they would crush the rebels.

On July 1, 1776, soon after the British fleet reached the harbor of Charleston, the Indians struck the unarmed and unprepared

Americans. Many settlers hurried to Salvador's house for shelter, hoping that the American militia would come to their rescue. But there was only one way in which the American troops could be notified—someone had to mount a horse and reach their camp, some thirty miles away.

Under the cover of night Salvador sneaked out of his home, and when he was certain that the Cherokees were out of earshot, spurred his horse on, to get help. The soldiers whom Salvador summoned rode back the next day and succeeded in driving off the Indian attackers, saving the community from probable destruction by the Cherokees.

One of those mortally wounded in the battle was Salvador himself. He was still alive when an army officer rushed to his side to see if he could help. Weakened by the loss of blood, Salvador only wanted to know how the battle was going, and when told that the Indians were fleeing, he smiled happily and died.

Through a series of circumstances that he could not have foreseen when he had been a young Englishman, Francis Salvador left his name in the annals of American and of Jewish history as one of the earliest patriots of the United States.

SAADYAH GAON

The Inspired Scholar

ABOUT ONE THOUSAND YEARS AGO Jews were scattered in various parts of the then known world. There were organized, active Jewish communities in Egypt, Palestine, Babylonia, Spain, and other areas centered around the Mediterranean Sea. The forced exile of the Jews from their homeland, which began in the year 70 when the Romans destroyed the Holy Temple in Jerusalem, continued to create great inner problems for the Jewish community. A new religion, Islam, had risen and had become very popular, and since many Jews lived in Arabic-speaking countries where the new faith flourished, there was great danger that many Jews would abandon Judaism and turn to Islam.

The sect of Karaites—Jews who insisted that they would obey only the laws of the Torah and totally rejected the commentaries and explanations enumerated in the Talmud—threatened to divide the community and to fragment it. What was needed, Jewish scholars felt, was a great Jewish leader who by force of his learning and qualities of leadership would help to reunite the Jews, and inspire them to remain true to their ancient faith as it had evolved through changing times. The philosophical works of the Greek thinkers had also begun to influence young Jews, and many began to question the basic principles of Judaism.

In Babylonia a large and well-organized Jewish community had flourished for many years, and it prided itself on two outstanding centers of Jewish learning, the schools at Sura and Pumbedita. The former school, which was more than seven hundred years old, had fallen on hard times, largely because of the lack of a suitable leader who set high standards of learning. Customarily, a member of a distinguished family of Jewish scholars would be named to the post of head of the school, but no one could be found in Babylonia and so the leaders of the ancient Jewish community selected a young scholar, Saadyah, born and raised in Egypt, and invited him to take up the prestigious position.

Saadyah did not come from a family of scholars, but he had already achieved a name for himself as a man of great wisdom who was completely devoted to the teaching of the Torah and Talmud, and who was at the same time a vigorous man unafraid to express his own ideas on controversial issues, even if they did not meet with the wishes of the leaders of the community.

Although the word *gaon* in modern Hebrew usually means "genius," it was reserved in those days as a title for the leader of a major school such as that of Sura. When he arrived to become the head of the school in Sura, Saadyah became Saadyah Gaon, and he set about his task of reviving the school to its past glory.

In a short space of time Sura once again became a major seat of learning, and Saadyah sought to teach the Jews of the time, in Babylonia and in other parts of the world, that the ancient faith of the Jewish people could not be equated with the new religious movements nor with the new philosophies that had begun to influence the younger generations. One of his chief targets was the Karaite sect, whose activities threatened to divide the Jewish people. He would address his students in Sura as follows:

"The Karaites claim that the laws of the Talmud have made observance of the Sabbath difficult to maintain. I say that it is the Karaites' narrow interpretation that has made the day of delight a day of darkness. The Torah teaches, for example, that we may not kindle a fire on the Sabbath, and so the Karaites sit in their homes on this day without warmth or light, and consume cold meals. But the rabbis of the Talmud understood the true meaning of the Torah laws, and said it was permissible to leave a fire burning through the day, so that the holy Sabbath can be a day of joy and rest.

"The same is true of the prohibition of making a journey on

the Sabbath—our Talmudic commentators explained that it is permissible to attend services, or to take a walk, or to pay a visit. The rabbis did not lay down new laws, but merely interpreted the Torah laws in keeping with the conditions of life as Jews knew them, and tried to show Jews how to live in full observance of the laws and traditions of our people."

Saadyah's campaign against a narrow, literal interpretation of the Torah laws helped to prevent a schism within the community. He turned the traditional retreats of the Babylonian Jews—the *kallahs*—into periods when thousands of men would gather to devote all their time to study, into vital, yearly gatherings when answers to religious questions would be offered and a renewed faith in Judaism would be assured.

Saadyah knew that there were at the time hundreds of thousands of Jews living in Arabic-speaking countries who had little knowledge of Hebrew, so he translated the entire Torah, with commentaries, into Arabic, a monumental achievement. He also organized a *siddur*, a formal prayer book, which included the traditional *Shma Yisrael* and *Amidah* prayers, to which he added special sections for the Sabbath and for specific holidays. A number of his own poetic prayers were also inserted into the service.

One of the most important works he wrote was called *The Book of Beliefs and Doctrines*, in which he tried to show that thinking people who sought to understand the Torah could do so on the basis of their own rational philosophy. He became in effect the first Jewish thinker of the Middle Ages who taught that the Bible and philosophy could both be accepted at the same time.

He taught the Jews of his time to believe in God as the Creator of the world, who gave to people three essential attributes—life, power, and wisdom. He also explained that the Torah laws and commandments could be divided into types—those that could be explained for their obvious logic (such as prohibitions against murder and stealing) and those that could be explained only as traditional, for which there were no rational causes but which were instituted for the inner benefit of people.

Another area in which Saadyah labored during his life was the development of a modern grammar of the Hebrew language, as well as a dictionary of the language as it was then known. Many of the works of this great Jewish scholar have been lost either in full or in part, and in recent years new fragments of his writings have been found indicating that he was busy responding to questions of religious interpretation sent to him by Jews from many corners of the world.

One of the things that Saadyah taught was that "God does not leave His people without a scholar whom He inspires, so that he can teach them and make them better." He could have been writing about himself.

BERNARD BARUCH

Adviser to Presidents

HE WAS BORN IN 1870 in a small town in South Carolina, the son of a doctor who practiced medicine in the difficult period in American history that followed immediately after the end of the Civil War. When he was ten, the young man moved to New York, where he was to become not only one of the great financiers in the country but also a unique adviser—to Presidents of the United States. That is how Baruch will always best be remembered: as an adviser, confidant, consultant, and close friend of Presidents.

The Baruch family came from the area that has sometimes been Poland and sometimes Germany, although originally the family traced its origin to refugees who fled from the Inquisition in Spain and Portugal in the fifteenth century. There had been a number of rabbis in earlier generations of the family. On his mother's side Baruch was descended from immigrants who came to the American colonies late in the seventeenth century, fleeing oppression.

There had not been a regular synagogue in his home town in South Carolina, but in New York young Baruch was able to learn Hebrew and attend synagogue regularly. He remained interested in his Jewish background throughout his lifetime, and always spent Yom Kippur in fast and prayer. On one such Day of Atonement when he was in the synagogue for the whole day, after he had become a very important stockbroker and financier, an aide rushed in

and whispered to him that there was a crisis in the market and that he should come at once and decide what steps to take. Baruch refused to budge. He said that he would not desecrate the holiest day of the Jewish year, and what would happen would happen. As things turned out by the end of the day, Baruch discovered to his amazement that his fortune had increased substantially precisely because he had not taken any action in the market.

Baruch studied at City College in New York and planned to follow his father's footsteps into medicine, despite the fact that his heart was not really in the decision. He had done some boxing in school, and was good at it and enjoyed the excitement of the ring. After a phrenologist—in those days a popular adviser to parents on what their sons ought to do—had examined Baruch's head, the advice had been to go into politics or finance, and Baruch's mother decided that the advice was sound. Bernard gave up all ideas of medicine and began looking around for a job. At the age of nineteen the only job he could find was as an office boy at a weekly salary of three dollars, and he decided to take it.

Through his mother Bernard was introduced to the head of a Wall Street firm who agreed to hire him as an apprentice, which meant he would work without salary while learning the business. The buying and selling of securities, the quoting of prices of various foreign currencies, and the art of investing in new enterprises that held promise of large earnings—this was to become the excitement that supplanted the boxing period, and at last young Baruch felt that he had found the kind of work he was most suited for.

Baruch once wrote about the stock market:

Above all else, the stock market is people, people trying to read the future. It is this intensely human quality that makes the stock market so dramatic an arena in which men and women pit their conflicting judgments, their hopes and fears, strengths and weaknesses, greeds and ideas. One could say that my whole career in Wall Street proved one long process of education in human nature.

Writing in his autobiography, *My Own Story*, Baruch added:

As I moved into public life I was to find that what I had learned about people from my speculator days applied equally to all other human affairs. Human nature remained human nature whether it stood bent over a stock ticker or spoke from the White House, whether it sat in on the councils of war or at peace conferences, whether it was concerned with making money or trying to control atomic energy.

Knowing human nature was not enough, however, Baruch felt. He quickly came to realize that, in order to succeed on Wall Street, he would have to study in depth the basic ingredients that went into the market—the histories, backgrounds, and special qualities of old and new raw materials that were making the wheels of industry spin. He became an authority on gold, copper, sulfur, rubber, and other commodities and applied his knowledge to speculating on stocks and bonds in the fields in which those commodities predominated. At the age of thirty-two, not much more than a decade after he had taken a job as an office boy at three dollars a week, Baruch had acquired a fortune of three million dollars.

In 1916, while World War I was being waged in Europe, President Woodrow Wilson took advantage of Baruch's know-how and appointed him chairman of the new Commission on Raw Materials, Minerals and Metals. It was the beginning of Baruch's entry into public life, and it gave him the opportunity he had always craved to carry out a service in behalf of his country. His parents had both been actively involved in various charitable undertakings as well as in a number of civic causes, and, until now, Baruch felt that he had been missing an opportunity to repay society for the good life he was enjoying.

When America entered the war in 1917, Baruch was named chairman of the War Industries Board, which made him a virtual czar over all of America's wartime industries. He joined the American delegation that took part in the Paris Peace Conference, acting as President Wilson's personal economic adviser. From that time on, almost until his death in 1965, every President of the United States sought out and received the benefit of his clear thinking on economic matters. During the Second World War, President Roosevelt named him to head a special committee to investigate the shortage of rubber and to recommend solutions for the problem. Later he became an adviser to the director of war mobilization, James Byrnes, and when the war ended—and atomic energy had become a reality—he became the American delegate to the United Nations Atomic Energy Commission.

Although he was a proud Jew who remained a synagogue member and worshiper all his life, Baruch did not agree with the Zionist program of building a Jewish homeland for the stateless and persecuted Jews. Instead, he thought that a refuge could be found for them in Africa.

In his revealing autobiography, the man who grew up in a small southern town where shoes were worn only on the Sabbath and whose financial advice was listened to by Presidents of the United States (as well as thousands of stock purchasers) wrote:

I believe in reason not because of the wisdom that men have demonstrated in the past but because it remains man's best tool for governing himself. It is not mere chance that, whenever society is swept by some madness, reason falls as the first victim. Neither perfection nor utopia are within man's grasp. But if the frenzy of soaring hope can never be realized, we can also avoid the panic of plunging despair—if we learn to think our problems through, decide what it is that we value most, and organize ourselves—both as individuals and as a nation—to see that first things come first.

JUDAH HALEVI

Poet of His People

ONE OF THE GREAT POETS of the Jewish people, some of whose works are classed alongside those of King David, who wrote the Psalms, Judah Halevi was also a physician, a philosopher, and a Jewish leader of his time who believed that Jews should return to their ancient homeland, for only there would they be able to live fully and wholly as Jews.

He was born in Spain in 1075 and died in 1141 in Egypt, where he had come en route to Jerusalem to fulfill his lifelong dream of returning personally to the Holy Land. He mastered both Jewish knowledge and the culture of his surrounding community, which at the time was largely Arabic, and became a physician, all the while producing poems. Some eight hundred of his poems have been preserved, some of which are included in the High Holy Day services. His poetic works were devoted to love of Judaism, love of God, expressions of mourning for the homelessness of the Jewish people, songs of yearning for Zion, and poems of love, nature, beauty, and the joy of life.

A lifelong friend and colleague was the Hebrew poet Abraham Ibn Ezra. Both of them spent much time wandering through the various cities of Spain and North Africa, visiting Jewish communities and examining the literary creations of the Arabic poets of the day. One of the great works that Judah Halevi produced was a book called *Kuzari*, which told the story of how the king of a small people in what is today southern Russia decided to convert his entire kingdom to Judaism after learning that both Islam and Christianity were religious movements that originated within Judiasm.

As he grew older, he found himself occupied with his duties as a physician, and he was also called upon to aid Jewish communities who often sought help as outbreaks of violence occurred in various parts of the then known world. He continued to write poems, and often gave his love poems to friends to offer to prospective wives as their own work.

Although he was very closely attached to his only daughter and grandson, he made up his mind that his deep desire to visit the Holy Land before he died was something he could no longer ignore. Despite the warnings of friends that the trip was dangerous, he set out for Jerusalem. When he reached Alexandria in Egypt, he was persuaded by the local Jewish leaders to stay with them, at least to recover from his difficult journey which had been made in a small vessel.

Legend says that he eventually reached Jerusalem and was killed by an Arab horseman as he bent to kiss the soil of the ancient city, but historians insist that he died in Egypt and never actually set foot in the Holy Land.

In the special service that is recited on the eve of the Tisha b'Av day of fasting and mourning for the destruction of the Holy Temple, there is included a poem by Judah Halevi, in which he bemoans the loss of the Temple:

> How shall it be sweet to me, to eat and drink while I behold
> Dogs tearing at thy lion's whelps?
> Or how can light of day be joyous to my eyes while yet
> I see in ravens' beaks torn bodies of thine eagles?

One of the best-known poems, recited even today by school children, refers to the fact that while he lived in Spain, his heart was in Zion. Part of the poem reads:

> My heart is in the east, and I languish in the far west.
> How can I enjoy my food? How can it be sweet to me,
> How shall I sunder my vows and my bonds, while Zion
> Lies in Edom's grip, and I remain in Arab chains?
> It would be a light thing for me to leave the bounty of Spain
> So that my eyes could behold the desolation of the Holy Land.

REB ARYEH LEVIN

The Tzaddik *of Jerusalem*

He was short of stature, a twinkle always sparkled in his eyes, and his full white beard indicated that he was a man of God. Aryeh Levin was born in a small village near Bialystok in 1885, in the Baltic region of what is today part of the Soviet Union. His father was a gentle, kindly man who had difficulty scraping out a living as a forester and who usually was away from home all week, returning home on the eve of the Sabbath.

Young Aryeh, in his late teens, became fearful that he would be conscripted into the hated czarist army, which usually meant servitude for at least twenty-five years. He left home and made his way to Odessa in the Ukraine, the major center of the early Zionist movement, and was soon recommended to become an employee of a fledgling bank in Palestine, forerunner of the present Bank Leumi of Israel.

In 1905 he arrived in Jaffa, where he established a lifelong friendship with Rabbi Abraham Isaac Kook, who was later to become Chief Rabbi of Palestine. In a short span of time Aryeh gave up all ideas of becoming a banker, set off for Jerusalem to continue his studies, and four years later was ordained a rabbi.

He soon became the supervisor and guiding light of the religious school Yeshiva Eitz Hayim in Jerusalem, enjoying the daily contact with young students, assessing their individual scholastic abilities, and guiding them in a path of righteous living.

Little by little there grew up around him a reputation of saintliness. Growing numbers of Jerusalemites became aware that there lived in their midst a self-effacing, dedicated, righteous man whose sole interest in life was to serve others. They began to call him, with deep affection, "Reb Aryeh," and no last name was needed to know whom they meant.

Material things meant nothing to him. As a young man, and even later, he often slept on a wooden bench in a synagogue school and joined a hospitable family for his meals. Whatever monies came his way, he quickly turned over to needy students—for bus fare, a pair of shoes, a hot meal. His wife, who shared his devotion to the performance of daily kindnesses, suffered a lifetime of undernourishment. Four of his children died in their early years. During World War I, when famine threatened to sweep through large sections of the Middle East, Reb Aryeh and his family nearly starved to death.

He lived in a tiny apartment, even after things eased up and money was available for more comfortable surroundings and a few of life's amenities. Menahem Begin, who became Prime Minister of Israel in 1977, admired him greatly, and a number of years ago offered to buy him a kerosene stove to help ward off the icy Jerusalem nights, but the offer was declined.

He never accepted a gift for himself or his family, always channeling such offers to those he felt were in far greater need. Together with his wife, he raised a number of children who were not his own.

One would think that such a *tzaddik* would look forward eagerly to spending the Sabbath day with his family, in restful enjoyment and contemplation, but for more than twenty-five years Reb Aryeh gave up his own Sabbath to spend the day with Jewish prisoners in Jerusalem.

He came to be known as the "Rabbi of the Prisoners." He conducted weekly services for them, attracting both the religious and irreligious prisoners, many of whom were incarcerated for political offenses against the British Mandatory government.

His weekly visits became a source of encouragement and inspiration, and very soon he was accepted by the prisoners as a true man of God, sent to succor them in their misery. He did not discriminate between prisoners who had been convicted of crimes and those who had been locked up for political offenses, treating them all with a heart full of compassion and understanding.

One of the services he carried out for his unusual congregation was relaying messages to and from the prisoners—messages that he memorized intact, for writing them down was forbidden by the laws of the Sabbath and by the prison regulations. His remarkable memory had been trained, it seemed, for just such a purpose by his long years of talmudic study.

Many of the hardened criminals came under his influence, and a number of them were eventually rehabilitated. They saw what all people saw in him—a loving, fatherly, selfless, and profoundly understanding person who related to each man on a one-to-one basis.

Once, when his daughter was deathly sick and the doctors had given up all hope, prison inmates called to the reading of the Torah in the prison services proclaimed their readiness to serve extra time if it would lead to the young girl's recovery. Contrary to all medical diagnoses, she regained her health.

He never lost faith in the innate decency of people, no matter what happened. Once a prisoner who had been released from jail came to him, asking for a few coins to tide him over until he found a job. Reb Aryeh gave him the money, persuaded him to spend the night with his family, and in the morning discovered that the man had fallen back on his old habits—he had disappeared during the night, taking with him the rabbi's Sabbath candlesticks and *kiddush* cup, the only valuables in the house. Reb Aryeh's immediate reaction was to summon his wife and make her promise that she would not let the incident influence her efforts, and his own, to help all those in need, including ex-prisoners.

He visited thousands of Jerusalem families during periods of personal tragedy. He and his wife helped arrange countless marriages between yeshiva students and daughters of local families. Once, a student came to him for advice about a certain girl he was interested in marrying. After listing the girl's many virtues, the young man added, "But she is extremely poor!"

Reb Aryeh's immediate rejoinder was, "Ah, you have just listed still another virtue of hers."

There was a section of a Jerusalem hospital in the early 1920s where lepers were kept in isolation from other patients. They had few visitors, but Reb Aryeh paid them regular visits, bringing food parcels and a word of cheer and hope.

When he died, religious and nonreligious Jews mourned him. He was known and loved by thousands of people, and on the day of his funeral the very air of Jerusalem seemed to drip with tears. Jerusalemites said they felt that one of the thirty-six saintly people in the world—for whose sake, tradition teaches, God allows the world to continue—had died. People wondered who would come along to replace him.

Reb Aryeh Levin died soon after witnessing the reunification of the city of Jerusalem. He was a unique personality, known far and wide by the religious and nonreligious as the *tzaddik* of Jerusalem, the truly righteous man of the holy city. He helped restore people's belief in the essential goodness that rests in every person.

ERNST BORIS CHAIN

Penicillin for Healing

Pronounced the Hebrew way, with the *ch* as a guttural, the name of this world-famous biochemist means "charm," but it would be more appropriate if his name meant "healer" since he and two other leading men of science shared the Nobel Prize for physiology and medicine in 1945 for introducing the drug penicillin, which has helped save countless lives.

Knighted in 1969, Sir Ernst was born in Berlin in 1906, the son of a chemist. Following in his father's footsteps, he studied chemistry and devoted a good deal of time to research on enzymes, working at the Charité Hospital in Berlin until 1933. In that year, when the Nazis rose to power, he left the country and settled in England, working first at the Cambridge School of Biochemistry and later at Oxford.

It was at Oxford that he joined forces with Sir Alexander Fleming and Sir Howard Florey (who shared the Nobel Prize with him) in investigating the antibacterial substances produced by micro-organisms. Chain and Florey were both of the opinion that a substance could be derived from a mold grown from spores either from soil or from the air which would fight infection and help cure serious illnesses. Fleming had already isolated a strain of the mold *Penicillium* which he had preserved for more than a decade.

The three men succeeded in extracting a tiny amount of penicillin out of Fleming's mold, and, although it was impure, it was the beginning of what was to become a veritable wonder drug. After experimenting on laboratory animals, the team decided to use it on a British police officer who lay dying of a blood infection. The minute amount of penicillin had a miraculous effect on him, but, although he was on the road to recovery, he died later when additional supplies of penicillin were simply not available.

A similar experience occurred with a young patient who was seriously ill with a streptococcus infection—but in his case, although it took many months to turn out the tiny amount of penicillin required, he was restored to good health.

By now, World War II had broken out. German bombs were raining on London, and the soldiers of the Allied forces were obviously going to need substantial amounts of this new life-saving drug. Every British plant was devoted entirely to one purpose: the production of badly needed war materiel with which to resist the Nazi enemy. The three scientists turned to the United States, which was still neutral, and urged American drug companies to do their utmost to manufacture mass doses of penicillin to help save the lives of military and civilian populations.

Three American drug companies, working closely with the U.S. government agencies, launched an all-out drive to find a way of mass producing the new wonder drug. Chain and Florey had managed to obtain one part of penicillin out of a million parts of their fermentation broth—it was estimated that one could extract more gold from ocean water than pure, life-saving penicillin from their primitive molds.

At first, American engineers and biochemists learned that they could increase the yield of penicillin by growing the cultures in large milk bottle-sized flasks, and then it was found that growing the mold in large, aerated tanks would produce much larger quantities. By luck, a researcher discovered that a mold on a cantaloupe produced a strain of penicillin that increased the yield to more than two hundred times that of the early method.

The drug manufacturers now set about manufacturing literally tons of penicillin in time to help save thousands of Allied soldiers wounded in battle. When the Allies invaded Normandy in June 1944, they carried with them ample supplies of penicillin.

Among the diseases that have responded to penicillin have been blood poisoning, pneumonia, meningitis, endocarditis, osteomyelitis, and syphilis. A synthetic penicillin known as syncillin, which did not lead to allergic reactions that sometimes accompanied treatment with the original drug, was developed in 1959.

Many countries and leading scientific institutions have honored Chain for his work. For a number of years he headed the Research Center for Chemical Microbiology in Rome, and in recent years he has served as professor of biochemistry at Imperial College in London.

Sir Ernst has been an ardent, activist Zionist all his life, a passion he has maintained second only to his search for scientific advancement. A firm believer in the ancient Jewish maxim *Lo hamedrash elah hamaaseh*—"Deeds, not words, count"—he has devoted considerable time and effort to the programs of the World Jewish Congress on a political level, and as a governor of the Weizmann Institute of Science he has guided the steady development of Israel's scientific achievements.

MENDELE MOCHER SEFARIM

Grandfather of Yiddish Literature

HIS REAL NAME WAS SHALOM ABRAMOVICH, but he became known during his lifetime by his pen name, Mendele Mocher Sefarim, or "Mendele the Bookseller." Today he is acknowledged as the grandfather of modern Yiddish literature and one of the truly great figures of modern Jewish writing.

He was born in a typical Russian *shtetl* in 1835, received an excellent Jewish and general education, and began to write both in Hebrew and Yiddish at an early age. Life became difficult for him when, at the age of thirteen, he lost his father. While still in his teens, he became a schoolteacher with a strong desire to help his people.

In the middle of the nineteenth century the vast majority of the Jews of the world lived in czarist Russia. Their life was harsh, for they were not allowed, without special permission, to leave certain defined areas reserved for them. Most of the Jews were extremely poor; few had an opportunity to advance themselves through education; and the fear of pogroms and attacks was always uppermost in people's minds.

Although he preferred to write in Hebrew and to revive the ancient language of the Jewish people, Mendele set about also to write books and plays in Yiddish that would show his fellow Jews that their only salvation lay in obtaining a better education for themselves and their children and in correcting the weaknesses that existed within the Jewish community itself. Although he was not a socialist nor a Zionist, and in fact the terms were not even known for most of his working life, he has been hailed as one of the early forerunners of both movements. Mendele saw himself as a man with the gift of writing, and he was determined to use it to encourage and uplift his people, who were then passing through a period of despair and hopelessness.

In his writings he stressed the importance of eliminating the corrupt practices that had dominated the Jewish communities for many years and of giving the great majority of the Jews an opportunity to decide on their own affairs. He also believed that the Jews should form alliances with outside political movements that would help to improve their lot in life. On the one hand, he fought the exploitation of the Jewish masses by groups of corrupt leaders who had been in control of their lives for many years, and on the other hand, he urged the Jews to turn away from superstition and join the modern forces of enlightenment that had begun to emerge in western Europe. He also urged them to fight against the tyranny of the Russian regime.

All this he did through his novels, plays, and articles. Because he chose to write in Yiddish in order to reach as wide an audience as possible, his books were enjoyed by large numbers of simple Jews, who sensed in his writing a deep love for the Jewish people and saw in him a champion who sincerely tried to help them out of their difficult lives.

Although he was not a political revolutionary, his books foreshadowed events that were to take place in coming years, including the co-operation of the oppressed Jews and the equally oppressed non-Jewish peasants and workers, all of whom endured great suffering under the regime of the hated czarist government.

He wrote that the anti-Jewish pogroms were nothing less than wars, and asked how it was possible for the instigators of such wars, the pogromists, not only to be let off free for their actions but even to be rewarded by forced payments of ransom by the Jews to prevent any further outbreaks of violence.

Many writers in Israel today attribute to Mendele the creation, almost singlehandedly, of the school of realistic writing that evolved in Hebrew in the last half century. And many literary critics describe Mendele as one of the truly great Jewish writers of the century and regret the fact that his work has not become as well known in English and other languages as that of other Jewish authors.

As a young man he also wrote books about nature and popular science, which were a great innovation for Jewish readers of the time. He traveled extensively, from one *shtetl* to another, always studying the ways of life of the Jews and observing how they and their non-Jewish neighbors got along. One of his most cherished ambitions was to translate the prayer book into Yiddish, but he never fulfilled this idea. He died in 1917, having seen the onset of the Russian Revolution and the early beginnings of the Zionist movement, both of which he hoped would bring an end to Jewish suffering.

SANDY KOUFAX

The Pitcher with a Mind

HE EMERGED AS ONE OF THE GREATEST PITCHERS baseball had ever seen, hurling his ball with such skill that few batters could even connect to make a single base. His record includes no-hitter games and many strikeouts, and for years before he retired as an active professional baseball player, the name of Sandy Koufax stood for superior skill coupled with an attitude toward America's national pastime that made all Jews exceedingly proud.

Sanford Koufax was born in New York in 1935 and grew up in a Long Island suburb. He attended religious school and was bar mitzvah. In his early years the six-foot two-inch athlete thought more in terms of professional basketball than baseball. In fact, he won a basketball scholarship to the University of Cincinnati, where he planned to study architecture.

Because he wanted to make a trip to New Orleans, he tried out for the baseball team and was accepted. He was switched from the position of first baseman to pitcher primarily because his batting was poor. A strange thing happened: He played thirty-two innings for the college team and struck out fifty-four men at bat. Scouts for the professional teams began to take notice of him, and before long he was being pressured to sign up with the Dodgers, the Giants, the Yankees, and other teams. Sandy signed with the Dodgers.

His professional career started out slowly, especially after he injured his arm. After a brief stint in the army, he began to make a name for himself as a pitcher who could strike out batters. By 1961 he established a new record by striking out 269 hitters. The next year he pitched a no-hit game. It was about this time that he developed a rare circulatory problem, known as Raynaud's phenomenon, that cut down on the flow of blood to his fingers. In 1963, after being saluted by newspaper sportswriters throughout the country, he received the National League's Most Valuable Player Award, the Cy Young Award, and the Babe Ruth Award.

When the Dodgers' manager scheduled Koufax to pitch on Yom Kippur in 1961, there were fireworks, and Koufax refused to do so, asking that the schedule be changed. At the last minute he was reassigned, and has never played ball on any of the High Holy Days. When he retired as an active ballplayer, he moved into a new profession, becoming a sports newscaster.

At the height of his fame Koufax was once asked by the Lubavitch organization, a group of Hasidic Jews, to pose for a photograph wearing a *tallit* (prayer shawl) and *tefillin* (phylacteries). Although he was a synagogue attendant only on the three Jewish High Holy Days, he readily agreed, and the photo of the popular baseball figure wearing the appurtenances of an Orthodox Jew appeared in newspapers throughout the country. The only change he insisted on in posing for the photograph was to wear a baseball cap rather than the traditional *yarmulke*.

Baseball historians have recorded him as the greatest left-hand pitcher in the annals of the sport. Before stepping down from the mound, he had pitched a total of four no-hit games.

One of Koufax's cherished ambitions is to see baseball introduced in a big way in Israel so that he could teach a future star pitcher the tricks of the game that he learned while he was one of America's leading players.

When asked the secret of his pitching skill, Koufax usually responded that he "pitched not only with my arm, but with my mind, too."

DAOUD/DAVID

He Walked to Jerusalem from Yemen

THERE IS A TEL AVIV LAWYER today from the Yemenite community whose first name is David, although as a small child he was known by the Arabic equivalent, Daoud. He shuns personal publicity, and for that reason his surname is omitted here.

He is married and has a nice family and a successful law practice, and he can point with pride to the fact that he celebrated his bar mitzvah in Jerusalem. But it is only after you talk with him at some length and check with his friends that the full story of how he celebrated his bar mitzvah in Jerusalem comes to light. It is not the average American thirteen-year-old boy being taken to Jerusalem on a modern airliner by his parents for the privilege of reciting the traditional blessings at the Western Wall who emerges, but rather a tenacious boy determined to fulfill his dead mother's wishes.

The story begins in the middle 1940s in the country of Yemen, in southern Arabia, where Jews had lived as second-class citizens for so many long centuries that it had become second nature for them. There one young Jewish family suffered a terrible tragedy: First the father died and, soon after, his wife, leaving behind a child of three, whose name was Daoud. On her deathbed the mother exacted a promise from her Moslem neighbor and friend to care for the child and when he was of age to tell him that he was a Jewish boy and that at the age of thirteen he should try to celebrate his bar mitzvah in the holy city of Jerusalem.

The Arab friend reared and cared for young Daoud, treating him like one of her own sons. Time passed, and in 1948 and 1949

71

virtually the entire Jewish community of Yemen was flown to Israel, from which they had been exiled two millennia earlier. Daoud's foster mother noted the events but kept silent because at the time he was only a child of seven.

Six years later, as he approached thirteen, totally unaware of the fact that he was Jewish, Daoud was summoned by his foster mother. She had him sit and, extracting a gold Star of David on a chain, handed it to him and for the first time told him about his true parents and their untimely deaths. She explained to him that he was approaching the age of bar mitzvah and told him of his mother's deathbed wish that he mark the event in Jerusalem. The Star of David had been left for him by his mother.

The young boy was transfixed by what she had said. He picked up the chain with the *Magen David*, kissed it reverently, and realized that somehow he had known all along that he was different from the other boys with whom he had grown up.

Within a matter of a few days, he told his foster mother he was setting out for the city of Jerusalem to celebrate his bar mitzvah. He realized that he had no money and no papers and did not know anything about Judaism, but something impelled him to believe he would overcome all obstacles and carry out his mother's wishes.

The foster mother gave him a few coins and some food and water. She had grown deeply attached to him but understood his need to make his pilgrimage to Jerusalem. She bade him be careful on the long journey and warned him to regard strangers with suspicion. It was a tearful farewell for both of them when Daoud left on foot, proceeding in a northerly direction.

One has to look at a map to understand what lay before the youngster. Yemen lies almost at the tip of the Arabian Peninsula. To reach Israel, one must traverse the entire Saudi territory—most of it hot, barren, and treacherous—and then cross a part of Jordan before even coming in sight of Israel. The distance to be covered was almost fourteen hundred miles.

Daoud started out and was soon picked up by a band of traveling Arab merchants. Taking his foster mother's advice, he hid his Star of David pendant and did not let on that he was a Jewish boy en route to Jerusalem for his bar mitzvah. Instead, he said he was going to the holy city of Mecca, which lies about midway between his point of departure and his destination.

Things went well. The merchants were kind and let him ride on their camels and share their supplies of food and water. After a few days he transferred to a group of pilgrims on their way to Mecca, and they journeyed together to the holy city of Islam on foot and on the swaying camels, camping out at night beneath the desert moon.

After more than a month of steady travel Daoud and his friendly caravan of Arab pilgrims reached Mecca. Daoud had become worried that one of the pilgrims in the party had grown suspicious of him, and so at the first opportunity he broke away from the group and soon lost himself in the crowds of thousands of Moslem pilgrims.

He remained in Mecca for a few days, begging for food, hiding at night for fear of being questioned by the authorities. Finally he was taken in hand by a friendly English couple who had obtained permission to visit Mecca and who had become aware of the boy's plight. He had broken down out of fear and hunger and had told them of his true identity and his plans to reach Jerusalem. They sneaked him out of the city and brought him to a point about five hundred miles south of Eilat, along the peninsula's coastline. There, all they could do was point him toward Israel and wish him well.

Daoud now took a deep breath and set out. He walked along what must have seemed like millions of miles of sand dunes, the Red Sea to his left and a vista of hot, shimmering sands to his right. From time to time he begged for food and water. In some small villages he was given hospitality and helped along the way. In others he resorted to pilfering food and drink.

His feet were blistered, his dark skin burnt a deep brown, but his determination to continue never flagged. When no one was in sight, he took out his hidden Star of David, kissed it, and in his own way offered a prayer. And then he continued to walk, his direction always north.

The long days became weeks, and the weeks months. And then suddenly he came across a road sign that indicated that the city of Aqaba, in southern Jordan, lay ahead. He had learned somewhere that this town lay close to the Israeli frontier, and he felt his pulse quicken. Almost at a run, he crossed the Jordanian border, and was immediately arrested by armed Jordanian soldiers, who took him to their headquarters.

He began to jabber that he was en route to Jerusalem and begged the soldiers to take him to the Israeli frontier. After months on the run, he was painfully thin and his clothes were in tatters. He conversed with the soldiers in his and their common language, Arabic. Something appealing must have gotten through to the Jordanian border patrol. Within a day, they escorted him to the frontier post guarding the entrance to Eilat, and turned him over to the Israeli soldiers there.

The Israeli soldiers were at first suspicious. Daoud's story did not make sense. How could this frail boy have traveled alone, on foot mostly, from Yemen to Eilat? How did he survive? But the more they questioned the boy, the more they became convinced that his story was incredible but nonetheless true.

They then began to outdo each other in trying to help. The soldiers gave him food, clothes, and gifts. They began to teach him Hebrew, and one offered to teach him the traditional bar mitzvah blessings.

After a while it was decided to take him to Jerusalem and to make arrangements for him to enter a supervised institution for young, homeless, and orphaned children. But when a car came to the apartment where he had been staying temporarily to take him on the eight-hour trip through the Negrev region of Israel to Jerusalem, David—he had had his name Hebraized—refused to enter.

"You have taught me," he explained, "that to go to Jerusalem, I must be an *oleh regel*—a pilgrim—I must go on foot."

Arguments were useless. And so young David took up his slow trek on foot from Eilat to Jerusalem. It took more than a week and a half, and he was accompanied all the way by a soldier. Finally he entered the city of Jerusalem, as had pilgrims on foot in days of yore.

David was taken in hand and raised in a religious children's institution. He was an exemplary student and went on to become a successful attorney. His bar mitzvah in Jerusalem was attended by scores of his fellow residents of the children's institution—and by the spirit of his mother's dying words.

Yes, David still has the Star of David she left for him.

ARTUR RUBINSTEIN

The Proud Pianist

FOR MORE THAN HALF A CENTURY Artur Rubinstein has been acclaimed as one of the greatest pianists of all time. He was born in Poland in 1886 and began to play the piano at the age of three, although he did not give his first professional concert until he was eleven.

The public at large and musical critics alike have long regarded him as a master pianist. He has performed all over the world, except in Germany, which he refuses to visit as protest against that country's brutality in both world wars. In Israel he refuses to accept payment for his concerts, and during the years when he was giving as many as 150 concerts a year, primarily in the United States, many of them were for the benefit of charity.

During a nationwide television interview on the occasion of his ninetieth birthday, the great musician spoke of his pride in being a Jew and of his attitude toward the Jewish people. He said, "I am very proud to be a Jew. I remember from my youth in Lodz the great struggles of the Jewish people. We are the only people who refuse to be defeated.

"I am very proud to have taken this characteristic and made it my own. For two thousand years, while the Jews were in exile, they did not know what it is to give up. My father was a very proud Jew. We were not Orthodox, but we had a nice meal on

Friday nights, with candles. We went to synagogue on Yom Kippur. I was bar mitzvah and I can say *Shma Yisrael* and *Baruch Atah*, but not much more.

"We are a people who would choose death rather than give in. In the Inquisition, Jews could save themselves by becoming Catholics, but they would not. We kept our faith and our laws, and for two thousand years we continued to say, 'Next year in Jerusalem.' That is what made it possible for us to come together after all those years.

"After Hitler we came together—three million Jews came together from all over the world, from Europe and North and South America, from North Africa, from Yemen, from all countries. Our faith made Zionism possible, and men like Weizmann and Ben-Gurion and the men who shed their blood made Israel possible.

"When I see Israel today I feel tremendous love for it and for our people. I am so deeply moved, I experience it double, for myself and for my father. I have performed there a good deal, and I have many, many good friends there. I love them and they care very much for me. I want to give all of myself to Israel.

"One day after the Six Day War I was at the Western Wall in Jerusalem and some of the Orthodox people came over and put *tefillin* on me, the little boxes on my head and arm. They said, 'Can you pray?' I said, 'I can,' and I did—for two days. But then I stopped. I realized that what matters is in my heart."

Rubinstein has never been an artist who hides behind the protection of the stage. He has spoken out against Soviet aggression in eastern Europe, against the outbreak of anti-Semitism in postwar Poland, against the Arab threat to Israel just prior to the June 1967 war.

He has been the subject of books, a film, and countless articles but takes special pride in the Artur Rubinstein Chair in Musicology established at the Hebrew University.

THEODOR HERZL

Founder of Modern Zionism

HISTORY HAS DESIGNATED HIM THE FOUNDER of modern Zionism. Towns, streets, schools—even a mountain in Jerusalem—are named for him. To look at his portrait today, one senses that behind the smoldering eyes and the regal beard there was something extraordinary about the man—and in a space of nine short years he proved that that was indeed the case. He said he had a vision of sorts; others said he simply dramatized what many generations of Jews had been praying and hoping for. But the fact remains that in that nine-year span Theodor Herzl succeeded in transforming a dream of the Jewish people returning to its ancient homeland in Palestine into the beginnings of a viable action.

Born in Budapest in 1860, Herzl was raised in a home where the Jewish content of his studies was downgraded. He studied law and earned a doctorate in the field, but turned his attention to literary pursuits. He wrote a column for a popular newspaper, and produced short stories, plays, and essays, with a modest success usually but nothing really earth-shaking.

At the age of thirty-four he was in Paris, the world's capital for the arts at that time and the home of the French Revolution a century earlier, which had done so much to alter the course of modern European (and American) history. A sensational trial was taking place in the French courts, and Herzl was assigned to re-

porting it. A French Jewish army captain, Alfred Dreyfus, was on trial for espionage, and the case had become a focal point of attention for millions of people around the world.

Eventually—more than a decade later—Dreyfus was exonerated and proved to have been completely innocent, the victim of trumped-up charges. What Herzl saw in and around the courtroom during the original trial, however, shook him to his very roots. He wrote at the time, "The Dreyfus case embodies more than a judicial error—it embodies the desire of the vast majority of the French to condemn all Jews in this one Jew. . . . Death to the Jews! the mob howled. In France—republican, modern, civilized France, one hundred years after the Declaration of the Rights of Man!"

For years Herzl had seen displays of covert anti-Semitism: his lawyer friends unable to move up the ladder of their profession because of their ethnic background, racial slurs directed at him when he was a student, stories of hostility to Jews because of their Jewishness that he had heard for years and had largely ignored.

But the Dreyfus case seems to have struck him with the impact of a lightning bolt. He wrote that until then "most of us believed that the solution to the Jewish question was to be patiently waited for as part of the general development of mankind" —but the trial in the French capital destroyed that sentiment. With the flair of a dramatist, he told himself that this was too long a period to wait. The time had come to do something.

Herzl sat down and wrote a booklet called *The Jewish State*, in which he argued that the only meaningful solution for the oppression and homelessness of the Jewish people was to re-establish the ancient Jewish homeland in Palestine. The next year, 1897, he succeeded in convening in Basel, Switzerland, the first World Zionist Congress, in effect launching the modern political movement called Zionism.

Many of those who participated in the historic gathering knew that Herzl was not aware that for a number of years there already had been a series of serious attempts to establish a Jewish homeland in Palestine. Throughout history, ever since their exile from their homeland in the year 70, Jews had been hoping to return to Zion. But Herzl had a magnetism about him that made everything coalesce and appear to be new and fresh.

From the time of the first Congress to his untimely death at the age of forty-four, Herzl was in effect the ambassador of the Jews to the governments of the world. No one knew what was the best way to proceed to turn the dream into reality, least of all Herzl, so he tried virtually everything.

He sent a copy of his *The Jewish State* to the heads of the Rothschild dynasty, appealing for financial support, but was rebuffed. A friend of Herzl who read the slim book feared that it was written as a result of a nervous breakdown.

He appealed for aid to the Turks, who then controlled the vast Ottoman Empire, in which the small area of Palestine was included, and here too he was rebuffed, despite having a number of meetings with the sultan. Obsessed by his vision, disregarding his health, Herzl proceeded to seek help from the German Kaiser, whom he met in Jerusalem, the heads of the Russian, British, and Italian governments, the Pope, but all to no avail.

At one time the British, then the greatest imperial power in the world, offered Herzl an opportunity to establish a Jewish homeland in Uganda, a proposal he was ready to accept, but he was overruled by his fellow Zionist leaders.

The early Zionist congresses over which he presided established some of the basic institutions of the Zionist movement that have helped to transform the Herzlian dream into a reality. To the Jews in Europe, especially the millions of poor village and *shtetl* dwellers in Russia and Poland, he was considered a royal figure, not only for his personal appearance and bearing but because he dared to call on the great leaders of the world and urge their support for the return of the Jews to Palestine. Although he had fired their imagination and kindled their hopes, they did not seem to be in as much of a hurry for the implementation of the program as he was.

Perhaps he knew that his time was short; perhaps he did not want to see even one more act of anti-Semitism if he could help it; but the fact is that he drove himself unsparingly. Suffering from a heart condition, he contracted pneumonia and died in 1904, deeply mourned by all Jews.

In his will he had asked that his remains be exhumed and reburied in the Jewish state that he dreamed of. In 1949, a year after the establishment of Israel, a group of Israelis escorted his remains from the Viennese cemetery for reburial in Jerusalem. The ceremony took place on Mount Herzl, named for him.

In a manifesto outlining his vision of the future Jewish state, he wrote:

> I believe that a wondrous generation of Jews will spring into existence. . . . We shall live at last as free men on our own soil, and die peacefully in our own homes.
>
> The world will be freed by our liberty, enriched by our wealth, magnified by our greatness. Whatever we attempt to accomplish there [in the Jewish state] for our own welfare will react powerfully and beneficially for the good of humanity.

David Ben-Gurion, the first Prime Minister of Israel, said, "Herzl was the first who was able to breathe a new spirit, the will to act, into the faith and nostalgia of the Jewish people yearning to be revived. He transformed the Jewish people for the first time since its exile into a political force, a fighting creative force, capable of reshaping its historic destiny by its own will and exertions. Herein lies his historical greatness."

Herzl wrote in his diary in 1897, referring to the first Zionist Congress, "At Basel I founded the Jewish state. In five years, perhaps, and certainly in fifty, everyone will see it."

He was off by one year. Israel was established in 1948.

ANNE FRANK

Unstilled Voice of the Holocaust

MILLIONS OF PEOPLE HAVE READ *The Diary of a Young Girl* or seen the film based on it, *The Diary of Anne Frank*. It is a moving account by a young Jewish girl who hid out with her family and several other Jewish people for two years, from 1942 to 1944, in a "secret annex," actually part of a warehouse belonging to her father, until the Nazis discovered them and sent them to a concentration camp. The *Diary* made it possible for millions of people to understand what the Nazi regime in Europe was really like and to grasp the great suffering that befell the Jewish communities in those countries seized by the Nazis.

Anne was born in Frankfurt, Germany, in 1929. When she was four, her parents took her and her sister, Margot, to Holland, for by then the Nazi regime had already come to power in Germany and the situation for the Jews looked very bleak. After World War II broke out in 1939, six million Jews were deliberately massacred by the Nazi authorities.

The Jewish community in Holland, which was overrun in 1940, did not suffer as much as Jews in other countries, at least in the beginning, because so many Dutch people were violently opposed to the barbaric ideas of the Nazis. But by 1942 the situation had become grim for the Jews, and the Frank family decided to hide out, hoping that the danger of the Nazi era would pass soon.

They moved into a secret part of a commercial building, together with another family, and later were joined by an older man —Jews in great danger of being arrested and deported to their death for no reason other than the fact that they were Jewish. Five devoted friends of the Frank family made it possible for the secret hiding place to succeed for a period of more than two years. These five non-Jewish men and women brought food, clothes, medicines, newspapers to the self-confined residents of the virtual prison, and sustained their hopes that the ordeal would soon come to an end.

When she entered the secret annex, Anne was about thirteen, a talented, sensitive girl who, together with her sister, had received a secondary Jewish education and who understood that, hard as it was for them to remain in hiding, things on the outside were far worse for other Jews, who were being rounded up and brutally murdered every day in every part of the European continent controlled by the Nazis.

She began to keep a diary, and in it she recorded her own observations of the impact of the close quarters in which her own family and the others lived for so long a period. She wrote of human weaknesses, including her own mother's standard of values; of the growing feelings of teen-age infatuation that she began to develop for young Peter, the son of the Van Daan family who lived with the Franks; of her own ambitions to survive the terrible ordeal that they were all passing through and to try to become a writer, a calling for which she believed she had a special talent.

Strangely, despite the conditions of their lives, Anne Frank retained a hopeful outlook on life and expressed her essential confidence in the decency of most people. She wrote that she hoped to live to see the day when the terrible nightmare of the Jewish people would come to an end and a time of peace and universal brotherhood would prevail.

In August of 1944, less than a year before the Nazis surrendered to the Allied forces, the hiding place was discovered and all of its occupants were sent to a death camp. Anne's father, Otto, survived. Two of the Gentile friends of the family who had helped them carry on for two years discovered Anne's diary when they went to inspect the site of the secret hiding place. It was published in 1947 in Dutch, and later appeared in many other languages, as well as in stage and film versions.

86

In the Nazi drive to annihilate all Jews, six million perished, among them more than one million children. Anne Frank, sixteen years old when she met her death, was one of the victims, but her name lives on, for through her diary she succeeded in making millions of people understand what happened to the Jewish people, by recounting the lives of eight Jewish men and women locked up for two years in a hiding place in a business building.

In her diary Anne Frank wrote:

I want to go on living even after my death. And therefore I am grateful to God for giving me this gift, this possibility of developing myself and of writing, of expressing all that is in me.

ROBERT SZOLD

Private Enterprise for Public Good

He had the humility of Moses and believed profoundly in the teachings of Maimonides, especially the dictum that the noblest form of charity was to help a poor man become a self-supporting individual.

Unassuming, gentle, self-effacing, blessed with a perpetual, mirthful twinkle in his eye, Robert Szold was a man unlike any other. The mold from which he was cast, and the times that helped make him the man he became, are gone.

Throughout his life he was living proof of the heights to which a man can rise, if he sincerely loves his fellow men. More than anything, he was a Jew with a deep conviction about the moral teachings of Judaism and the Jewish heritage.

He was born in 1889 in Streator, Illinois, and grew up in the heartland of America. He was a small child as the twentieth century unfolded. His father was a merchant who maintained a life-long devotion to his Jewish faith, despite the difficulties of doing so in a preponderantly Gentile atmosphere. Across the continent, in Baltimore, his cousin, Henrietta Szold, was destined to make her own mark in the history of the Jewish people.

As a teen-ager he helped in the family business, learning the importance of daily toil. He graduated from Knox College and went on to earn a law degree from Harvard, from which he graduated with honors in 1912. From his earliest years he was attracted to public service for his country, and for the embryonic Zionist movement that was just beginning to develop. He helped found a Zionist organization, and in the same year was named assistant attorney general for Puerto Rico, working closely with the United States solicitor general.

He was deeply stirred by the sight of small children in those early years of the twentieth century working in factories, and drafted legislation that eventually led to outlawing child labor in the United States. When World War I ended, he entered private law practice, keeping up an active Zionist role and gradually influencing his lifelong friend Louis D. Brandeis, who was later to become Supreme Court Justice, to share his views about Zionism. In 1919 he made the first of many trips to Palestine, and for a short period served as administrator of Jerusalem. His ideas about the economic development of the Jewish homeland crystallized.

Szold had been raised in a country that believed wholeheartedly in the free-enterprise system, and he came to the conclusion that the same system would help make the nascent Jewish state strong and viable. He coined a phrase that was to become his lifelong motto: "Private enterprise for the public good." To him that meant that free, individual enterprise would bring out the best in people but that this economic way of life had to be channeled toward helping the public at large.

For the next half century he led an American company that invested in all kinds of businesses in Palestine, seeking to expand agricultural production, encourage industrial undertakings, and promote banking, insurance, and shipping. Investors included the very wealthy and the not-so-wealthy who shared Szold's vision of a Jewish homeland that would prosper if it were built on a sound economic base. Over a period of years, the Palestine Economic Corporation (PEC) poured many millions of dollars into Palestine and later Israel, taking risks that few others would even consider. After seeing that a particular enterprise was productive, well run, and on the road to success, the American investors would transfer to other enterprises, starting the process all over again.

Agricultural collectives, including those committed to socialist principles, could always count on the PEC for low-interest loans.

Major plants in Israel were established by large American companies in the paper, chemicals, and rubber industries, in conjunction with the PEC, because they were confident they would be carefully guided and managed. A small staff in New York and in Tel Aviv conducted the multicompany business and industrial network, aided by a corps of top-level business executives who gladly volunteered their time and expertise. Szold led and inspired the entire operation for several decades.

One of the most innovative steps the company took under Szold's leadership was the establishment of large, modern industrial plants in scattered parts of Israel. These were subdivided into smaller units and offered to small businessmen at modest rentals, helping them to get started and develop thriving businesses.

All this time Szold continued his own law practice, and also became a prime mover of the concept of low-cost co-op housing in the United States. He had married Zip Falk in 1917, and had a family of four daughters, and quickly came to realize the importance of decent housing for every working family. Always opposed to government-subsidized housing projects, he argued for the co-operative concept, in which each family would invest some of its capital and develop a sense of pride and ownership. A whole series of co-op housing developments, many of them sponsored by unions, were put up in various parts of New York and in other cities, and Szold's thinking was proven right, for the tenant-owners maintained their apartments with great care, while the vast majority of government-backed low-rental housing units often developed into slums.

Szold hated pompousness and dishonesty, and admired a keen mind and a good heart. It was not unusual to see him paying the mail clerk at the PEC office a few cents for a postage stamp to mail off a personal letter. Once, he was late for an appointment with a job applicant, a man thirty years his junior. Szold apologized profusely, and when the interview was over walked out of the office with the applicant, intent on escorting him back to his own office as a sign of contrition.

The PEC has been absorbed by a larger Israeli conglomerate, but the principles laid down by Szold continue to guide its work. Another organization that he established, Palestine Endowment

Funds, continues to transmit charitable funds for educational, social service, medical, and humanitarian needs in Israel. It is conducted almost entirely by volunteers.

From his appearance Szold might have been the descendant of a long line of Vermont-dwelling early settlers. His English was rustic, and he knew little Hebrew or Yiddish. When friends and admirers got together to establish an institute at the Hebrew University in Jerusalem in his name, he insisted that it be practical and useful, and the Robert Szold Institute is now dedicated to applied science.

When he died at eighty-eight, the American Jewish community lost a great son.

ENZO SERENI

Emissary of His People

HE WAS THE SON OF A DISTINGUISHED PHYSICIAN who served as the personal doctor of the king of Italy, Victor Emmanuel. He grew up in an affluent home, surrounded by people of culture and wealth—and he chose to settle in a forsaken spot of land in Palestine and devote his life to building a homeland for the Jewish people.

He died a hero's death. After parachuting behind enemy lines during World War II to help speed the Allies' victory and to bring a message of hope to his fellow Jews, he was caught by the Nazis and sent to the infamous Dachau concentration camp. Like so many other Jews in that horrible place, he was gassed and his remains burned in a crematorium.

But during the not quite forty years of his life he succeeded in filling the world with his own sense of commitment, dedication, and idealism. In Israel his name is synonymous with the highest concepts of personal and utter dedication to humanity.

Enzo Sereni was descended from a family that had lived in Italy for many centuries; some believe that the family could trace its ancestry to the years immediately following the Roman destruction of the Temple in Jerusalem, when thousands of Hebrew slaves were forcibly brought to Rome, where Jews have continued to live for nearly two millennia.

He was born in Rome in 1905 and knew nothing of Zionism until he heard of the World Zionist Congress in Karlsbad in 1921.

93

The idea of the Jewish people returning to their ancient homeland captivated his imagination: Although he was still in his teens, he sensed that this was what he had been waiting for, and, always a person of action, he set about making preparations for a new life in Palestine.

He graduated from the University of Rome with a doctorate in philosophy, studied Hebrew with a private tutor, served his time in the Italian army, emerging as an officer, and even before he and his young wife, Ada, set sail in 1926 for Palestine, had already organized a number of Zionist youth groups in Rome and Florence, urging them to leave the Diaspora and make a new life in Zion.

Most of his acquaintances in Italy, including his family, thought that his enthusiasm for the Zionist cause was a passing fancy, but they were wrong. In a speech prior to his departure from Italy he said, "It is the duty of able bourgeois Jewish youth, sons of merchants in the Diaspora, to be transformed into the working class that Israel requires. There is no remedy for Jewish life except in Israel. Bodies and souls will be lost in the transplantation to Israel—but come, and we will go with the full consciousness that the sacrifice must be made."

When Enzo and his wife and infant daughter, Hannah, arrived in Palestine, it could not have been at a worse possible time. Unemployment in agriculture and in the building industry was widespread, and there was hardly any other industry to speak of in the country at the time. The young family lived for a while in Rehovot in the most primitive of conditions, but Enzo was an enthusiastic, dynamic person, and before long he had assembled a group of young people and led them to a tract of land not far from Tel Aviv, announcing that they would become squatters unless the area was officially leased to them as the site of a future kibbutz.

The stratagem worked, and before long Givat Brenner was established with practically no funds or resources except an overwhelming desire to fashion there a self-supporting agricultural commune in which the law of social and economic equality would rule supreme. Before long, the dream began to become reality, and as waves of Jewish refugees from Germany began to arrive in Palestine, substantial numbers joined the kibbutz, which today is one of the showplaces of Israel.

Throughout his life Enzo Sereni had the ability to generate enthusiasm for anything he undertook, and to undertake several challenging tasks simultaneously. His warm, outgoing, contagious personality led the Zionist leaders to send him abroad as an emissary, seeking to persuade Jews to come to Israel and to help support its various institutions financially. He was sent to Germany in 1929 and created a stir, four years before the ascendancy of Nazism, by warning the German Jews that they were sitting on a volcano and urging them to emigrate immediately before it was too late. Not many listened to his warnings, but those who did owe their lives to him.

As the years of the Nazi era developed, before the outbreak of war in 1939, Enzo was sent on missions to Holland, Belgium, Switzerland, France, Egypt, and Iraq, urging all who would listen that time was short and they should pack up and leave for Palestine. He became adept at languages, including Yiddish, and wherever he went, he was admired and respected, but only small numbers of Jews took his words at face value, most choosing rather to believe that he was a well-meaning alarmist.

His long absences from home and from his growing family (a second daughter and a son were born in Israel), troubled him always, but he felt obsessed by what he was trying to achieve. In a letter to his elder daughter, he wrote:

> Perhaps I was mistaken not to have tried to make you understand the core of my soul and my work. When you grow up, and maybe I will no longer be with you, you will understand someday why your father traveled so much, was always among strange people, and sometimes didn't even find time to talk to you.
>
> Your father goes from place to place and tries to heal the wounds of an unfortunate people that no one loves, a people persecuted all over the world.

He returned to Germany after the Nazis' rise to power, at great personal risk, begging Jews to leave and to wake up to the grave danger that surrounded them. At times he carried large sums of cash on his person to help a prospective immigrant family reach Israel with whatever they could salvage.

Whenever he came home to his kibbutz, Enzo was immediately questioned by everyone in the settlement. He became a living bridge between Jewish communities overseas and the Jews living in Palestine. The children of the kibbutz delighted in his arrivals, for he always found time to take them on picnics, talking, joking, entertaining, and trying to imbue them with his own enthusiasm for a life based on ideals.

He was at heart a pacifist and at one time expressed great admiration for Ghandi's nonviolence philosophy, but when war came in 1939, he knew that the time for fighting the Nazi enemy was at hand. He returned to Europe—to France, Italy, Holland—months or sometimes only weeks before the Nazi armies invaded, trying even in those last few hours to persuade Jews to leave at once for Palestine. In Paris a few months before the Germans defeated the French in June 1940, he wrote that "anti-Semitism has penetrated French society. The sky is becoming darker, and the approach of war gives the opportunity for provocation against Jews."

Upon his return to Palestine, he was among the first to enlist in the British army. He became part of the British counterintelligence network, and at the same time continued to carry out his own intelligence vis-à-vis the entrapped Jewish communities.

In 1944 the British agreed to a daring plan in which volunteer Palestinian Jewish parachutists, all of whom had lived in various European locales, would be dropped behind enemy lines so as to provide vital information in the war effort and also to aid, as best they could, the decimated Jewish communities.

Although he was nearing forty, whereas the other volunteers were mostly in their early twenties, Enzo insisted on being one of the parachutists. At the time, southern Italy was almost entirely in Allied hands but the northern part of the country was still held by the Nazis.

By virtue of his seniority and because of his natural traits of leadership, Enzo became the leader of the parachutists. He always seemed to be bubbling over, always confident of what the future held in store. He advised his fellow Palestinians to appear at all times self-confident, which would help them survive the double life they were about to enter. To prove his point, he removed his British army uniform, complete with captain's insignia, and walked right past a guard at the entrance of a military post, wearing only a rumpled civilian suit. Nobody stopped him, he explained to his young compatriots, and they learned the lesson well.

Most of the other parachutists took off for a base in Yugoslavia, but Enzo's mission was northern Italy. He was accompanied by an Italian officer who was to serve as his radio operator. The pilot took off on the night of May 15, 1944, and made a fatal navigational error; he dropped them in the wrong spot, and Enzo and the Italian officer never saw each other again after the flight.

The details of what happened after that are hazy. It is believed that Enzo was caught almost immediately by the Germans and was at first imprisoned in a camp called Mildorf, together with other Italian prisoners. He had been given the right by his British commanders to select a British or American alias but chose to use a Hebrew name, Shmuel Barda. In the prison camp with the Italians, Enzo came to be known and respected and often was called on to settle petty arguments. The prisoners called him affectionately and simply "the Captain."

Sometime later he was moved to Dachau, where his coreligionists could hardly believe he was a Jew from Palestine who had voluntarily come to help. He seemed more like an angel from another planet.

According to records subsequently found in Dachau, "Shmuel Barda" was taken to a special interrogation cell on November 17, 1944, and died the following day.

Earlier, Enzo Sereni had written, "If we wish to live, we must be prepared to die. Even in death, the seeds of life are contained. If we know how to live as required and to die as required, the light will not be lost to us."

ALBERT A. MICHELSON

America's First Nobel Laureate

He was born in a small village in Germany in 1852, brought to the United States at the age of two, and grew up first in Nevada and later in San Francisco. At the age of seventeen, alone and without funds or support from government or political figures, Albert Abraham Michelson made the long journey on the newly inaugurated railroad from California to Washington, D.C., to try for an appointment to the U. S. Naval Academy at Annapolis. The son of poor parents, he knew that he had no other way of obtaining a higher education.

Annapolis at first turned him down, although his high school grades were excellent. He was told there was no vacancy. But Michelson was anything but a quitter: He went to the White House, asking for an appointment to see the President, and eventually President Ulysses Grant did see the young man from far-off California, heard him out, and decided that he was the kind of able student Annapolis needed. He appointed him to the Academy, from which Michelson graduated four years later.

During the next few years Michelson became an instructor in physics and chemistry at Annapolis, and found that he was fascinated by the phenomena of the speed of light. In 1878 he computed the speed of light to be 186,508 miles per second, a discovery that won for him instant acclaim and invitations to devote his time to research rather than to teaching.

After a few years attending lectures and seminars with the eminent physicists of Europe, Michelson returned to the United States and devoted himself to developing an instrument known as an interferometer, which could measure tiny distances more accurately than the strongest microscope. He was intrigued by the question of whether there was independent motion by the earth, and carried on his experiments at the Case School in Cleveland, where he discovered that there was no drift in the ether surrounding the earth as had generally been assumed to be the case. His discovery proved of inestimable value to the development of the science of optics and helped lay the groundwork for Einstein's subsequent experiments in relativity.

Astronomers began to use Michelson's interferometer to determine the size of stars. The first recorded measurement of a star utilizing Michelson's invention took place in 1920 at the famous Mount Wilson Observatory in California.

Another device that Michelson created was the echelon spectroscope, which enabled a viewer to see molecules in the act of vibration when a given substance was heated. Michelson was also anxious to determine the rigidity of the earth, and he developed a test involving the laying of long pipes half-filled with water at a depth of six feet underground and determining the strength of tidal pulls, the earth's size, and that of the sun and the moon, and proving that the interior of the earth was both strong as steel and simultaneously elastic.

Later he devised a method of utilizing the speed of light as a method for measuring the entire world. Michelson's pre-eminence as a scientist led to his election to the presidency of the American Association for the Advancement of Science and of the National Academy of Science. He was honored by many other scientific bodies around the world, and in 1907 received the highest award from the Royal Society of London—the oldest scientific body in history—which bestowed the Copley Medal on him.

In that same year, Michelson was awarded the Nobel Prize in physics, which was a great tribute not only to him but also to the United States since he became the first American ever to receive a Nobel Prize.

He died in Pasadena, California, in 1931, still experimenting, still trying to unlock the earth's secrets for the benefit of mankind. Like Einstein, he loved to play the violin, and also enjoyed relaxing with a paintbrush and easel. His book *Light Waves and Their Uses* has been acclaimed a modern scientific classic.

Had an ambitious seventeen-year-old immigrant boy from California not pressed the President of the United States for an interview and won an appointment to Annapolis, who knows whether the world as we know it today would be quite the same?

JOSHUA LEDERBERG

The Extraordinary Bacteriologist

HE WAS BORN IN MONTCLAIR, NEW JERSEY, but was raised in the Washington Heights neighborhood of upper Manhattan, not far from Columbia University. His father was an Orthodox rabbi, and young Joshua received a traditional Jewish upbringing.

His early interest in the world of science led him to attend the Stuyvesant High School, where the natural sciences and mathematics are stressed. At the age of nineteen he graduated from Columbia, and soon enrolled in the medical school attached to the university.

Lederberg's probing mind came to the attention of one of the leading bacteriologists of the time, Edward L. Tatum, who invited him to come to Yale and help in research—specifically genetic research of bacteria.

It was a happy choice for both Lederberg and Tatum, and the young scientist soon found his life's work in microbiology research. After receiving his doctoral degree in microbiology from Yale, Lederberg went to the University of Wisconsin, where he set up a department of medical genetics. Later he became head of a similar department at Stanford University in California.

In 1958, at the age of thirty-three, Dr. Joshua Lederberg was awarded the Nobel Prize in physiology and medicine together with Dr. Tatum and Dr. George Beadle. The award was bestowed for the work the three had done in discovering that all biological

reactions, including those in bacteria, are the result of genetic influence.

Working with powerful microscopes, the researchers found that even among the tiny cells of bacteria there is a system of genetic inheritance, just as there is in higher plant and animal life.

Subsequent studies conducted by Dr. Lederberg and others led to the discovery that where viruses invade bacteria, they often transmit additional characteristics, thus in effect leading to the development of a new strain of bacteria.

Although this may seem to be of marginal interest to the average person, it is of vital importance to cancer-research specialists since it means that a virus is capable of changing a normal cell into a malignant one.

Dr. Lederberg's pioneering work in the genetics of bacteria has helped to open up a whole new area of study, which it is hoped may one day help to find a cure for the scourge of cancer.

Always anxious to have the general public made more cognizant of new medical and scientific developments, Dr. Lederberg for a number of years wrote a weekly newspaper column titled "Science and Man," which was widely syndicated.

He has also taken a strong, personal interest in the scientific achievements of Israel's universities and research centers, reflecting perhaps his own genetic background: Not only was his father a rabbi but his family's genealogy shows a long line of rabbis, many of whom lived in Palestine long before the establishment of modern Israel.

In recent years Dr. Lederberg has expanded his studies to include the chemical origin and evolution of life, space biology, and the social consequences of genetic changes in humans. From 1961 to 1978 he directed the Kennedy Laboratories for Molecular Biology and Medicine.

In 1978 he was elected president of Rockefeller University in New York, the crowning achievement of his distinguished career. When the announcement of Dr. Lederberg's elevation to that prestigious post was made, Rockefeller University said that he was one of the pioneers who has transformed the "genetics of micro-organisms into a comprehensive field of research" that is invaluable for biomedical research. The scientific community is hopeful that one of the youngest Nobel laureates will continue to make vital contributions to mankind's knowledge of itself.

MORDECAI ANILEWICZ

He Led the Warsaw Ghetto Uprising

VISITORS TO ISRAEL have heard of a kibbutz named Yad Mordecai, but not everyone knows that it was named for a twenty-four-year-old Polish Jew whose heroism has been compared to that of the ancient Maccabees.

Mordecai Anilewicz was born in Poland in 1919. In his youth he was attracted to the Zionist movement and dreamed of the day when he and his friends could settle in Israel and help build a Jewish homeland based on the principles of social and economic justice. Those who knew him as a student, when he was about eighteen or nineteen, described him as a soft-spoken, gentle, and scholarly person who always showed an intense interest in economics. He was convinced that if the world's economic structure could be turned around, if poor people would have more funds to improve their lives, the world would be a better and more peaceful place to live in.

On the morning of September 1, 1939, the world awoke to learn that the Germans had launched a massive attack on Poland, which was the beginning of World War II. Mordecai tried to escape across the Polish-Rumanian border, hoping to reach Palestine, but he and his friends were stopped at the border and sent back to Warsaw. The Germans very quickly succeeded in reducing Poland to a state of virtual enslavement and soon turned their attention to the Jews.

There were at the time more than three million Jews in Poland, one of the largest communities in the world. Large segments of the population were unable to believe that the Nazi announcements of "death to the Jews" were real, but within a relatively short time, hundreds of thousands of Jews had been imprisoned in walled-in ghettos, labor camps, and concentration camps. When the Russians seized part of the western sectors of Poland in advance of the German invaders, thousands of more fortunate Polish Jews were rescued.

When young Mordecai found himself in the Warsaw ghetto, together with scores of thousands of other Jews, he knew that he had to do everything he could to help the inmates of the huge prison survive. He organized a system of food and clothing rationing, and set up classes for the small children. In mid-1942, nearly two years after the Nazi conquest of Poland, he and other Warsaw ghetto leaders learned what was happening to the Jews of Poland under the new German regime—they were being systematically murdered.

Plans were made to organize some kind of resistance movement, despite the obviously difficult obstacles. Anilewicz was named commander of the new, secret Jewish Fighting Organization, which was made up of people who were determined to fight back if the Germans tried to ship the Jews to death camps, as they knew they would.

Obtaining arms was a major problem, with some members of the Polish resistance movement willing to co-operate with the Jews but others utterly opposed. Gradually some arms were smuggled into the ghetto, and utmost secrecy had to be maintained about the whole operation since it was suspected, correctly, that there were informers among the ghetto inhabitants.

Mordecai Anilewicz, in his twenty-fourth year of life, in early 1943, had taken over the command of the resistance movement within the ghetto. He was no longer a studious type but a tough commander in a situation that called for resolute action. He and his fellow resistance leaders deeply regretted that they had waited some three years to organize their campaign of resistance to the Germans. They now knew that the only fate that awaited the vast majority of Jews in Poland and other parts of Europe under

Nazi domination was deliberate annihilation, and they were determined to fight back and to take as many of the enemy with them as possible to their graves.

Young men and women were taught how to fight with homemade weapons, as well as with the pitifully small number of real guns that had managed to reach the Jews inside the ghetto. On April 18, 1943, the first night of Passover, the resistance fighters under Mordecai's command were on the alert. There were more Jews in the ghetto at that time than normally since a number of Warsaw Jews who had been living outside the walls had sneaked back in in order to celebrate the Passover in a more Jewish environment.

Early in the morning of April 19 a heavily armed German force, including Latvian collaborators, invaded the ghetto and were met by a "hail of grenades, bottles, bombs, and rifle shots—and the only machine gun did not err," a report of the event noted, adding that the Nazis quickly withdrew from the ghetto area.

More military forces were thrown into the attack by the Germans, who also brought in artillery, which the Jews of course did not have. The battle raged for many hours, and at nightfall the Germans withdrew, giving the Jews a brief respite. At sundown some of the more observant Jews sat down to the traditional Passover Seder celebrations, which were conducted in bunkers.

The tempo of the fighting continued all through the balance of the month of April, and Jews and Germans lost their lives daily. On May 8, after weeks of fierce fighting, the Germans succeeded in learning the location of the command bunker from which Anilewicz and other leaders conducted the battles. To this day no one knows how they learned of the secret headquarters.

Surrounded by the Germans who had thrown gas into the bunker, the Jewish resistance leaders took their own lives rather than fall into the hands of the Nazis. One account says that Anilewicz committed suicide and another reports he died fighting. The German commandant of the battle against the ghetto regretted that he could not interrogate the leaders of the revolt, including Anilewicz.

The young Polish Jew was described by Emmanuel Ringleblum, who kept an invaluable diary of the events of the Warsaw Ghetto Uprising, as "one of the finest and noblest warriors, who from the beginning put his life at the service of his people."

The courage that Mordecai Anilewicz displayed served as a source of inspiration to other Jews caught in the Nazi trap, and later to the Israelis when they fought against invading Arab forces. A kibbutz in the northern part of the Negev in Israel, Yad Mordecai, was named for him—and, during the crucial battles between the beleaguered Israeli forces and the far larger Egyptian army attacking from the south in 1948, the kibbutz stood fast, preventing the planned assault on Tel Aviv.

A statue of Mordecai Anilewicz near the museum dedicated to the Warsaw Ghetto Uprising located in kibbutz Yad Mordecai shows him standing on the alert, grenade in hand, ready to resist any attack on his people.

CHAIM WEIZMANN

First President of Israel

EVERY CITY AND TOWN IN ISRAEL has a main street named for him. His name is synonymous with modern Zionism. He was the first President of Israel, serving for four years until his death at the age of seventy-eight. He was one of the few fortunate people in the world who dreamed of a great event and lived to see it come to fruition. His name was Chaim Weizmann, and today one of the foremost scientific research centers in the world bears his name, the Weizmann Institute of Science, located in Rehovot, Israel.

He was born in 1874 in a small town near Minsk, in Russia, one of fifteen children. Few Jewish boys (and practically no girls) had an opportunity to study beyond the simple classroom of the village, but young Chaim was determined to obtain a higher education. He went to Germany and studied biochemistry, and soon became caught up in the revolutionary new movement that Theodor Herzl had established—Zionism. Living in Germany, he could not forget the squalor and misery that existed for millions of Jews in eastern Europe, and he believed that only if there were a Jewish homeland would the persecution of Jews come to a permanent end.

He threw himself into the political, educational, fund-raising, and organizational work of the new movement, and soon his leadership qualities were recognized and he became one of the new, young leaders. Meanwhile, he continued to work in his chemistry

laboratory, and a few years later he was invited to come to England—a country he greatly admired—to teach at the University of Manchester.

In Palestine, then under Turkish rule, small groups of Jewish colonists had set up agricultural settlements and were struggling to turn the long-neglected land into fertile, productive soil. Weizmann realized that the country was small and poor in natural resources and that its chief hope for emerging as a modern, self-supporting nation lay in its becoming scientifically and technologically advanced, taking advantage of the many new technical breakthroughs that were beginning to transform all segments of society. His dream of a major scientific institution, in which skills and brain power would supplant large masses of land or great financial resources, took years to implement, but it was created and has grown into the prestigious Weizmann Institute. He was a practical man who also understood the need for creating a sound agricultural and industrial foundation for the future Jewish state and preached the need to devote great efforts toward these twin goals.

Most Zionist efforts were suspended when World War I broke out in 1914, although most Jews hoped for an Allied victory, while most Arabs wanted to see the German-Turkish side triumph. During the years that he was in England, Weizmann had made friends with a number of British political figures, including David Lloyd George, who became Prime Minister of England, and James Balfour, who served as Foreign Minister. He won them over to the idea of a Jewish state and made them understand that the Zionist movement would welcome England's help and protection in its formative years.

By 1917, while the war was still raging and England was having a difficult time producing munitions, Weizmann had discovered a way of manufacturing vital acetone (from ordinary chestnuts, which abounded in England), and the discovery helped immeasurably in the war effort. His influential friends were deeply grateful and said they would recommend that he be knighted. Weizmann declined the honor, pleading instead that the British government proclaim its readiness to support the idea of a Jewish homeland in Palestine. In November of that year the British issued the famous Balfour Declaration, which announced to the world that they were ready to help in the formation of a Jewish homeland—an announcement that Jews throughout the world saw as a major step forward in their nearly two thousand years of never-ending yearning for the re-establishment of their ancient homeland.

Weizmann became the world leader of the Zionist movement and devoted all his energies to realization of the dream of a modern, viable Jewish state. He traveled throughout the world, explaining his organization's work to world leaders, addressing mass meetings of Zionists, urging all-out support for the building up of the ancestral homeland. He especially emphasized the need for setting up modern schools and universities in Palestine and raising the intellectual levels of the small but growing Jewish population in the country.

The rise of Hitlerism saw an increase in the number of German Jews arriving in Palestine, and Weizmann and his fellow Zionist leaders were fearful that the numbers of uprooted and oppressed Jews would increase. They tried to alert the Jewish and world leaders of the day to the long-range menace of Nazism, but few chose to listen. After World War II began, one of Weizmann's sons volunteered for the Royal Air Force and was lost in combat. It was a black period for all Jews, but Weizmann did not allow himself to despair.

When the war ended and the realization of the calamity of the Nazi era impressed itself on the world, Weizmann journeyed to America, seeking the help of President Truman. The country he had admired and come to love, England, had issued a ban on further Jewish immigration to Palestine, and he was shattered. At the White House he succeeded in persuading Truman that the only humanitarian thing to do—following the deliberate destruction of six million Jews in Nazi-occupied Europe—was to throw the gates of Palestine wide open to the survivors. Truman agreed, and pleaded with the British to rescind their ban, but his appeal fell on deaf ears.

In 1947 the United Nations voted to partition Palestine (which had already been divided earlier, with the area east of the Jordan River going to the new kingdom of Jordan) into a Jewish and an Arab state. The United States supported the partition plan, thanks to the influence of Truman, who spoke in glowing terms of Weizmann, for whom he had developed a great affection.

Minutes after Israel proclaimed its statehood on May 14, 1948, the United States announced its recognition of the new nation. Weizmann went to Washington a few days later and told the President, "You will never know what this means to my people. We have waited and dreamed and worked for this moment for two thousand years. By recognizing the State of Israel, you have helped us take our place among the nations of the world. Your act will never be forgotten." A day earlier Weizmann had been elected the first President of Israel, and when the two Presidents now met in Washington, the Israeli leader presented Mr. Truman with a Scroll of the Law, a Torah, which was later placed in the Truman Library in Independence, Missouri.

During the four years that he served as President, Weizmann was in poor health, but he did everything he could to help the young nation in its first difficult years. Much of his time was devoted to the new scientific research center in Rehovot, which now became a center for the study of cancer research, nuclear physics, immunology, electronics, mathematics, and other new fields of scientific exploration.

When he died in 1952, he was buried near his home in Rehovot, within sight of the institute bearing his name, and the area has become a national shrine for the people of Israel. Although he had many disagreements with Zionist leaders over a period of nearly half a century, he was universally admired and loved for his complete dedication and for his lifelong role in bringing about the fulfillment of the Zionist dream.

One of the great disappointments of his life was his inability to reach a friendly understanding with the Arab leaders on future co-operation between the two peoples. He conferred with the outstanding leader of the Arabs, Emir Feisal, but could not win him over to a plan for a real accord between the Jews and the Arabs.

REBECCA GRATZ

A Life Dedicated to Others

SHE WAS LIKE AN AMERICAN PRINCESS, residing in a palatial home in Philadelphia soon after the establishment of the United States. Her beauty became world-famous, and many believed she was the model for Sir Walter Scott's heroine in the famous novel *Ivanhoe*.

Rebecca Gratz left a rich legacy of great works, and her name shines forth from the pages of American Jewish history. Yet despite her great beauty, comfortable circumstances, and the good works she established for the education and support of those in need, she had to overcome personal unhappiness to live a life of devotion to others.

She was born in 1781, just a few years after the infant United States of America came into being. She belonged to a large family, with many sisters and brothers, and her home was filled with excitement and happy times. Her father, Michael, had grown rich as the new nation grew and prospered. There was never a lack of anything in the Gratz household. The family home in Philadelphia was a center for Jewish and non-Jewish families, and tutors, servants, friends, and relatives were always coming and going.

The family was deeply devoted to the Jewish way of life, supporting religious education, giving comfort to the poor and needy, observing the Sabbath and the holidays and all the laws of a traditional Jewish household.

One day when Rebecca returned home from school, she found everyone in a mournful mood. Her mother's father, who lived with the family—an elderly man whose small *yarmulke* never left his head—sat in a corner, tears streaming down his bearded cheeks. Soon she was told what had happened: Her aunt, her mother's sister, had married a Gentile. For the Gratz family, it was as though the world had collapsed. Rebecca's mother made no attempt to hide the pain and grief she felt. The scene was imbedded on Rebecca's memory for all time. From that moment on, Rebecca's mother never mentioned her sister's name again; it was as though she had never existed.

As one by one Rebecca's sisters and brothers married and began to raise families, she devoted more and more time to caring for her growing number of nieces and nephews and enjoying the role of Aunt Rebecca. She felt confident that she would one day marry and have a family of her own.

Meanwhile, the Gratz family continued to prosper. Every morning Rebecca's father would recite his prayers, adding a small blessing for the bounty of America. He now owned a general store, traded in land and furs, and ran a kosher meat business that provided for the needs of the Jews in Philadelphia and up and down the coastal cities of the new nation.

In the course of time Rebecca met a young lawyer, Samuel Ewing, who loved to write and recite poetry. He was tall, handsome, gentle, and good company, and she enjoyed going to balls with him, much to the distress of her parents. They all knew that with all his fine qualities, he was not of their faith.

When he proposed marriage to her, confessing that he was madly in love with her, Rebecca knew that they could not see each other again. She told him as simply and as forcefully as she could that she could not abandon her religion, and that marriage was therefore out of the question. It was a painful thing for her to say, because she found herself, each time they went to a dance or a performance together, liking him more and more. But the memory of the deep hurt that her aunt had inflicted on her parents, especially on her mother and grandfather, could not be erased.

Years later, after Ewing had married and raised a family, he died at the age of thirty-nine. Rebecca went to the funeral and left three roses on his casket. His widow told her that he had told her a long time ago of his love for Rebecca and of how their difference of religion had prevented them from marrying.

Rebecca eventually got over her feelings for the young lawyer-poet and began to immerse herself in charitable works, serving as secretary for the Female Association for the Relief of Women and Children in Reduced Circumstances. Later she organized the Female Hebrew Benevolent Society and established the Philadelphia Orphan Asylum. She is perhaps best remembered for having founded and led the first Jewish Sunday school system in America.

As she grew older, Rebecca found satisfaction in helping others. She remained carefully observant of all the Jewish religious laws, and lived through the painful years of the Civil War, in which many of her nephews were involved. She suffered in the knowledge that her nephews were fighting against each other, since some were Union soldiers and others fought on the side of the Confederacy.

She was grateful when the war ended and the bloodshed finally came to an end. She felt that she had lived a full life, helping many strangers who needed help, giving much love and joy to her family.

She died at the age of eighty-eight, greatly mourned and always to be remembered as a beautiful lady with a noble spirit. Before she died, she wrote:

> I, Rebecca Gratz, of the city of Philadelphia, being of sound health of body and mind, advanced in the vale of years, declare this to be my last will and testament. I commit my spirit to God who gave it, relying on His mercy and redeeming love, and believing with a firm and perfect faith in the religion of my fathers.

Hear, O Israel, the Lord, our God, the Lord is one.

MOSHE DAYAN

Hero-Soldier Turned Diplomat

THE ONE-EYED MILITARY HERO whose eye patch has helped make him one of the best-known Israeli personalities in the world is a complex person, widely respected for his daring on the battlefield and for his unorthodox methods of dealing with the Arab populations, both those outside Israel and those living in territory occupied by Israel for more than a decade.

Moshe Dayan has served as Foreign Minister of Israel and as Minister of Agriculture, Minister of Defense, and Chief of Staff—but he despises diplomatic niceties and inevitably speaks his mind freely on all issues of the day, no matter how unpopular his opinions make him. For nearly three decades the people of Israel have loved and admired him and at times have turned against him, blaming him for their troubles. He is first and foremost a man of boldness, who insists that his own early years among Arab populations have given him an understanding of Israel's neighbors superior to that of most other Israeli leaders.

Dayan was born in Deganyah Aleph in 1915 and raised in the agricultural colony of Nahalal. When he was only twelve, he was already standing guard against Arab marauders, but that did not prevent him from forming lasting friendships with Arab youngsters in the area, from whom he learned to speak Arabic. Like most young Palestinian Jews of the time, he joined the underground

Haganah defense organization, where his natural qualities of leadership were quickly recognized. During an outbreak of Arab rioting in 1936 he served as a special policeman in the Galilee and Jezreel Valley sectors, helping to guard isolated Jewish settlements. By 1938—at the age of twenty-three—he commanded a group that had been trained in nighttime fighting tactics by the British general Orde Wingate, who had become a dedicated supporter of the Zionist cause. A year later, he and forty-two other Haganah men were arrested by the British authorities for illegal arms possession, and he was sentenced to ten years' imprisonment in the Acre jail. Two years later, however, the British released him and his fellow inmates, on condition that they lead a scouting expedition into nearby Syria, where pro-Nazi Vichy French forces were threatening to invade Palestine from the north. It was during this period, when he held a telescope to his eye while on duty in Syria, that a once-in-a-million shot penetrated the telescope, driving shattered pieces of glass into his left eye and blinding him in one eye for life. (He has worn the eye patch since then because of an inability to wear an artificial eye.)

In the 1948 War of Independence that followed Israel's proclamation of statehood, Dayan became commander of a mechanized battalion that helped liberate the area around Lydda and later stopped the Egyptian forces attacking from the south en route to Tel Aviv. Later he was named commander of the vital Jerusalem front, where he managed to achieve a cease-fire with the Arab Legion. In the ensuing years he was named to head the southern and then the northern front, and took some time out to study military strategy in England. In 1953, at the age of thirty-eight, he was appointed Chief of Staff of the Israel armed forces.

In the course of the next two years terrorist attacks against Israeli settlements began to increase. Children in school and worshipers in synagogues lost their lives in these sneak raids, which were carried out by Arab guerrillas, or *fedayeen*. Dayan organized a series of reprisal attacks against known terrorist bases, but the raids continued.

In 1956, a week after Egypt, Syria, and Jordan signed an agreement pledging their united armed forces to the goal of destroying Israel, Dayan mounted the Sinai Campaign, which swept the Egyptian forces out of the Sinai. Heavy pressure from the

United States, however, forced the Israelis to give up the area they had seized. Two years later Dayan resigned from the military leadership of Israel and decided to enter political life.

After studying at the Hebrew University, he was elected to the Knesset and later was named Minister of Agriculture under Prime Minister David Ben-Gurion. By 1964, in a disagreement with the new Prime Minister, Levi Eshkol, he resigned his cabinet post but remained a member of the Israeli parliament. He spent many months of 1966 as a military correspondent for a Tel Aviv newspaper in Vietnam, observing the hard-fought battles that were being waged in that part of the world between the Americans and South Vietnamese against the Viet Cong. His dispatches were translated and distributed to newspapers throughout the world.

In May 1967 a new threat loomed over Israel. The Egyptians had massed heavy concentrations of tanks on Israel's southern border, while bellicose warnings were simultaneously coming from the Syrians in the north. Prime Minister Levi Eshkol, who also held the post of Minister of Defense, ordered a full mobilization of Israel's reserves, and for days tens of thousands of Israeli troops waited for the promised attack. Public opinion in Israel was not happy however with having Eshkol as Defense Minister, and there was a spontaneous outbreak of clamoring for Dayan to be invited back to the cabinet to assume that key post. About a week before the outbreak of the Six Day War, Dayan was named Minister of Defense, which restored public confidence in the country's ability to resist the expected attack.

Together with the Chief of Staff, Yitzhak Rabin, Dayan conducted the Six Day War, which began with a devastating attack on Arab air forces on June 5; and before the week was out, the Egyptians had been routed in the south, the Syrians in the north, and the Jordanians in the west. It was one of the most brilliantly executed military achievements in history. Almost as soon as the fighting ended, Dayan became administrator of the territories occupied by the Israelis, and he set up a military government that gave as much autonomy to the local Arab populations as possible. He also instituted the program whereby travel and trade between the Arab countries and the administered territories was encouraged.

Dayan also promoted free movement of Arab visitors to Israel from the occupied territories, believing that Arab tourists who would see Israel for themselves would come away with a determination to break down the enmity between the Arabs and Jews and begin to move toward reconciliation.

In the 1973 Yom Kippur War, in which Egypt and Syria attacked Israel, causing large numbers of casualties, Dayan was among those blamed for the heavy loss of life. The true sequence of events prior to the war, when Prime Minister Golda Meir was advised not to order a full-scale mobilization, will probably never be known, but the Israeli public turned its fury on Dayan as well as on a number of other military and political leaders in Israel. In the two years that followed the 1973 war, Dayan hardly appeared in public in Israel, so bitter was the animosity against him of Israeli families who had suffered casualties.

In 1977, when a new government led by Menahem Begin came to power in Israel, Dayan was named Foreign Minister despite the fact that he had been a lifelong member of an opposition political party. Although he continues to avoid the typical diplomat's methods of carrying out his duties, he is credited with having helped reduce tensions in the Middle East through secret meetings with top Arab representatives.

Dayan has said repeatedly that war cannot bring peace to the Middle East and that only a face-to-face political agreement with the neighboring Arab countries will achieve true peace. He now seems to be dedicating all of his remarkable talents to that end, and has been visiting the world's leaders to try to enlist their support for the creation of a new, peaceful era in the Middle East.

LOUIS D. BRANDEIS

Supreme Court Justice

PRESIDENT FRANKLIN ROOSEVELT used to call him affectionately "Isaiah," and there was about him an aura of the ancient
prophet. Many compared him—in manner, appearance, views—to
Lincoln. As a young attorney in Boston, he came to be known as
the "people's advocate" because he always seemed to be defending
the rights of the poor, the downtrodden, and those who could
never hope to approach high-priced lawyers for help.

Despite stiff opposition in the Senate, which debated the issue
for four months, he became the first Jew to serve on the Supreme
Court, a position he filled with distinction. Many believed that,
had he not been Jewish, he would certainly have been named Chief
Justice. He was without a doubt one of the great Jewish personalities produced in America.

He was born in 1856 and raised in Louisville, Kentucky, and
as a small child remembered seeing his mother helping in the local
canteen, providing food and drink to Union soldiers during the
Civil War. His parents had been immigrants from Bohemia (part
of Czechoslovakia today), and he grew up in a home where the
needs of the impoverished and the ill-treatment of many social and
economic groups were genuine sources of concern.

After graduating from a local high school at fifteen, Brandeis
entered Harvard Law School and at the age of twenty became a

lawyer. Together with a classmate, he started practicing in Boston, and by the end of a decade he had achieved a reputation as a clear-headed, courageous attorney who cared deeply about such issues as shortening workers' hours, child labor, and workmen's compensation. He and his wife, Alice, lived simple, frugal lives, and he was happy to be able to help those less fortunate than he.

He loved everything American, particularly after having spent a few years studying in a school in Germany. Although he admitted that the scholarly levels in Germany were high, he hated the disciplinary methods employed. "In Louisville," he once said, "you could whistle." He never denied that he was Jewish, nor did he ever personally feel any exposure to overt anti-Semitism. He contributed to local Jewish charities on a purely philanthropic basis, but until past the age of fifty he was isolated from the mainstream of the Jewish community.

All that changed in 1910, when he was asked to come down from Boston to New York and arbitrate a major clash in the garment industry between the employers and workers. For the first time in his life, he got to know East European Jews, most of whom spoke Yiddish, many of whom declared themselves to be Zionists, and most of whom he came to admire for their passionate interest in the welfare of their coreligionists.

He began to read Jewish history, and made inquiries about the then brand-new Zionist movement launched by Theodor Herzl at the first World Zionist Congress in Basel, Switzerland. An early Zionist leader, Jacob de Haas, who was the editor of a Jewish newspaper in Boston, helped influence Brandeis' thinking, too.

In the course of time, Brandeis announced that he was a Zionist, explaining, "My approach to Zionism was through Americanism. In time, practical experience and observation convinced me that Jews were by reason of their traditions and their character peculiarly fitted for the attainment of American ideals. Gradually it became clear to me that to be good Americans we must be better Jews, and to be better Jews we must become Zionists. Jewish life cannot be preserved and developed, assimilation cannot be averted, unless there be established in the fatherland a center from which the Jewish spirit may radiate and give to the Jews scattered throughout the world that inspiration which springs from the memories of a great past and the hope of a great future."

When World War I broke out, he became head of the Zionist movement in the United States. He was a close friend of President Woodrow Wilson and high American officials, and is credited with securing support for the Balfour Declaration and for the British Mandate over a territory with adequate boundaries.

Despite his judicial bearing, he was essentially a man of action and of logic. In 1915, while the war raged in Europe, a threat of famine hung over the people of Asia Minor. He organized a nationwide campaign, appealing to all people to help stave off a disaster. By March, two months after the drive had been announced, a mercy ship filled with nine hundred tons of food sailed for Jaffa from Philadelphia, preventing a great loss of life.

As the war drew to an end and the defeat of Germany was in sight, Brandeis addressed a large Zionist meeting, urging his audience to look ahead to the peace. "By battling for the Zionist cause," he declared, "the American ideal of democracy, of social justice, and of liberty will be given wider expression. By concrete action, the prayer of twenty centuries will be made to come true."

He visited Palestine soon after the war ended and came away with mixed feelings: The spirit of the idealistic pioneers exhilarated him, but the sight of the disease-ridden malaria swamps filled him with sorrow. He returned to the United States more determined than ever to turn the Zionist movement into an instrumentality of practical support for the early pioneering efforts, and stressed the need for modern capital investments in industry as well as in agriculture.

As a justice of the Supreme Court, he gave enormous prestige to the Zionist movement in the United States and did not hesitate to debate the wealthier elements of the community who feared that their overt support for creating a Jewish homeland would subject them to criticism from non-Jewish Americans.

He asserted, "I have been to a great extent separated from Jews. I am very ignorant in things Jewish. But recent experiences, public and professional, have taught me this: I find Jews possessed of those very qualities which we of the twentieth century seek to develop in our struggle for justice and democracy, a deep moral feeling which makes them capable of noble acts, a deep sense of the brotherhood of man, and a high intelligence, the fruit of three thousand years of civilization.

"These experiences have made me feel that the Jewish people have something which should be saved for the world, that the Jewish people should be preserved, and that it is our duty to pursue that method of saving which most promises success."

On the bench, Brandeis became famous as a moralist and teacher. Even during periods in American history when members of Congress were working to defeat new social legislation, he and his close friend and colleague, Chief Justice Oliver Wendell Holmes, explained that the U. S. Constitution was not restricted to a single economic credo and that therefore prevention of progressive social legislation was contrary to the spirit of the Founding Fathers.

His judicial decisions not only backed such measures as minimum wage laws, price controls, and protection of labor unions against injunctions but also emphasized the need for sharing power between the federal government and the individual states in the Union.

At the age of eighty-five, Brandeis retired from the Supreme Court, having left an indelible mark on American history. In Israel a kibbutz, *Ein Hashofet* ("Spring of the Judge"), was named for him, and in Waltham, Massachusetts, not far from Boston, where he began his career, a Jewish-sponsored university bears his name.

LENA KUCHLER

"Mother" of a Hundred Children

THERE IS A WOMAN LIVING IN ISRAEL who is looked upon as the mother of some one hundred children—and the grandmother of many more scores of young Israeli children. Indeed, she also has "children" and "grandchildren" in the United States and in other parts of the world.

And yet, in point of fact, this remarkable woman is the mother of only one lovely young lady, Shira. The woman's name is Lena Kuchler, and in the annals of the Jewish people she will always be remembered as a true heroine of an era that was marked by unparalleled brutality.

The story begins at the time of the outbreak of World War II, in 1939. Lena Kuchler was a young Jewish wife and mother when Hitler's army invaded Poland, where she and her family lived. She was an educator, specializing in child psychology.

The panic that followed on the heels of the German invasion, the roundups of Jews and their imprisonment in camps and ghettos, the attempts to hide from the ruthless enemy, the systematic massacres—all these have been well chronicled. It was a disastrous time for all people in Poland, but for the Polish Jews it was a time of utmost peril: The Nazis were bent on carrying out their threat of extinction of all Jews in Europe.

Lena and her family sought refuge in a small village, most of whose residents were not Jewish. At one point she left her small child with a Gentile family for safekeeping; her husband decided to try to evade the Nazis by hiding out in the woods, and she herself opted to live as a Christian maid. Her blond hair and Slavic appearance led her to believe that this was the best way to outsmart the Germans.

She found employment with a family living in a distant rural area, where she came to be regarded as a Christian Polish woman who did her job well.

This was how she spent the early years of the war, afraid to breathe the truth about her identity, constantly worried about her small child, wondering about the fate of her husband, her family, her friends. Although she was in an isolated community, she nevertheless began to hear of the unceasing massacre of Jews throughout Nazi-occupied territories, including Poland. She found herself living as though in suspended animation. She waited for the nightmare to come to an end.

Alone, at night, she would lie on her cot, tears filling her eyes, wondering, worrying, knowing that she could do nothing except what she was doing—remaining in hiding from the angel of death who wore a swastika on his uniform.

The days stretched into months, the months into years—and then, one day, from the west, Russian troops began to overrun the farm where she had been living in limbo, a self-imprisoned survivor, and at last she was free to look for her family.

With incredible difficulties she made her way back home, while all around her the fighting continued, although gradually it became clear that it was only a matter of time before the Nazi war machine was destroyed and the Nazi reign of evil and terror came to an end.

She returned home and found devastation. Her parents, her husband, her child—all had "disappeared" in the giant graveyard the Nazis had dug in the territory they seized. She was thrown into deep shock—physical, mental, emotional. Lena became a broken person, hating herself for having survived while virtually everyone else had perished.

But there were some other survivors after all, the so-called *shearith hapleitah*. Children of varying ages, who had been kept hidden and alive in monasteries and convents by kindly priests and nuns, now emerged from their hiding places, proclaiming in their own way that they were Jews. Other children, who had been hidden on remote farms by peasants who had hoped to be rewarded handsomely for their lifesaving, now found themselves thrown out once it became known that the parents—and the parents' funds— would never be seen again.

These sick, emaciated, destitute children were brought together in a Jewish communal residence, and an effort was made to heal them. Funds and supplies were made available by a number of Jewish relief organizations, but the situation was desperate and called for much more than money.

The surviving children had ceased being children. They did not sing or laugh or play. They looked forlorn, abandoned, hopeless. Many were ill, suffering from a wide variety of diseases. All of them were undernourished. Some of the older ones had taken to stealing, and felt no compunctions about doing so.

It was around this time that the local aid organization discovered Lena. She was, after all, a child psychologist and an educator. She knew about children. She had suffered too. The group's leaders persuaded her to try to help the children in any and every way she could.

Reluctant at first, she slowly overcame her inner sense of hopelessness and bitterness and began to work, trying to rebuild the lives of the children put in her care. Instinctively she knew that if she could help them, she would be rebuilding her own life, too.

She organized classes, recruited medical help, found a clean mountain-resort residence in the Zakopane area where the children could breathe fresh air and eat nourishing food, and where—she hoped—they could begin to learn, and to sing, to play, to hope.

By 1946, nearly a year after the war ended, the miracle had begun to work: Some one hundred children in her care were living in Zakopane, and each day saw them gaining daily, in their health, in their minds, in their spirits.

And then one day the little private world they had created in the Zakopane mountain resort was shattered when news arrived of an outbreak of a postwar series of pogroms against the surviving Jews in Poland. This was still two years before there was an Israel, but Lena decided that the best hope for her children was to get them, somehow, to Palestine.

A few weeks after the first pogroms erupted in Poland, the

children's residence in Zakopane was attacked, with Lena and a number of the older children defending themselves and the younger children until help arrived.

Soon after, without requisite official documents, Lena led her children, stealthily and unofficially, across the border into Czechoslovakia, and eventually to southern France, from where shiploads of Jews were being smuggled to Palestine despite the ban on any new Jewish immigration imposed by the British Mandatory power.

Eventually, Lena led her family of one hundred children to Palestine, shortly before the Jewish community there established the State of Israel. The vast majority of the children have grown up in Israel, have found jobs, married, and look upon Lena Kuchler as their mother—and *their* children regard her as their grandmother.

Lena remarried in Israel, where she gave birth to a daughter. She works in her profession of child psychology, seeking to help children who need guidance and support. Nearly every day the mail brings news from her children, none of whom can ever forget that she led them across the threshold of despair to hope and a new life.

NAHUM SOKOLOW

Journalist Turned Politician

NOT TOO MANY JOURNALISTS become great political leaders, but Nahum Sokolow did just that. He was a prolific writer and a passionate speaker, and devoted his entire life to the dream of the Jewish people restored to their ancient homeland.

He was born in Poland in 1859 and received a traditional Jewish and a general education. As a teen-ager he was already contributing articles and essays to the new Hebrew daily *Ha-Tzfira*, and soon he was named its editor. His large following of readers included those who did not agree with him on Zionism, and he constantly sought to convert them to his thinking. He also discovered that he could deliver talks before large audiences that would stir his listeners and win them over to the Zionist cause, and soon he became a Zionist orator much in demand, meanwhile continuing to produce not only newspaper articles and reportage but also books, including a Hebrew-language biography of Spinoza and the beginnings of a massive Hebrew dictionary.

In Palestine the early settlers in Jaffa had decided to establish a new, modern Jewish city nearby and asked his help in choosing a name. Having recently translated Herzl's idyllic novel *Altneuland* ("Old-New Land") into Hebrew under the title *Tel Aviv*, which means "Hill (or mound of ruins) of Spring," symbolizing the old and the new, he proposed that the new city carry this name, and the suggestion was accepted. Tel Aviv today, of course, is Israel's largest city.

One of the great achievements of Sokolow's life was helping win over the British Government to the support of the Zionist movement, which was expressed in the issuance of the Balfour Declaration in 1917. Negotiations with the British authorities were carried on by Chaim Weizmann, at the time head of the Zionists in England, and by Sokolow, who then represented the World Zionist Organization. Sokolow first had to obtain assurances of support from France, Italy, and the Vatican before the British would issue their declaration, and he succeeded in doing so.

Soon after the death of Herzl, Sokolow became secretary-general of the World Zionist Organization and remained at that post until 1931, when he was named president of the organization, a position he held until his death in 1936. As his efforts to expand the Zionist movement continued, Sokolow gradually emerged as a leading statesman of the growing organization. His home in London became a center for British diplomats favorable to the Zionist cause, and among his friends were Artur Rubinstein, the pianist, who practiced in his living room, and the painter Leonard Pasternak (father of the Nobel laureate Boris Pasternak), whose portrait of Sokolow has remained a centerpiece of the London home where Sokolow's daughter still lives.

In tribute to Sokolow's journalistic background, the Tel Aviv press center has been named Beit Sokolow. For a number of years there has been a movement under way to set up a special archive in Jerusalem to house Sokolow's writings and his library. Chaim Nachman Bialik, the great modern Hebrew poet, once said of Sokolow's work that it was so vast it would take three hundred camels to assemble it all in one place.

After the establishment of Israel, Sokolow's remains were transferred to Jerusalem and reburied near the final resting place of Herzl and other founding fathers of Israel.

GERARD SWOPE

For Israel's Future Engineers

NOWADAYS THERE ARE JEWISH ENGINEERS GALORE. Jewish young men and women interested in entering virtually any branch of the vast world of engineering know that the doors of MIT, Cal Tech, and scores of other important educational institutions specializing in the engineering sciences are wide open to them, and admittance is based on ability and academic standing.

But this was not always so. Eighty or ninety years ago (and until even more recently than that), the field of engineering did not take kindly to Jewish applicants. Some students, like their colleagues in medicine, went abroad to study; some fought valiantly to be admitted, and eventually won their battle; some changed their names in the hope that their Jewish origins would escape notice; and some went to the Hebrew Technical Institute in New York, which flourished for a period, and is still active in providing scholarships for needy students.

One of these would-be engineers was a brilliant young man born in Missouri in 1872, the grandson of a rabbi. The boy's name was Gershon Schwab. There was no doubt in his mind what he wanted to do with his life—engineering, especially the growing new field of electrical engineering, was his passion, and he was determined to attain his maximum potential.

He left his home and went east, to Cambridge, Massachusetts, the home of MIT and Harvard. In the course of the move, he altered his name, and his MIT application was approved. The student from Missouri known now as Gerard Swope turned in first-rate work, and when he graduated from MIT as an engineer, it was with top honors. A brilliant future was predicted for him.

He found a job in a small company, and very soon began to rise to ever-increasing levels of responsibility. The fact that he was a Jew had been all but erased from his mind. He concentrated on building his promising career. The young engineer's talents as an administrator were soon revealed, as was his ability to speak before audiences of investors and businessmen.

One day he found himself in a courtroom defending his company in an industrial dispute, arguing his case against the giant General Electric firm. When the trial was over and GE had lost, a strange thing happened—the General Electric people offered the young engineering executive a bigger job than he held at the time in his own firm. He decided to accept.

He rose quickly in the ranks of General Electric, and in the course of time became its president and chief executive officer, a position he was to retain for many years, leading the company upward and onward in the expanding fields of energy, and machinery and appliances based on electrical power. The young man, born Gershon Schwab but now known only as Gerard Swope, had certainly made it big. For all intents and purposes, he lived the life of a non-Jew.

He married a Gentile woman. Children were born and reared; everything was fine and everyone was happy. But there is an old saying that truth is stranger than fiction: Who could really know what went on in the heart and mind of this major American industrial executive?

One wonders how this grandson of a rabbi reacted to scenes of Yiddish-speaking Jewish refugees fleeing from eastern Europe, trying to make a new life for themselves in America. How did he feel when he picked up his newspaper in November 1917 and read that the British government had proclaimed its readiness to support the establishment of a Jewish homeland in Palestine? And in the early 1930s, when the scourge of Nazism threatened to take over all of civilization, how did he respond to scenes of his fellow Jews being driven into concentration camps or locked up in ghettos? We shall never know precisely, because he is dead now, but something must have stirred within him; somehow the tiny spark of his

Jewishness must have remained alive, even though practically no one knew that this powerful figure in American economic life was himself a Jew.

And then on impulse he went one evening to hear a talk by a New York lawyer, Abraham Tulin, a lifelong Zionist, on the geopolitical possibilities that confronted the world after the end of World War II. The speaker wove into his talk the hopes that then existed for the new, barely two-year-old State of Israel. Something in that talk fanned that tiny spark of Jewishness in the executive's heart, making it glow just a little brighter.

He invited Tulin to lunch; they talked at length and became friends. The president of General Electric then told his new friend what almost no one knew—that he was himself a Jew. Now in his late seventies, with his children grown and on their own, he felt he would like to "do something" for the people he belonged to and from whom he had estranged himself for most of his life.

The attorney was an active leader of a small American group that was providing support for a small, still struggling engineering school in Israel, the Technion–Israel Institute of Technology in Haifa. Cautiously, he suggested that his particular institution was perhaps a vehicle through which Swope could provide greatly needed help to Israel, which was in urgent need of a steady stream of modern, well-trained engineers.

The idea appealed to Swope, and soon wheels began to turn. He paid a visit to Israel in the early years when food rationing was in force, new immigrants were still living in tents, and the chief assets of the country were hope and courage. He visited the small campus of the Technion and was shown land that had been set aside for construction of a new network of classrooms, laboratories, workshops, libraries, and dormitories for a vastly enlarged campus. He met with David Ben-Gurion, the Prime Minister, and talked with fellow engineers, students, and Technion faculty members.

He toured the country, seeing with his own eyes places that he dimly remembered hearing about in his early youth—Jerusalem, Beersheba, Galilee, Ashkelon. He spent time visiting the new immigrants, among them survivors of the concentration camps, whose arms remained tattooed with the numbers burned into their flesh by the Nazis.

He returned to the United States, his mind made up about what he was going to do. He told his lawyer friend that he did not want to have any buildings named for him; he wanted instead to help students acquire an engineering education. He had become a very rich man, and he had decided to provide amply for his children (his wife had died) and then to leave the remainder of his estate to the Technion to become a perpetual source of aid to needy students and to attract the very best faculty members possible.

There was no lack of complicated legal tax problems in the decision, but these were overcome under Tulin's guidance as a legal adviser. Eventually a fund of more than eight million dollars was established, which became the basis of the Technion's scholarship fund. It is now valued at many millions of dollars, and has already provided help for many hundreds of students.

There is no doubt that in the course of time thousands of students in future generations will be aided to obtain an engineering education at the Technion because a stilled Jewish voice cried out in the heart of one man.

HERMAN WOUK

Literary Luminary

THE NAME OF HERMAN WOUK is known and admired in every part of the world. His books have been translated into numerous languages, and he was awarded the Pulitzer Prize for his memorable novel of World War II *The Caine Mutiny*.

He is not only an observant Jew but one who has returned to a traditional Jewish way of life after having been exposed to a secular, irreligious environment in his college years and while he was active as an advertising and radio writer. He has been a visiting professor of English at Yeshiva University and has actively supported synagogues and educational institutions both in the United States and Israel.

In addition to his best-selling novels, he has written a book titled *This Is My God*, in which he undertakes to explain his own faith in the Jewish way of life—a book that has remained in print for nearly a generation and that has undoubtedly influenced Jewish men and women to take a new look at their religious heritage.

Wouk was born in New York in 1915. He was a successful radio writer for some six years before entering the Navy in World War II. He served in the Pacific for four years, an experience that he used to produce *The Caine Mutiny*. Among his other books are *Marjorie Morningstar, Youngblood Hawke, The Winds of War,* and *War and Remembrance*.

He has declared himself to be a religious Jew, aware of the fact that his vast reputation as a novelist may influence some members of the current and newer generation of Jews, especially in the United States. In *This Is My God* he wrote:

> Judaism is part of my life and of my family's life. . . . Religious people tend to encounter, among those who are not, a cemented certainty that belief in God is a crutch for the weak and the fearful. It would be just as silly to assert that disbelief in God is a crutch for the immoral and the ill-read. . . . I believe the survival of the Jewish people looks like the hand of Providence in history, and I also believe in the law of Moses as the key to our survival. . . . I believe it is our lot to live and serve in our old identity, until the promised day when the Lord will be one and his name one in all the earth. I think the extinction of Jewish learning and Jewish faith would be a measureless tragedy.

Wouk has established at the religiously oriented Bar-Ilan University in Israel a student scholarship in memory of his grandfather, Rabbi Mendel Leib Levine, whom he has described as follows:

> His lifetime of ninety-four years stretched from the last days of Abraham Lincoln to the first years of the nuclear era. He served as a Jewish jurist and minister under czarism and communism, in the freedom of America, and in the reborn land of Israel, where his bones lie.

Compared with other well-known authors, Wouk is a relatively private person. He is a daily worshiper at an Orthodox synagogue in Washington, where he lives, and devotes time each day to the study of the Talmud. He does not enjoy the lecture circuit and does not usually like to address large gatherings, even if they are for worthy causes which he fully supports.

On the rare occasions when he consents to speak to a Jewish fund-raising meeting, the only condition that he stipulates is that the food served be strictly kosher. At the time of their marriage, his wife was a Gentile, but she has since become a convert to Judaism and shares her husband's strong convictions about traditional Judaism.

ISRAEL BAAL SHEM TOV

Master of the Good Name

HE WAS BORN IN 1700 in a small *shtetl* in Poland, the kind of community in which very small boys, sometimes no older than five or six, could be seen at the break of dawn rushing off to their daily religious-school classes. When he was himself no more than about twelve, and an orphan who was cared for by the community as a whole, Israel ben Eliezer—who many years later was to become known as Israel Baal Shem Tov—used to escort the young boys to class every morning (except, of course, on the Sabbath, when everyone went to services in the synagogue).

People in the town noticed something different as soon as the young man became the official escort of the young students. The boys, even at an early hour, before they had had much more than a morsel of bread and a few swallows of tea, would march down the unpaved road to school singing, smiling, laughing as though they were going to a party. It seems that young Israel had begun to teach the students that everything around them—the rising sun in the early hours of the day, the singing of birds along the way, the smell of fresh-cut hay in the nearby fields, indeed everything in the world—was beautiful, God-given, and deserved to be greeted with joy and song. This is how he had begun to understand the world around him, and he began to explain his ideas to the boys in his care—and apparently they liked what they heard and preferred to sing and smile rather than proceed to school in a somber, serious manner as they had been taught to do previously.

This philosophy that the young man developed remained with him all his life, and in the course of time he became the founder of a Jewish religious movement which stressed that the blessings of the world around us should be seen and appreciated, and admired in song. The movement eventually became known as the Hasidic movement, and those who belonged were known as Hasidim, or "Pious Ones." There are today followers of the Hasidic philosophy in all parts of the world, who have shown that song and dance can make people as appreciative of Judaism as a lifetime of study. The Hasidim do not believe in fancy clothes or expensive homes or cars, but rather that every Jewish family should have the minimum needed for a decent standard of life, and should devote some time to study and much time to joyous song, prayer, and enjoyment of life. Of course, they also stress the importance of observing each and every commandment of Jewish religious life, and have even added a few customs and practices of their own.

When he was about eighteen, Israel ben Eliezer was given the job of *shamash* or sexton of the local synagogue. His job was to take care of the books used for study and worship, to call people to the various sections of the reading of the Torah, and to welcome strangers who would drop in and find a resting place in the synagogue for the night.

He was not a scholar by nature, and some people also said he was "strange," for he never tired of talking of the beauty and wonder of nature and of the foolishness of trying to make money so as to have a bigger house or a newer carriage. A few years passed, and he tired of his job as a *shamash* and began to wander around the countryside, sleeping in various synagogues, dressed as a woodcutter, and making friends of the Christian peasants whom he met and with whom he sometimes camped.

Eventually he married the daughter of a respected rabbi, even though he himself was not a learned man and it was against tradition for a rabbi's daughter to marry someone who was relatively uneducated. But there was something in the eyes of the young man that attracted the girl's father when he first met Israel, and Hannah, the bride-to-be, agreed to her father's wish that they marry. Deep in her heart she believed that her husband, despite his rough clothing and simple ways, must really be a righteous, saintly person.

For a few years the young couple lived in a poor hut in the mountains, hardly able to scrape out a living. Later, Hannah's brother, Rabbi Gershon, bought an inn for the young couple so they they could live more comfortably. Both Israel and Hannah were well suited to their new business, making the guests who stayed with them as comfortable and welcome as possible. Most of the work, however, fell on Hannah's shoulders, because her husband often spent long hours in the nearby woods, deep in thought, and sometimes praying alone in the fields for hours at a time.

There was one thing that people began to discover in Israel—a sympathetic listener. They came to him from the nearby countryside, explaining their troubles and problems, asking for his advice and guidance. Everyone seemed to find in him a source of wisdom and comfort, and his own strong faith in God helped many people overcome their own personal and family troubles.

Gradually he came to be known as Israel Baal Shem Tov, or "Israel, the Master of the Good Name." He began to visit nearby communities, to encourage Jews who were downhearted, to assure them that they were all holy and loved in the eyes of God, and so long as they lived as good, God-fearing people, all would be well. Soon the reputation of the Baal Shem Tov spread far and wide, and before long those who agreed with his views had organized the Hasidic movement.

Although there were many Jews who disapproved of the group's emphasis on joy in study and prayer, the movement grew very quickly. Visiting a service of the Hasidim meant seeing men and women profoundly immersed in prayer, singing and swaying with a sense of closeness to God that was quite different from the more formal services of most other Jews. The Hasidim looked upon the Baal Shem Tov as a *rebbe,* a truly righteous leader whose personal example inspired them to seek to lead lives of simplicity and afforded them an opportunity to become more and more in tune with the spirit of the Torah.

Israel Baal Shem Tov never wrote any books, but everything he ever said was remembered and repeated, so that every Hasid after a while could cite his words of wisdom as a source of guidance.

When the Baal Shem Tov died in 1760, he left behind him a movement of tens of thousands of Hasidic followers, and soon there grew up other Rebbes who preached the importance of personal commitment to God and who denied that intense study was the only way for Jews to attain the highest rung on the ladder that would lead to a fully rewarding life.

One of the leading Hasidic leaders in the world today is the Lubavitcher Rebbe, whose headquarters are in Brooklyn, New York. There are several hundred thousand Jews who are known as Lubavitch Hasidim scattered throughout the world, and although they now encourage study to a far greater degree than did the early followers of the Baal Shem Tov, the basic philosophy of the group has not changed. That is why a visit to a Hasidic synagogue or to a *farbrengung*, a kind of lecture on the Torah accompanied by much singing, is a very special experience.

The followers of the Hasidic movement managed, during more than sixty years of the Soviet Union's determined campaign to wipe out all forms of religion, to continue to live as observant Jews, although they had to do so in complete secrecy. Several thousand of these Soviet Hasidim have managed to reach Israel and the United States, where they now follow their traditional way of life without fear of interference.

One of the frequently quoted phrases of Israel Baal Shem Tov is, "Whoever lives in joy does his Creator's will. It is the goal of my whole life on earth to show my brethren, by living example, how one may serve God with merriment and rejoicing. He who is full of joy is full of love for his fellow men and all fellow creatures."

AVRAHAM YOFFE

Keeper of the Animals

ALTHOUGH JEWS AS A GROUP are not usually known as an animal-loving people, Jewish tradition has always kept a careful eye out for the welfare of all creatures. The Talmud teaches that you "should not eat before you have fed your animal." The Bible orders that "you shall not muzzle the ox when it treads corn."

In Israel today there is a man obsessed with a mission: to protect the country's wildlife. A former general in the Israeli army, he has persuaded the government to set aside four per cent of the scarce land area of that small country to provide natural reserve areas for animals that might otherwise become extinct. One could say that Avraham Yoffe has put down his sword and replaced it with a network of nature reserves, where rare animals are encouraged to live and flourish.

In the vast Negev region in the southern part of Israel, a tract of ten thousand acres of land known as Hai-Bar South has been cordoned off for animals, including such rare creatures as the Nubian ibex. Antelopes, gazelles, and other animals are provided with food and are carefully protected from hunters.

Yoffe heads Israel's Nature Reserves Authority, which is dedicated not only to safeguarding the country's wildlife but also to protecting anything else of nature—such as plants, flowers, trees, and birds—that are considered in need of special guarding. A placard from the Authority warns all people against interfering with the natural growth and development of a particular object—in some cases, only a single tree standing alone in the desert.

While the huge Sinai Peninsula is strictly speaking not Israeli territory, it has been under Israel's occupation for more than a decade, and Yoffe has instituted many steps to assure that the area is not allowed to become a hunter's paradise. Like the Negev, the Sinai too has a limited number of rare animals, such as the Sinai leopard, and Yoffe is determined to help the animals thrive and multiply.

Caring for the fauna and flora has led Yoffe to become deeply involved with ecology. A government plan to establish a large electric power plant on a lovely stretch of Mediterranean coastline was defeated thanks to a campaign that he led against it.

The pollution of water resources has become a new worrisome issue for Yoffe, and he has organized a nationwide drive to prevent additional spoilage of water sources by industrial and municipal wastes.

Yoffe has a strong historical feeling about his work. In ancient times, he says, Israel was a "land flowing with milk and honey," lush with foliage, with large numbers of animals who lived in peace in their protected surroundings. He wants to see Israel, despite the advent of the industrial age, become again a verdant, unpolluted, beautiful country in which there will be ample room for all of nature's creatures.

Yoffe often visits the Sinai, where he has appointed scores of Bedouin Arabs members of his Nature Reserves Authority enforcement teams. He has inspired them to emulate his efforts to let the endangered species of animals in that huge wasteland live peacefully.

Whenever he visits the Biblical Zoo in Jerusalem, which contains animals mentioned in the Bible, he feels somewhat saddened. Animals should be allowed to roam freely, he believes, and not be caged for people to stare at. He feels his work is succeeding: Two decades ago there were only some eight hundred gazelles in Israel; now an estimated five thousand enjoy life in the special nature preserves he has established.

One of the most beautiful spots his agency has developed is the 1,100-acre site near Ein Gedi, not far from the Dead Sea, which was a famous retreat in the days of King David. Filled with springs, waterfalls, and pools, Ein Gedi is visited today by more than 200,000 people every year.

DAVID SARNOFF

Communications to Unite the World

THE NAME OF DAVID SARNOFF has become synonymous with modern radio and television communications. During World War II, when he served as a special consultant to General Dwight Eisenhower, commander of all Allied military forces in Europe, he devoted his expertise in communications to helping win the war against the Nazis. He was decorated by both the United States and French governments, and was elevated to the rank of brigadier general for his important contributions to Allied victory.

Sarnoff's life story reads like a Jewish version of a Horatio Alger tale. He was born in a small village, a traditional *shtetl*, in Russia in 1891 and was brought to the United States at the age of nine. He had learned English and was just beginning to feel part of the bustling Lower East Side scene in New York when his father died, and young David had to become the family's chief supporter.

He sold newspapers, found work as a delivery boy, and at the age of fifteen landed what was considered a good job—as a messenger for the new Commercial Cable Company. He saved his meager income, used the money to buy a simple telegraph key, and soon mastered the Morse code. The new concept of "wireless" communications fascinated him; he sensed that here lay a major new field of endeavor, and he strove to become part of it. He sought work as a telegraph operator with the Marconi Wireless Telegraph Company, but settled for an office boy's job on the theory that he would at least get his foot in the door. His weekly salary was five and a half dollars.

When he was seventeen, the company offered him an operator's job in a lonely station on Nantucket Island, off the Massachusetts coast. The increased pay (sixty dollars a month) plus the chance to read the station's large library of technical books convinced him to accept. For a few years after that he worked as a wireless operator aboard ships sailing between Boston and New York, and on one occasion he sailed on an expedition that reached the Arctic ice fields.

He returned to New York, working for the company in Brooklyn while attending an engineering course in the evenings. In April 1912 Sarnoff picked up a distress signal from the S.S. *Titanic*, a giant vessel en route from England to New York that struck an iceberg and sank with a loss of 1,517 lives. He remained at his post for seventy-two continuous hours, relaying the names of the survivors to an anxious world. President Taft ordered all wireless stations along the Eastern Seaboard off the air so as not to interfere with Sarnoff's reception. Overnight, David Sarnoff became a household word.

He was promoted by the Marconi Company and by 1915 was assistant traffic manager. A year later he sent a memorandum to the chief executive of Marconi, proposing development of a "radio music box" to receive broadcasts for public information as well as entertainment. He wrote that radio would become a "household utility in the same sense as a piano or phonograph. The idea is to bring music into the home by wireless." It was the beginning of a revolutionary new era in world communications.

In 1921 Sarnoff became general manager of the newly formed Radio Corporation of America. In the next two years the company sold $83 million worth of radio sets. A few years later RCA set up the National Broadcasting Company to provide programs for some five million homes already equipped with radios. In 1930 Sarnoff became president of RCA, and in 1947 he was named chairman of the board.

Sarnoff early on believed in bringing quality programs to his vast audience of radio listeners. Outstanding musicians and educators were invited to counsel the new medium and to help set up worthwhile entertainment and educational programs. In 1939 at the New York World's Fair Sarnoff launched the new medium of television, announcing to the world, "Now we add sight to sound —this miracle of engineering skill brings the world to the home."

Sarnoff was honored by the governments of the United States, France, Italy, Japan, Poland, and Israel, the latter conferring its Medallion of Valor, Commendation Award on him in 1960. Countless industrial organizations and social service agencies paid tribute to him for his work and his contributions to the advancement of mankind, among them B'nai B'rith, the YM-YWHA, the American Technion Society, the Jewish Theological Seminary of America, the American Committee for the Weizmann Institute, and the National Conference of Christians and Jews.

When he died in 1971 at the age of eighty, the little immigrant boy who sold newspapers and delivered messages was universally honored for his leadership in the world of communications and for having made the world a better and more enjoyable place to live in.

YITZHAK NAVON

Israel's First Sephardi President

THE FIFTH PRESIDENT OF ISRAEL is the first occupant of that position born in Israel. He is also the first Israeli President from the Sephardic, or non-European, sector of the population. Like his predecessors, he is a man of letters and learning.

Yitzhak Navon was born in Jerusalem in 1921 to a Moroccan Jewish family. From his earliest years he was a typical *sabra*, or native-born Israeli, who shunned formality and always liked a direct, straightforward approach to all problems.

He studied Hebrew literature and Moslem culture at the Hebrew University, from which he graduated and became a teacher. During the period prior to the establishment of Israel he joined the underground Haganah movement (for a while he was a member of the Irgun), and he headed the Arabic department of the Israeli army in the 1948 War of Independence.

Soon after Israel proclaimed its independence, Navon joined its diplomatic service and served in a number of South American countries. In order to establish better ties with the local Jewish communities of Argentina and other Latin American nations, he mastered Yiddish, the lingua franca of most of the Jews of that area.

Upon his return to Israel in the early 1950s, he became a chief adviser to the then Foreign Minister, Moshe Sharett. Soon after, Sharett asked him if he would undertake to teach the Prime Minister, David Ben-Gurion, Spanish. It seems that Ben-Gurion was anxious to read Spanish classics in the original and felt the need for a private tutor. Not only did Navon teach Spanish to the Israeli leader, but his role was expanded to that of political adviser, and he was in effect a right-hand man to Ben-Gurion for more than a decade.

Ironically, while he was an aide to Ben-Gurion, Navon sent a telegram to Albert Einstein, inviting him to become President of Israel, an invitation which the famed scientist turned down. Navon also acted as the Prime Minister's emissary in transmitting an invitation to Zalman Shazar to serve as President, which led to Shazar's becoming Israel's third President.

Navon has long been identified with Israel's Labor party, and served as a Labor member of the Knesset, the Israeli parliament, from 1965. In the Knesset he was at various times a deputy speaker and a member of various important committees, including the vital Defense and Foreign Affairs Committee. He became Israel's fifth President in 1978, following the resignation of Ephraim Katzir.

Navon has always felt strongly that no time must be lost in helping to bridge the social-economic-educational gap that separates the two main bodies of Jews in Israel, the Sephardim and the Ashkenazim. He said once that "there is no community in Israel that does not have a contribution to make, nor is there any which has historically failed to make a contribution. . . . if there is no change in the environment, in housing conditions, in the level of schooling, and the general atmosphere in which the Sephardi child is raised, then there is a strong possibility that the son will follow in his parents' footsteps."

The Israeli leader has written extensively about Sephardic life, including a popular play that has had many performances in Israel. One of his most ambitious literary efforts was a play called *The Sephardic Garden* which seeks to portray the high cultural levels of Sephardic Jews during the Golden Age in Spain, and in the period of the Inquisition and expulsion that followed. Navon is a gentle, soft-spoken man who delights in amusing children with sleight-of-hand tricks. He can become enraged, however, when he talks of the "stereotypes of the Moroccan Jew—the waiter, the gangster, the delinquent. Moroccan Jewish life is full of beauty and wisdom," he maintains, "for those who understand it."

The common denominator for the people of Israel, Navon has declared, "must be Jewish tradition—that adhesive force that keeps all sectors and factions in this nation together. Any culture that cuts us off from the roots of Judaism will always be a foreign element in our midst."

It was not until he was in his forties that Navon married, choosing as his wife a former Miss Israel beauty contest winner. They have two small children, and the Israeli President has let it be known that the duties of his office will not be allowed to interfere with his parental role.

Shortly before his death, Ben-Gurion wrote to his former aide, "I believe the Jewish people will yet see you as the President of Israel."

ERNEST BLOCH

Composer of Biblical Themes

WHEN HE WAS TEN YEARS OLD, Ernest Bloch knew exactly what he wanted to be: a composer. Always a person of strong will, he wrote his ambition down on a slip of paper and symbolically burned it over a stone mound filled with small twigs. At the time of his death in 1959, just before his eightieth birthday, he had written numerous musical compositions, both for specific Jewish use and for secular use, and had carved a place for himself in musical history.

He was born in Geneva, Switzerland, and was raised in a traditional Jewish home. At sixteen, in the face of his parents' strong objections, he left home and studied music in Germany, France, and Belgium. While still in his early twenties, he wrote his Symphony in C-sharp Minor. He went home to work in the family clockmaking business, but busied himself weekends and evenings writing music. When he was thirty, his opera *Macbeth* was produced in Paris and was very well received.

It was around this time that he began to remember the songs he had heard as a child, sung by his grandparents. He wrote later that, although he himself was not traditionally observant, he was always deeply conscious of his father's chanting during study of the Talmud, and of the unforgettable Passover Seder melodies. He produced seven works that reflected his profound emotional preoccupation with the themes of the Bible, including the famous *Shlomo Hebrew Rhapsody*. A New York *Times* music critic said that this work "has an ancestral grandeur, an intense bitter seriousness without parallel—the music is Hebraic in all that the word profoundly and superbly implies."

Bloch said later, "I am a Jew, and I aspire to write Jewish music—this is the only way I can produce music of vitality and significance." On another occasion he wrote, "It is the Hebrew spirit that interests me—the complex, ardent, agitated soul that vibrates for me in the Bible, the vigor and ingenuousness of the Patriarchs, the violence that finds expression in the books of the Prophets, the burning love of justice, the sorrow and grandeur of the Book of Job, the sensuality of the Song of Songs. All this is in us, all this is in me, and is the better part of me. This is what I seek to feel within me and to translate in my music—the sacred race-emotion that lies dormant in our souls."

Bloch's career encompassed not only composition but also conducting, teaching, and writing on music. He lived and worked for short periods in New York, Cleveland, and San Francisco, and then returned to his native Switzerland to compose *Sacred Service*, a musical work that took him three years to complete and that is suitable both for vocal and orchestral performances. To prepare himself for this master work, he memorized the entire service in Hebrew, stating, "I now know its significance, word by word. It has become mine as if it were this very expression of my soul—it has become a 'private affair' between God and me."

Bloch returned to the United States shortly before the outbreak of World War II and lived for many years in Oregon. In recognition of his works with a distinctly Jewish theme, including the *Israel Symphony* and *Three Jewish Poems*, the Jewish Theological Seminary of America bestowed an honorary doctorate on him in 1954.

When he learned in 1958 that he required urgent surgery for cancer, he postponed the operation until he had finished a number of his works in progress and wrote the words for *Funeral Music*, composed for the violin. He died less than a year after his surgery.

Although he directed the Cleveland Institute of Music and the San Francisco Conservatory of Music, and demonstrated his love for his adopted country by writing *America*, an epic rhapsody, Ernest Bloch will best be remembered for having composed Bible-inspired music that spanned the centuries from the earliest days of the Jewish people to his own.

MENAHEM BEGIN

Militant Prime Minister

MENAHEM BEGIN, SIXTH PRIME MINISTER OF ISRAEL, was born in Poland in 1913 and was educated at Jewish schools and the University of Warsaw, from which he earned a law degree in 1935. While still in his teens, he became active in Betar, a Zionist youth movement that emphasized nationalism and activism. In 1939, the same year that the Nazis launched World War II by invading Poland, Begin was named head of the Betar organization in Poland, a country which at the time had a Jewish population of three million.

The first time he was imprisoned was in 1937 when he led a group of Jewish youths in a demonstration against the British legation in Warsaw, protesting Britain's restrictive immigration policy in Palestine. When war erupted in the fall of 1939, he was arrested by Soviet authorities and sent to a Siberian labor camp, where he remained until 1941. After the Germans attacked Russia, the Soviets allowed imprisoned Poles to be released to join a Polish army, with which Begin was able to reach Palestine in 1942.

The underground Irgun Zvai Leumi in Palestine, which had been waging guerrilla war against the British Mandatory authorities, invited Begin to leave the Polish military force and lead it in its attempt to wrest control of Palestine from the British. For six years, until the British withdrew in May 1948, Begin directed the Irgun's activities and was one of the most sought leaders of the Palestinian underground movements. At times he was disguised as a bearded rabbi, a role he was able to carry off easily since he had

been raised in an Orthodox milieu. Once, when British troops were searching every nook of Tel Aviv for him, he remained hidden behind a secret panel in his apartment for three days, without food or water, almost dying of dehydration.

He became an active political leader in Israel immediately after the creation of the state, and for more than a quarter of a century was the chief opposition leader in the Knesset. He served on various Knesset committees, and for three years was a member of the cabinet, during a period when Israel was run by a national unity government. In 1977, in an upset election, he became Prime Minister.

Begin is a man with clearly defined tastes and views. Although he is completely uninterested in material possessions and he and his wife, Aliza, maintain the same modest Tel Aviv apartment they have had for many years, he is polite and courtly to the point of sometimes being described as an old-fashioned European diplomat. It is not unusual for him to kiss the hand of a woman when he is introduced. A nonsmoker, he has issued strict orders that he will not permit smoking during meetings of the Israeli cabinet.

Begin is a religious man, and he has said that "faith creates reality." When anyone refers to him as a former terrorist, he bristles with rage. Terrorists, he explains, are murderers who do not hesitate to kill innocent women and children, while the men and women whom he led in the Irgun were "freedom fighters" intent on dislodging a government that they believed had no right to rule Jews in their own homeland.

The Israeli leader, a frail man with a history of heart disease, is a fiery orator, and despite an obvious accent he has mastered English well enough to be able to conduct himself well in extemporaneous exchanges with journalists and various audiences. In all his speeches, including those he has directed to world leaders, he has reminded his listeners that, had there been a free Jewish state in the 1930s or 1940s, the Holocaust, in which one third of the Jewish people were annihilated by the Nazis, might not have taken place. He has maintained that the underground Jewish groups that operated before Israel statehood came into being in 1948 "fought valiantly for our people."

He has written:

It was our aim to save our people from utter destruction. We were only a small minority in Palestine; about two thirds of the population were Palestinian Arabs. All of us would have been murdered; the Arabs were notoriously pro-Nazi. Israel is ours by right; we are the indigenous civilization. Our enemies must realize that we are indestructible—then the day of peace will come.

Some people have described him as a blend of soldier and prophet. He is said to be influenced by nearly mystical beliefs, combined with a tough will to attain his goals. Although he believes wholly in democracy, he rules his own party with a touch of authoritarianism. His autobiographical books reveal his inner strength during years of hard labor in Siberian camps and the years when he remained in hiding from the British until Israel was created.

Begin is well versed in the Bible and Talmud and often quotes classical Jewish sources in his talks. His greatest task, he has said both before and since the President of Egypt, Anwar Sadat, made his historic trip to Jerusalem, is to find a way for establishing a secure peace for Israel and to usher in an era of friendly relations with Israel's Arab neighbors.

HERMAN BRANOVER

Physicist with a Yarmulke

ONE OF THE WORLD'S LARGEST Jewish communities has always been that of Russia. Before the outbreak of the First World War, when Jews in Russia lived under a cruel and hated czarist regime, hundreds of thousands made their way out of the country, most of them finding new homes and new lives in the United States and South America, and a smaller number in Palestine, then beginning to develop as an embryonic Jewish homeland.

Toward the end of World War I, in 1917, revolution erupted in Russia and the czarist regime was overthrown, replaced by a Communist government that preached full equality. Another strong principle that guided the new Soviet authorities was total opposition to religion, including of course Judaism. For more than sixty years the Jewish population of Russia has been denied an opportunity to practice the basic tenets of the ancient Jewish faith. Owning a copy of the Bible became a punishable offense. Any interest in the Zionist movement or in the Hebrew language was strictly forbidden. The prospects for the continuation of the Jewish community as a religious or cultural entity in the Soviet Union looked very dim. Soviet Jews were not permitted to maintain any ties with organized Jewish groups abroad, and even individual correspondence between Russian Jews and relatives abroad was frowned upon.

Hundreds of thousands of Russian Jews were massacred by the Nazis when they invaded the Soviet Union in the summer of

1941. When the war ended, there were estimated to be some three million Jews in Russia, saved from the Nazis but gradually beginning to be totally assimilated, their religious and cultural heritage fading with each passing day.

There were a few notable exceptions to the general rule. The Hasidic movement, which had had large numbers of followers in Russia, struggled to keep up a semblance of religious life. Everything had to be carried out in total secrecy; anyone caught observing the Jewish holidays or studying a Jewish religious work could be arrested and shipped off to a Siberian labor camp. At the same time, the deeply rooted anti-Semitism that had existed from czarist days was still far from dormant. Despite the new Soviet laws proclaiming liberty and equality, Jews were often singled out for harassment and persecution.

The news of the establishment of Israel in 1948 kindled a spark among many Jews in the Soviet Union. Notwithstanding the fact that they had been cut off from the mainstream of Jewish life for many years, many Soviet Jews began to take heart that a Jewish state had been created and that Jews could live as Jews freely and openly there, as well as in other democratic countries. One such Jew who was deeply moved by the events around him was a physicist who had achieved a lofty reputation—Dr. Herman Branover, attached to the Academy of Science in Riga.

Born in Riga in 1931, he grew up in a nonreligious home that nevertheless had strong, positive feelings about Jewish culture. At the age of twenty-one he was studying in Leningrad and saw the Soviet authorities relegate more than twenty thousand books on Judaism to a public fire. It was a traumatic event for him. Secretly, he began to study Jewish history, religion, and philosophy. Five years later, at the age of twenty-six, knowing that he was taking a very dangerous step, he committed himself to leading the life of an observant, traditional Jew. He attached himself to the Hasidic movement in Riga and became one of them.

All this time he continued to pursue his scientific career, specializing in the field of magnetohydrodynamics. He wrote more than one hundred scientific papers in the field, about a third of which were translated into English and other languages, establishing his reputation as a world authority in this highly specialized field. At the same time, he translated the entire *Kitzur*

Shulḥan Aruch, the abbreviated code of Jewish laws, into Russian. His fellow Hasidim called him Rabbi, and indeed he was duly ordained after he was tested by overseas phone calls from leading rabbis in Israel and England.

In 1972 he embarked on a daring course: He began to teach Bible to young Jewish students, shrugging off the warnings from the authorities that he would be imprisoned if he persisted. Soon thereafter he applied for permission to emigrate to Israel, and it was only after the intervention of top world scientists, as well as leading American officials, that he and his family were allowed to leave.

Professor Branover today teaches physics at both the Tel Aviv and Ben-Gurion universities in Israel. He has formed an organization of Soviet Jewish academicians now living in Israel, seeking to teach them the basic tenets of Jewish religious life. He is also active in widespread educational programs in Israel aimed at bridging the information gap among the Russian immigrants who had been cut off from Judaism for more than half a century.

Professor Branover, who believes that "science helped me find my religious faith," has written, "Knowledge means setting up a world view that is free of contradictions, understanding the goodness of the world, and recognition of God. One must possess, in addition to intellect, logic and imagination. . . . the ancient but still ringing words of the Torah express a wisdom that every man must strive to acquire for himself."

LEO BAECK

The Comforting Rabbi

IN FEBRUARY 1948 a rabbi named Leo Baeck rose in the House of Representatives in Washington and invoked a special prayer marking the birthday of Abraham Lincoln. He was the first non-American rabbi so honored. Every congressman in the great chamber listened attentively to the slightly accented words. "For the sake of this land," Rabbi Baeck said, "Abraham Lincoln became witness and testimony of humanity, the herald of God's command and promise, to the everlasting blessing of this country and of mankind."

The words were especially apt, for the stooped, frail rabbi had himself been a witness only a few years before: He had been confined in a Nazi concentration camp, and through his kindliness, strong will, and exemplary behavior had helped many hundreds of other internees not to give in to despair and to continue their struggle to remain alive in the face of savage cruelty.

Leo Baeck was born in Poland, the son of a rabbi. He grew up in a peaceful town, entered a rabbinical seminary, and led a small congregation for a decade before he was invited to become the rabbi of one of Berlin's large congregations. He became a very effective and influential rabbi, scholar, and author of theological works, the most famous of which is *The Essence of Judaism.* During the First World War he served as a chaplain with the German army. He became an active leader of B'nai B'rith, and was named head of the organization of German rabbis.

In the late 1920s and early 1930s Nazism evolved in Germany, and in 1933 the leader of this vile movement seized power. It was the beginning of the end of the German Jewish community, which had existed for nearly a thousand years and which numbered some 600,000 people. German Jews began to emigrate from the country, fearful of the climate that had been established and of the terrible events they were afraid would ensue. Rabbi Baeck, as the leading rabbi in the country and a scholar of international renown, could easily have left, and indeed was invited by various organizations and institutions to join them, but he rejected all such offers. He felt his place was with the German Jews.

The situation in Germany gradually grew worse. In 1935, after passage of the infamous Nuremberg Laws that virtually barred Jews from all occupations, Dr. Baeck composed a special prayer to be recited on the eve of Yom Kippur as part of the service. It said:

In this hour every man in Israel stands erect before his Lord, the God of justice and mercy, to open his heart in prayer. . . . We will publicly confess the sins we have committed and beg the Lord to pardon and forgive. Acknowledging our trespasses, both personal and communal, let us despise the slanders and calumnies directed against us and our faith. Let us declare them lies, too mean and senseless for our reckoning.

It was a dangerous prayer to write, but Dr. Baeck was not afraid. The Nazis prevented the worshipers from using the prayer and arrested Dr. Baeck for questioning but released him a day later. Soon after, news of the Nazi concentration camps and their bestial conditions began to circulate, and Dr. Baeck, unafraid of the consequences, wrote a sharp letter of protest to the Nazis, condemning the conditions.

By 1938 the future for the German Jews had deteriorated; the outlook was bleak. Rabbi Baeck's daughter and family had gone to England, and she urged her father to join them, but again he refused despite the fact that his wife had died and she was his only child. He insisted that he had to remain behind and help in any way he could. An adventurous Scotsman arranged for a private plane to fly Dr. Baeck out of Germany, but he refused, saying, "I will go when I am the last Jew alive in Germany."

Shortly before the outbreak of war in 1939 Dr. Baeck became chairman of the World Union of Progressive Judaism, the international body of Reform Jewish congregations. The Nazis were enraged by the fact he had been named to so high a post; they arrested him and kept him under detention five times but in the end released him. Unwillingly, they had come to respect the aged rabbi—he was then a man of sixty-six—and seemed eager to see as little of him as possible. Dr. Baeck went about his work: to comfort those in despair, and to aid those able to leave.

He was also deeply heartened by occasional displays of friendship and support from Christian Germans. From time to time he would find a basket of fruit or vegetables outside his door, delivered anonymously. Once a stranger dropped something, picked it up, and handed it to Dr. Baeck, saying that the rabbi had dropped it. It was an extra book of food rations, invaluable in those difficult days.

Dr. Baeck was elected president of the Representative Council of German Jews, and was called to Gestapo headquarters frequently to receive orders for the Jews in Germany. In 1943 the Nazis sent Dr. Baeck to a concentration camp. At first he was chained to a wagon hauling garbage, and later, at the age of seventy, he was permitted to wander in the camp, helping those in need. He organized lectures in the camp, and sometimes as many as seven hundred people—starving, in tatters, ill, with hope all but gone—would crowd into a wooden barracks to hear him lecture on the Bible, on Jewish philosophy, on Maimonides. Children were not allowed to receive an education, but Dr. Baeck encouraged the inmates to teach the youngsters in secret the basics of reading and writing. Every morning and evening Dr. Baeck recited prayers, noting later that the experience in the camp showed him more than he had ever realized "how utterly dependent man is on faith."

During the two years he was in the Theresienstadt concentration camp, he helped those who were condemned to die to face death with a measure of dignity; at the same time he succored those who fought to live on to continue their struggle and not give up. When the Russians liberated the camp, they offered the surviving Jews an opportunity to take vengeance on the German guards who had been captured, but Dr. Baeck forbade it.

Two months after the camp was liberated, only after he was satisfied that the survivors were being well cared for, he left Germany and rejoined his daughter in England. He began at once to busy himself with Jewish affairs: He organized a council of European rabbis, lectured at the Hebrew University in Jerusalem, and taught at the Hebrew Union College in Cincinnati. He became a British subject and lived to see his great grandchild—the son of his granddaughter, who had married a rabbi. Visitors to his home in a London suburb included Albert Einstein and Albert Schweitzer and scores of neighborhood youngsters who sensed that he was their friend. He died at the age of eighty-three, a heroic rabbi of modern times.

EMMA LAZARUS

"Give Me Your Tired, Your Poor, . . ."

MOST NEWCOMERS TO THE UNITED STATES nowadays arrive at bustling JFK Airport in New York, which is a great pity, for thus they miss the chance to be greeted by that beautiful lady in the harbor, the Statue of Liberty, which has been offering a wordless welcome for nearly a century to many millions of immigrants to America.

It is usually only after the new arrivals—including the several thousands of recently arrived Russian Jews—have become reasonably ensconced on American shores that they find time to pay a visit to that majestic symbol of freedom.

Visitors from far and wide—newcomers, tourists, and native-born Americans—read the glorious lines engraved on the pedestal of the statue, and each person reacts in a personal way. The lines seem to have a life of their own, and have remained stirring to this day. They begin, of course:

> Give me your tired, your poor,
> Your huddled masses yearning to breathe free . . .
> I lift my lamp beside the golden door.

American Jews who know their history are rightly proud of the fact that the poetic message engraved at the foot of the statue is that of a devoted Jewish woman, but who knows how strange was her own life story?

Born into an affluent Jewish family in 1849, Emma Lazarus from her earliest days displayed a flair for the gentle, the artistic, and the spiritual. Unlike her siblings, she was forced to remain at home a good deal because of frail health and received her education from private tutors.

Somehow she never seemed to mind. She spent long hours reading the novels and poetry of England and of the new authors in America who were beginning to make their mark on a new generation of readers. From time to time she would jot down her own innermost thoughts, often in verse, but was too shy to share them with anyone. She seemed content to lead a quiet, sedentary existence, surrounded by great books and great minds whose voices seemed to speak directly to her from between the book covers.

Emma was Jewish, but in her home that fact seemed to matter very little. On Passover there was a large family gathering, with lip service paid to the reading of the traditional Seder Haggadah. On the High Holy Days she accompanied her rather stern father to the synagogue, where being seen in one's finest seemed more important to most of the worshipers than becoming part of the congregants intent on prayer and meditation.

Her family was of Sephardic origin. Her great grandfather had reached America even before the American Revolutionary War. From occasional snatches of conversation at the dinner table she learned that he was descended from the fortunate few Spanish and Portuguese Jews who had succeeded in fleeing before the full impact of the Inquisition had spread its tentacles over the Iberian peninsula, causing the violent deaths of thousands of Jews, the expulsion of many thousands of others, and the forced conversion to Catholicism of still many thousands of others.

As Emma grew into young womanhood, her early literary talents began to blossom, and she put pen to paper in earnest and began to create poetry, no longer too shy to have it published. Ralph Waldo Emerson, the foremost literary figure in America at the time, liked her work and encouraged her to continue.

It is said that sometimes a single book can change the life of a reader, and this happened in the case of Emma Lazarus. She obtained a copy of a novel written by George Eliot in England, entitled *Daniel Deronda*, which portrayed a Jewish family's aspirations to return to the ancient Jewish homeland in Palestine and to put an end to exile and concomitant suffering and persecution. The book stirred her deeply, and her poetic mind began to imagine a homeland where Jews would once again live as a sovereign people as in ancient biblical days.

Realizing that she was greatly deficient in Jewish knowledge, Emma began to study Hebrew, and soon mastered it well enough to begin translating the classic Hebrew poems of the great literary figures of Spain's golden age, including the works of Judah Halevi, Ibn Ezra, Alharizi, and others. A number of her beautiful translations have found their way into the prayer book. For the first time, Jews and non-Jews alike who did not know Hebrew were given an opportunity to enjoy the work of some of the greatest Hebrew poets who ever lived.

The translation of the poetry led her to undertake a study of Jewish history and religious practices, and she began to see herself as a Jewish woman rediscovering her long-suppressed roots.

In 1881 some six thousand miles away in czarist Russia a wave of ugly pogroms broke out, in which Jews were slaughtered for no reason other than the fact that they were Jewish. Reports of the wild butchery of innocent men, women, and children slowly reached New York. The hands-off policy of the Russian government enraged Americans. Within a short time boatloads of refugees from Russian pogroms and hooliganism began to arrive in America, survivors of a wave of modern barbarism. Many of the newcomers accused the Russian authorities of direct collaboration with the pogromists.

This was a time when America was busy rebuilding itself after a tragic civil war a generation earlier. The frontiers were being pushed ever westward; gold had been discovered in California; land was being offered to all settlers for the asking; and the industrial revolution was transforming the United States into a strong, modern nation in which democratic traditions had remained steadfast.

Emma Lazarus read the news accounts of what had taken place in czarist Russia, and her heart trembled with grief for her fellow Jews. A gentle girl, never having seen to what extent depraved men can sink, she felt her whole world crumbling as she read of one group of human beings being deliberately murdered by another—in this case, Russian illiterates, goaded by leaders who sought power and influence and did not mind if in the process thousands of Jews were put to death.

She began to visit the port of entry, wishing to see for herself the Jewish refugees who were coming ashore in America. She never left the pier without tears welling in her eyes, grateful that her coreligionists had reached haven—and uncomprehending about the brutal nature that lurked in men's breasts. Soon she began to help in the relief and resettlement programs organized by the Jewish community for the benefit of the refugees. For a while she stopped writing poetry and threw herself into the program of aiding the new arrivals make a new life for themselves in America.

Around this time the French government presented the Statue of Liberty to the people of the United States. A contest to select a suitable inscription to be engraved on the base of the statue was announced. Emma Lazarus determined that she, as a Jew who understood deeply the meaning of persecution and homelessness, would write the winning poem.

The theme of freedom, the memory of the Jewish refugees whom she had seen and helped as they reached America's shores, the symbolism of the great lady in the harbor for all decent men and women—she felt all these deeply. She seemed to have been preparing all her life for this one great task.

She sat down and wrote her unforgettable poem, which was selected as the most suitable and in time was engraved on the statue's base.

Through the poetic voice of Emma Lazarus, the American Jewish community seems to say to the world: This is a blessed land, a haven for the oppressed, a shining example of what a decent country ought to be.

MOSES MONTEFIORE

Guardian of His People

Sir Moses Montefiore was born in 1784 in Italy but lived most of his life in England, having immigrated there as a youngster. When he was knighted by Queen Victoria, he became the first Jew to be so honored. When he died at the age of 101, he had given a lifetime of remarkable leadership to the Jewish people.

His beginnings were humble. At a very young age Moses Montefiore became an apprentice in a company of food and tea merchants. Later, after he had learned the business, he struck out on his own and after considerable effort he and his brother, who was a partner in the company, became respected and successful merchants.

At the age of twenty-eight he married Judith Cohen, who was related to the Rothschild family, and through her he was brought into close contact with that famous dynasty. His fortune began to grow, in the best rags-to-riches tradition. At the age of forty he retired from business and decided to devote himself to charitable and civic works—which he kept at for the next sixty-one years.

He and his wife did not have any children, but whenever he met a child during his frequent visits to orphanages, schools, and various charitable institutions, he would try to pass on the motto that had guided him all his life. "Think and thank," he would say— meaning, use the mind that God has given you, and show your thankfulness that you have a good mind and are well by helping all those less fortunate than you.

Montefiore was an imposing looking man, standing six feet three inches tall. With the designation "Sir" appended to his name, with his habit of straightforward talk, and with a fortune at his disposal to use as he saw fit, he came to be looked on as a modern Moses who would help lead his people out of their misery into an era of peace and plenty.

As a young man he paid little attention to the Jewish religious laws, but after the first of seven visits to Palestine, he became a strictly observant Jew, seldom seen in public without a head covering and often taking along a personal *shohet*, a ritual slaughterer, on his long journeys, to ascertain that the meat and poultry he ate was strictly kosher.

On the coat of arms that Queen Victoria gave Montefiore when she knighted him was engraved the word "Jerusalem" in gold letters. The vision of the Jews returning to their ancient homeland in Palestine had taken hold of Sir Moses, and he did everything he could to make the dream a reality.

He tried to buy large tracts of land in Palestine for the future use of Jewish settlers. He helped in the establishment of a number of the early agricultural colonies, and brought a printing press into the country to help spread Jewish culture. He built a windmill in Jerusalem—which still stands—in an effort to introduce a source of energy to the holy city.

The Yemin Moshe quarter of Jerusalem, which he helped develop, was named in his honor, and the old-fashioned horse-drawn carriage that he used to take him around the country is still a tourist attraction to this day. He endowed a Jewish-oriented college in England in his wife's memory.

Perhaps his greatest achievements were the prevention of pogroms and bloodshed among threatened Jewish communities. In 1840 in Damascus a group of Jews were arrested on charges that they had killed a Christian monk to obtain his blood for the preparation of the Passover unleavened bread, the *matzah*. The accusation was utterly false, of course, but there was a grave danger of Arab mobs running amok and killing many hundreds of innocent Jews.

Sir Moses hurried to Damascus, met with the authorities, demonstrated to them how absolutely vile the charge was, and a pogrom was averted. He brought with him not only the authority of a leading British personality, which he was acknowledged to be, but also the moral indignation of one of the ancient biblical prophets.

A few years later he visited czarist Russia, where assaults on Jewish villages had become commonplace, and again succeeded in his mission. The Russians toned down the attacks, and for a time at least there ensued a period of relative peace.

Jewish communities in Morocco and in Rumania were also faced with the very real danger of mob attacks, and he went to the rulers of both countries, pleading for an official policy of greater tolerance and compassion, and again his visits were fruitful.

In Rumania, where large crowds of peasants and townspeople threatened to attack the Jews, Sir Moses ordered an open carriage and told his driver to move into the circle of maddened would-be rioters. Rising to his full stature in the carriage, he shouted at the crowd, "Plunder and kill if you choose—I have come here in the name of justice and humanity. I have faith in God—He will protect me!" As though they had been listening to a Mosaic voice thundering at them from the heights of Mount Sinai, the mob shrank back and eventually scattered. Another potential pogrom against Jews was averted.

In 1884, at the age of one hundred, Sir Moses was honored for his leadership and charitable works by Jewish communities all over the world. When he died the next year, mourners included kings, princes, sultans, and the entire Jewish people.

ARTHUR KORNBERG

Synthetist of DNA

WHEN ARTHUR KORNBERG WAS A MEDICAL STUDENT at the University of Rochester, he became ill with hepatitis. Rather than allow the disease to waste his time in pursuit of his studies, he made careful notes of the symptoms and progress of the disease as he experienced it and, when he recovered, wrote a paper entitled "The Occurrence of Jaundice in Otherwise Normal Medical Students."

The pursuit of knowledge—especially medical knowledge to benefit mankind—has been a lifelong characteristic of Dr. Kornberg, who shared the Nobel Prize in physiology and medicine in 1959 with Dr. Severo Ochoa. The prestigious award was given to them for "discoveries in the biological synthesis of ribonucleic acids and deoxyribonucleic acids"—in other words, for creating in a test tube the huge molecules of RNA and DNA, the key substances that are believed to be the very basis of life itself.

Arthur Kornberg was born in Brooklyn, New York, in 1918. At the age of sixteen he was admitted to City College and three years later earned a bachelor of science degree. He studied medicine in Rochester and did his internship there. In 1942, while the United States was engaged in the war effort in Europe and the Pacific, he donned the uniform of a U. S. Public Health Service officer, remaining with that agency for eleven years and eventually becoming its medical director.

He began to carry out medical research studies while still a United States health officer, at New York University and later at the Washington University School of Medicine as well as at the National Institute of Health in Bethesda, Maryland. He has directed the department of chemistry of Stanford University's school of medicine since 1959. His wife, Sylvia, a biochemist, has worked with him for a number of years, carrying out research at the Stanford laboratory.

Dr. Kornberg's achievement in synthesizing DNA is expected to lead to significant understanding both of heredity and of the way in which cancer cells are transmitted. The potential importance of his work may be seen in the possibility that DNA may be transplanted into animals or man, introducing desirable characteristics. It is also hoped that Dr. Kornberg's discoveries will lead to the development of chemicals that will either prevent cancer or make future generations completely immune to it.

Like a number of other Nobel Prize-winners, including I. I. Rabi and Ernst Boris Chain, Dr. Kornberg has continued a lifelong interest in the medical and scientific research work being carried out in Israel, where he has visited a number of times.

ALBERT EINSTEIN

Science with True Freedom

ALBERT EINSTEIN IS UNIVERSALLY ACCLAIMED as one of the greatest scientists who ever lived. Although he is credited with having helped immeasurably to open up the era of the nuclear age, he was unalterably opposed to war and violence throughout his lifetime, and until his death he continued to urge that the atomic bomb be outlawed.

He was born in Ulm, Germany, in 1879, grew up in Munich, lived for a while in Italy with his parents, settled for a number of years in Switzerland, and then, as the wave of Nazism began to rise, left for the United States, where he lived in Princeton, New Jersey, carrying on his research at the Institute for Advanced Studies. He died in 1955, gratified that the dark forces of Hitlerism had been defeated, happy that Israel had been created, and fearful of the misuse of the atomic energy he had helped to unlock.

When he was a young student, some of his teachers thought he was backward, for he hated the regimented system of the German school, much preferring to stare into space and wonder about the world about him or to read poetry, philosophy, and books on mathematics. Games with toy soldiers, which were very popular at the time in Germany, more than bored him—they annoyed him. He explained once that he felt sorry for the soldiers because they *had* to do what they were told. This abiding passion for freedom remained with him always.

For a while his father worried that the boy was mentally deficient. One day he bought him a pocket compass and a book on geometry, and these small gifts were all that were needed to demonstrate once and for all that Albert was far from mentally weak. He developed an early interest in physics and began to devour everything he could find on the subject, reading books that were meant for specialists and seeming to understand them.

At twenty-one he graduated from the prestigious Zurich Polytechnic Institute, took a job in the Swiss patent office to provide for his needs, and began to concentrate on his research work. In 1905 he published a scientific paper on relativity, and in 1921 he was awarded the Nobel Prize in physics for his work. He had by then already achieved worldwide fame as a scientist and had been honored by many countries, including Germany, where a special research institution was set up so that he could devote full time to his work there—but his deep interest in peace and in Jewish affairs did not slacken.

At the invitation of Dr. Chaim Weizmann, the world Zionist leader, Einstein went to the United States in 1921 on a fund-raising visit in behalf of the nascent Jewish state. Later he spent two years as a visiting professor at the California Institute of Technology. He paid a visit to Palestine in the 1920s, meeting with scientists at the Hebrew University in Jerusalem and at the Technion–Israel Institute of Technology in Haifa, expressing the hope that important scientific developments would be forthcoming from those institutions. A tree he planted on the Technion campus is known to this day as the Einstein tree.

Although he was not a formally religious man, he used to say, when asked, that he believed in a "Supreme Intelligence" and that he had the feeling, as he carried out his experiments, that God "does not play dice with the world." In his home he always featured a menorah, the candelabrum that is symbolic of Judaism and that has become the official emblem of Israel.

One of the great moments of his life, he wrote, came when the State of Israel, after the death of its first president, Chaim Weizmann, invited him to become its second president. He declined because he did not feel he was qualified for the role but said the invitation had touched him deeply. Whenever he could, he urged support for Jewish education for the young, and for financial contributions to Israel. Himself a refugee from Nazi Germany, he could never forget the specter of armed Nazis roaming the streets of Germany, harassing and imprisoning Jews.

The world of science acknowledged that his work did more to revolutionize scientific thinking than that of any other single man. Numerous inventions and practical applications based on his theories and experiments led to television and sound motion pictures. None of these useful inventions really interested him, since he was concerned with the basic laws of the universe—time and space, mass and energy, gravity and space and time. He did not believe that the world had developed by happenstance and said instead that because of human inadequacy man has simply not yet learned to understand the fundamental law of nature.

In 1939 the Nazis launched World War II, and although Einstein was a confirmed pacifist, he concluded that the defeat of the Third Reich and its allies was more important than his espousing of pacifist philosophies. With the war raging in Europe and one European nation after another falling to the seemingly invincible Nazi armies, Einstein wrote a letter to President Franklin D. Roosevelt, saying in effect that it was now possible to release atomic energy—a possibility he dreaded, but he felt it was far more important for the United States to construct an atomic bomb before the Germans did.

Einstein's letter was the catalyst that helped initiate the secret American program to develop atomic bombs and usher in an era of nuclear power. Sending the letter had been a matter of profound inner turmoil for him: At the age of twenty-six he had announced the equation of mass with energy, and now, at sixty, he realized that his recommendation to the President of the United States could lead to a weapon that could imperil the future existence of mankind.

Despite all the honors that were thrust at him, he remained a humble and unassuming man all his life. He enjoyed a simple walk in Princeton, where he would chat idly with neighborhood youngsters. The money he received for the Nobel Prize was donated to charity. A story is told that a check for $1,500 sent him by a research foundation served for months as a bookmark—until he lost both the book and the bookmark.

He found great enjoyment in playing the violin and listening to music. Just prior to his death he was invited to attend a fund-raising dinner arranged by Yeshiva University in New York to help launch the projected Albert Einstein College of Medicine affiliated with the university. Surprising everyone, since he studiously avoided all public functions, he came to the dinner, as a result of which many millions of dollars were raised and the new medical school got off to a flying start.

His melancholy, philosophical face has appeared on the postage stamps of several countries, and the number of books and pamphlets written about him and his work is legion. Jewish schools, hospitals and other institutions bear his name.

He was deeply concerned for the survival and well-being of the new State of Israel, and agreed to go on a nationwide radio and television program in 1955—scheduled to coincide with Israel's seventh anniversary—to express his support for the Jewish state. But he became ill a few days before the program and died soon after.

He once said in a speech, "If we are to resist the powers that threaten intellectual and individual freedom, we must be very conscious of the fact that freedom itself is at stake—we must realize how much we owe to that freedom which our forefathers won through bitter struggle." That was in 1933, the year Hitler seized power in Germany.

Chances are that, if Einstein were alive today, he would voice the very same sentiments. Scientific progress without true freedom seemed meaningless to him.

CHAIM NACHMAN BIALIK

Poet Laureate of Israel

He is considered the greatest poet of the Hebrew language in modern times. His poems have been set to music and sung by young and old. Students have memorized them and retained them throughout their lifetimes. He wrote of nature, of love, of sadness and joy, of the troubles of the Jewish people, of poverty, and of the rebirth of Israel.

Even among those who knew no Hebrew, Bialik came to be known as the modern poetic spokesman for the Jewish people, who expressed his people's great sorrows and at the same time offered them hope for a better tomorrow. His poems touched a special response in the hearts of Jewish men, women, and children, and he was acclaimed the poet laureate of the Jewish people of the twentieth century.

Bialik was born in a small village in czarist Russia in 1873. His father, a scholar who struggled to earn a living, died when Chaim was seven, and the young boy was sent to live with his grandfather, where he began to pursue the study of Talmud. The study of the Jewish Law did not satisfy him, however, and secretly he began to read Russian literature (an activity sharply condemned at the time by most traditional Jews).

As he grew up, he learned that other Jews in other parts of the world were planning to resettle the ancient Jewish homeland in Palestine and were reviving the use of Hebrew as a spoken and

daily language. Still in his teens, he journeyed to the city of Odessa, on the Black Sea, then a principal center of Zionist activity. He had in the meantime written a poem, *El Hatzipor*—"To the Bird"—which he kept on a crumpled piece of paper in his pocket for months, too shy to share it with anyone.

With the help of a rabbi, his friend's father, he was introduced to Ahad Ha'am, the leading Zionist writer and editor of the day, who realized—after hearing Bialik's first poetic effort—that the shy young man was a natural writer and poet, and encouraged and helped him. Bialik's poem was published in a Hebrew magazine and this gave him the encouragement he needed to start producing many more poems. To support himself, he gave private lessons. Soon he met a local girl, fell in love, and was married.

Bialik was obsessed by the beauty of nature, and many of his poems were tributes to the simple joys of the outdoors. For a time he worked in his father-in-law's lumber business and used the long stretches of time he spent alone in the woods to read widely and to write.

When Theodor Herzl convened the first World Zionist Congress in Switzerland, Bialik greeted the event with a new poem. A few years later, when violent waves of pogroms broke out in Russia, he sat down and wrote bitterly of the slaughter and massacre. His words became an echo of what so many thousands of Jews in all parts of the world were feeling but could not articulate—and they were deeply grateful that Bialik could say it for them.

The spark of prophetic indignation burned in Bialik too, and when he felt that his people were not doing enough to defend and help their coreligionists who were being killed and oppressed, he spoke up sharply and clearly—in poetry. Gradually he became the voice of the Jewish people.

He began to embark on a career as a publisher, concentrating on the production of modern textbooks to teach Hebrew that incorporated the latest innovations in teaching methods. He was a rather poor businessman, but somehow he continued in his profession, preferring to live in the world of words and ideas rather than in any other world. Although as a younger man he had at one time thought of enrolling in a modern rabbinical seminary in Berlin, he abandoned the idea in favor of writing and publishing.

In 1917 Russia became the battleground for a revolution that saw the overthrow of the hated czarist regime and the installation of the new Communist government. One of the first steps taken by the new government, which was violently antireligious, was to outlaw the teaching of Hebrew, which was regarded as a language of the decadent Bible. Bialik and his fellow Hebrew writers, many of whom were concentrated in the Odessa area, realized that they could no longer remain in Russia. Through the intercession of the famous author Maxim Gorki, Bialik and his wife received permission to emigrate from Russia, and in 1923 he arrived in Palestine, settling in the new all-Jewish city of Tel Aviv, where he remained until his death in 1934.

Surrounded by fellow Jews who spoke Hebrew, in an atmosphere of hope and confidence in the future of the Jewish people, Bialik continued to write poems, expressing his own and his people's longings and reactions to the events of the day. He established a new publishing house to replace the one that had been closed down in Russia, and together with a lifelong friend and partner, Y. H. Ravnitzki, he produced a massive anthology of long-forgotten Jewish legends and fables that has become a modern classic.

In Jerusalem a new institution of higher learning—the Hebrew University—was scheduled to open, and Bialik was invited to deliver the principal speech at the dedication exercises. It was a great honor that he always remembered with profound gratitude. Speaking to a crowd of several thousand spectators and guests, many of whom sat on the grass on soil that was permeated with Jewish history, Bialik said, "The eyes of tens of thousands of Israel are lifted from all parts of the world to this hill, shining with hope and comfort. Their hearts and their flesh are singing a blessing of thanksgiving to the living God who has preserved us and sustained us and let us live to see this hour. We must hasten to light here the first lamp of learning and science and of every sort of intellectual activity in Israel, before the lamp grows dark for us in foreign lands."

Bialik's home in Tel Aviv became a center for Jewish leaders from all parts of the world who came to visit Palestine. Although he had broken away from many of the traditional ways in which he had been brought up as a small child, Bialik believed that there were many practices in Jewish tradition that were very worthwhile and deserved to be retained and strengthened.

He introduced the concept of the *Oneg Shabbat,* the "Sabbath delight," and it has become an accepted practice in Jewish communities throughout the world—the idea of spending a few hours on the Sabbath afternoon to come together with friends and neighbors, to learn together, sing a little, and enjoy some light refreshments.

Bialik described his arrival in Palestine as giving him an opportunity to become one of a "first generation of free men."

One of the many beautiful poems he composed is entitled "My Poem":

Would you know from whom, and where I learned my song?
A lonesome poet had settled in my father's house;
Ever modest, retiring and hidden,
He dwelt in the darkness of cracks and crevices.
One melody only this poet knew, one lone song, in one familiar
    style.

But whenever my heart grew sad and speechless,
When my tongue clove to my palate in pain,
And a suppressed cry froze in my throat—
He came and filled my empty soul with his song.

For he was a cricket, the poet of the poor.

VLADIMIR JABOTINSKY

His Warnings Went Unheeded

His enemies accused him of being fascistic and militaristic, but his friends and followers said there had never been a gentler, kinder man. Photographs show him always wearing a serious expression, for he seemed to carry the weight of the Jewish people on his shoulders for many of the sixty years of his life. He was brought up in a home where both Hebrew and Yiddish were frowned on, but in later life he mastered both languages, and some of his translations into Hebrew have been acclaimed as masterpieces.

The story of Vladimir Jabotinsky is one filled with "might have beens"—but with the passage of time, scholarly historians and laymen alike now begin to see that he was a man of enormous talent and of unparalleled devotion who never lived to see the fulfillment of his dreams. Menahem Begin, who became the Prime Minister of Israel in 1977, has hailed Jabotinsky as his mentor and spiritual guide.

He was born in 1880 in Odessa, Russia, to a partially assimilated family, was educated in Russian schools and, unlike most Jewish young men of the time, did not receive the traditional Jewish education replete with biblical and talmudic study. He began to write poetry and fiction while still a very young man.

When he was seventeen, he translated Edgar Allan Poe's work into Russian, causing the noted Maxim Gorki to hail him as a new literary luminary. He went to Switzerland and Italy to study and continued to write, this time as a newspaper correspondent. When he returned to Odessa in 1901, he joined the editorial staff of a leading newspaper, producing brilliant essays and literary criticism.

In 1903 a bloody pogrom erupted in Kishinev, in which many Jews lost their lives and which changed the course of Jabotinsky's life. He seems suddenly to have become aware at this time of two Jewish problems—the danger of physical attacks by frenzied mobs on the one hand, and the assimilationist tendencies of the young Russian Jewish intellectuals on the other.

One of the first steps he took while still living in Odessa was to organize a self-defense unit for young Jews, and the idea spread to other Jewish communities in Russia. Jabotinsky translated Chaim Bialik's noted poem about the Kishinev massacre, "City of Slaughter," into Russian. All of his interests and attention now focused on the condition of the Jews, which he admitted later in autobiographical essays he perceived for the first time.

That same fateful year, 1903, the Odessa Zionist organization sent Jabotinsky to the sixth World Zionist Congress as its delegate. He was only twenty-three at the time, but his great gifts for leadership and oratory were immediately discernible. The violent anti-Semitism of czarist Russia and the drift of educated young Jews away from the Jewish community had turned Jabotinsky into a Zionist overnight.

He embarked on a career of Zionist propaganda immediately, as speaker, editor, pamphleteer, negotiator, traveling constantly throughout Europe and organizing Zionist groups wherever he went. Five years after he had become a Zionist, he was invited to join the World Zionist Executive, and his immediate assignment was to proceed to Turkey, then the Ottoman power that controlled Palestine, and publish four magazines designed to spread the Zionist message.

Like a man obsessed, he worked day and night at his new calling, all the time mastering new languages in order to communicate better with his audiences. In addition to his native Russian, he became fluent in Hebrew, Yiddish, English, German, Italian, French, Spanish, and Ladino, and could get through to people in Turkish, Swedish, Polish, and Portuguese. It was while he was in Turkey that he visited Palestine for the first time, and he came away convinced of the importance of making Hebrew the lingua franca of the Jewish people.

Jabotinsky was not, however, a typical "organization man." In a few years he resigned his position in Turkey because of a disagreement with the Zionist leadership and went back to Russia, addressing hundreds of Jewish gatherings in behalf of Zionism and against the principles of Communism which had come to be attractive to growing numbers of young Jews.

When the First World War broke out in 1914, he became a roving correspondent for a Moscow daily and traveled extensively in the Allied countries. When Turkey announced its decision to enter the war on the side of Germany, Jabotinsky was in Egypt and concluded that it was in the best interests of the Jews to ally themselves openly with the Allies (most Zionists of the time had preferred taking a neutral position). He and a young Palestinian Jew, Joseph Trumpeldor, who had lost an arm as an officer in the czarist army during the Russo-Japanese War, were agreed that a Jewish military force fighting alongside the Allies should be organized to help defeat the Germans and Turks and to strengthen the Jews' claim to a homeland in Palestine.

There were at the time some six hundred Russian Jews in Egypt who had fled from Palestine as soon as word of Turkey's alliance with Germany was made known. They had become "enemy aliens" overnight, and they formed the nucleus of the Jewish Legion that eventually fought alongside British units, notably in Gallipoli, helping to defeat the Turks. Jabotinsky himself some years later was to lead a Jewish unit across the Jordan River in a charge against the fleeing Turks.

But the Zionist leaders, who had not been consulted, were at first wary of any such idea as a Jewish Legion. Jabotinsky persisted, and in 1916 Trumpeldor and Jabotinsky reached London, where they eventually formed a unit that consisted of Jewish volunteers from the United States, England, and Palestine, which saw service under a Jewish banner.

While he was in London, Jabotinsky, who at the time was still a private, used to correspond with the British War Office, and often would be the recipient of official documents sent by messenger. The standing joke at the time was that a "message had arrived for Jug-o-Whiskey," which is the way his name came to be mis-pronounced.

When the war ended, Jabotinsky was in Palestine, in conflict with the British authorities and with large segments of the Jewish leadership. The British now thought of him as a troublemaker since he demanded that the Jews be allowed to organize and maintain a self-defense organization openly; and the Jewish leaders of the time not only wanted such a unit to be clandestine but also could not reconcile themselves to Jabotinsky's antisocialist philosophy and insistence on militance.

In 1920 Jabotinsky organized the Haganah in Palestine and let his men train openly. After an outbreak of Arab rioting several of the Haganah men were arrested, and when Jabotinsky came to their defense—insisting to the British authorities that, if they were guilty of any offense, so was he—the British obliged and arrested him too. The fifteen-year jail term imposed was later reduced to a few months.

He continued to work within the world Zionist movement in the 1920s and early 1930s, but he could not acquiesce in policies that he thought were detrimental to Zionism, and in 1935 he formed the revisionist New Zionist Organization, whose delegates were chosen on the basis of votes by some three quarters of a million people, mostly in central and eastern Europe.

The storm clouds had by now begun to hover over Europe, and even before the Nazis took power in Germany, Jabotinsky had been traveling up and down through the Baltic states and Poland, Rumania, and Hungary, urging the Jews to pack up and leave, warning of an impending holocaust. He continued to preach this way after the rise of Nazism, and at one time even worked out a plan whereby one and a half million Jews from east European countries would be helped to leave their homes for Palestine, at the rate of ten per cent annually. The plan was opposed, however, not only by the British authorities in Palestine but also by Jewish leaders who claimed that it would look as though the arguments of the anti-Semites were right, namely, that the Jews could not be integrated into the lives of those respective countries.

Between 1936 and 1940 a clandestine movement of "illegal" immigration into Palestine from eastern Europe was organized by Jabotinsky and his followers, resulting in the prewar rescue of several thousand Jews. The movement was continued and expanded after the war by the Haganah.

During a trip to the United States in 1940 Jabotinsky visited a summer camp where youthful followers of his organization were receiving military training. After greeting them, he retired to a bungalow and died, causing considerable shock waves of grief to echo throughout the Jewish community.

In Palestine, where he had been opposed by large numbers for his allegedly militaristic views, the entire Jewish community went into mourning. Reports said that Jews already detained in Nazi camps in 1940 grieved for him. In 1964 his remains were brought from a Long Island cemetery and reinterred on Mount Herzl, near those of Herzl.

His credo, often cited by his followers, never changed. Speaking of a Jewish state, he said, "I want a state with an army. I don't want a 'national home' for the Jewish people in Palestine. The Jewish people are not ready to retire to a home for the aged and the obsolete. The Jewish people are coming of age. They have work to do. They have a house to build. They have enemies to be swept aside."

ALEXANDER GOODE

He Gave Up His Lifejacket

OF THE MORE THAN THREE HUNDRED RABBIS who served as chaplains during World War II, seven lost their lives in service. One of the most unforgettable acts of selflessness and heroism involved Alexander Goode, a rabbi from York, Pennsylvania, who died together with a Catholic priest and two Protestant ministers in an incident that took place in the stormy Atlantic in February of 1943.

The war between the Nazis and the Western world had been going on since 1939, but it was only in December 1941 that America had entered the war, determined to join in the crushing of the Nazis and their Pacific-area partners, the Japanese. In early 1943 the outcome of the war was still in doubt, although the prospects for a victory by the Allies were improving steadily. The Germans were now fighting a two-front war, against the Russians in the east and against the Allies in the west, but they showed little inclination to put down their arms. American transports filled with men and urgently needed supplies formed massive convoys as they steamed into the North Atlantic, intent on providing arms and manpower to the British and, way up north through the port of Murmansk, badly needed supplies for the Russians.

One such transport was the S.S. *Dorchester*, filled to capacity with American troops. On the night of February 3, 1943, a Nazi U-boat fired a torpedo into her side, and within a brief span of time the vessel began to sink. Although all on board had been trained what to do in such an emergency, pandemonium broke loose. Many of the men could not find their lifejackets in the dark, and confusion, fear, and hysteria broke out.

In one corner of the vessel four chaplains—Rabbi Goode, Father George L. Fox, Rev. Clark V. Poling, and Rev. John P. Washington—wearing their lifejackets, were preparing to board the lifeboats that offered them a chance for survival. And then, almost simultaneously, they realized that scores of young soldiers were running around, bewildered, terrified, because they could not find their own lifejackets, and the ship appeared to be ready to sink at any moment. Without any discussion, almost as though they were divinely inspired, all four of the religious leaders removed their lifejackets and handed them to the nearest soldiers.

Survivors of that horrible night recall seeing the four men standing on the deck of the doomed vessel, their arms interlocked, almost smiling, not even wishing to take up any room in the crowded lifeboats.

After the war the U.S. government commemorated their action by issuing a postage stamp dedicated to the four chaplains, and one of the permanent exhibits in the Soldiers and Sailors Liberty Memorial Building in Washington comprises the first sheet of the postage stamp. A memorial fountain paying tribute to them was built in the National Memorial Park in Falls Church, Virginia. And a Boy Scout camp in Dillsburg, Pennsylvania, where Rabbi Goode had camped when he was a boy, has erected a memorial chapel.

The heroic four chaplains, including Rabbi Alexander Goode, who gave up their lives so that others might live have become an example of self-sacrificing courageousness that has seldom been matched, an everlasting symbol of faith and heroism above and beyond the call of duty.

YONATAN NETANYAHU

Casualty at Entebbe

THE NAME "ENTEBBE" has come to signify extraordinary courage, heroism, and superior planning and execution. It is the name of an airport in Uganda, in the heart of the African continent, which the world remembers as a place where a few dared to pit their skill and bravery against very heavy odds and emerged triumphant in an unprecedented effort to rescue innocent people in great peril.

The story began to untold in late June 1976, as the United States was getting ready to celebrate its Bicentennial, the two-hundredth anniversary of the founding of the American republic. An Air France airliner was hijacked soon after it took off from Athens on the last leg of what should have been a routine flight from Tel Aviv to Paris. The hijackers were terrorists, mostly Arabs and Germans, and their hostages were Jews and Gentiles. The plane was flown to Entebbe, where the hostages were kept in a virtual prison in an unused airport building. After a few days, the non-Jews were freed and permitted to resume their trip to Paris. The Jews were promised their freedom if the Israel government would free imprisoned Arab terrorists who had been captured in earlier acts of terror.

The world watched with bated breath while the deadline neared when the hostages in Entebbe would either be freed or exe-

cuted, depending, according to the terrorists, on what the Israel government would do. While some high-ranking diplomats tried to bargain for the release of the hostages and the Israel government reluctantly considered the idea of exchanging their imprisoned terrorists in order to save the lives of the civilian hostages, a top-secret plan was being developed for a daring landing at the airport itself and the swift release of the hostages.

To mount such a rescue seemed at first glance almost impossible. Entebbe lay 2,500 miles away from Israel. Reaching the area meant passing through unfriendly territory. Touching down secretly and quickly, snatching the hostages from the hands of their armed captors, and bringing them back safely to Israel—it all seemed more like a fictional plot in a suspense novel than something that could realistically be carried out.

Among the military planners in Israel there were some who believed it could be done and others who thought the idea suicidal. One of the Israeli officers who believed that the plan could work, and that it was well worth the risk in order to save the more than one hundred hostages, was a young lieutenant, Yonatan Netanyahu.

The son of a well-known Israeli scholar, thirty-year-old Yonatan had been born in New York but returned with his family to Israel when he was a small child. Later he returned to New York, and celebrated his bar mitzvah in a Long Beach, New York, synagogue. In the 1967 Six Day War he was an Israeli soldier and was wounded in the fierce fighting on the Golan Heights. Later he chose to enter officers' training school, and during the 1973 Yom Kippur War he was decorated for bravery under fire. It was his unit, under his personal leadership, that was chosen to carry out the daring Entebbe rescue mission, a mission that he felt would succeed and that he also thought had to be carried out, no matter how dangerous, for otherwise it would mean that the State of Israel had turned its back on a group of endangered Jews, who had been spirited off for no reason other than the fact that they were Jews.

The Entebbe rescue mission, which took place in the morning hours of July 4, America's Bicentennial Day, has become a legend. The small convoy that set off from Israel managed to land at the faroff airport, rescue the hostages, and bring them back safely to

Israel. Only one member of the rescue team was lost in the raid—Yonatan Netanyahu.

More than four thousand mourners attended the funeral of the young Israeli commando when he was buried at the Mount Herzl Cemetery in Jerusalem. People of good will throughout the world were saddened to learn of his death. In an editorial honoring Israel for its rescue, the New York *Times* said that "it will serve as an inspiration to other countries that, when the occasion demands and if they have the steadfastness and the will, they can do as much."

A book dedicated to young Yonatan's grandfather, a rabbi who died in 1935, spoke of his "life work for Zionism and nobility of spirit." The hero of Entebbe must certainly have inherited some of that dedication to Israel and a measure of that noble spirit.

S. Y. AGNON

Nobel Author with Yarmulke

IN 1966 A MAN WEARING A YARMULKE and a full dress suit stepped forward as his name was called out and accepted the Nobel Prize for literature—for his own work, and in the name of the people of Israel. Although there had been many Jews who had won the world's most prestigious prize—for physics, chemistry, medicine, and literature—this was the first time an Israeli had been so honored, and it was a day of great rejoicing for Jews everywhere.

Shmuel Yossef Agnon at the time was seventy-eight years old, and he had been writing novels, short stories, poems, and essays almost from the time he was a teen-ager. Only a few of his books had been translated into English, but the members of the literature prize committee honored Agnon for emerging as a "giant among Israel's writers."

The gentle expression on the old man's face as he received the Nobel Prize was caught in photographs that appeared in newspapers and on television. The expression was a mixture of humaneness, awe, and wonder, blended with his own unique commitment to the ancient principles of the Jewish faith. Agnon, who died a few years later in 1970 in his beloved Jerusalem, personified the man of spirit who sought all his life to illumine the mystery that has guided the destiny of the Jewish people, and the mystique that has dominated the relationship between the Jews and God and between the Jewish people and the Land of Israel.

He was born into a family renowned for its learning, and grew up in a small town in Galicia. The family's name was Czaczkes, but the pen name of Agnon that he adopted later became his permanent name. He studied in local schools, concentrating on traditional biblical and talmudic texts, and was also tutored by his father, who was a fur merchant with a penchant for scholarship. Putting words to paper, in Hebrew and Yiddish, came easily and early to him; and by the time he was fifteen, he had already published a number of poems in both languages. At the age of eighteen he became assistant editor of a Yiddish weekly; and before he was twenty, he set sail for Palestine, settling in Jerusalem, and began to write in earnest.

A year before the outbreak of World War I, in 1913, feeling himself lacking in formal education and sensing the need for greater contact with other literary men, he went to Berlin, where he remained for a decade, returning to Jerusalem in 1924, where he resided the remainder of his life. When he left for Jerusalem, he was accompanied by his wife and two young children. He had studied and worked in Germany, arousing the admiration of various literary critics and winning the support of Zalman Shocken, a distinguished Jewish publisher, who provided him with a steady income so that he could devote all of his time to writing.

Over a span of years his work began to appear in magazines, newspapers, and books, and the students of the Jewish community in Palestine, and later Israel, were taught to read and study his work, which was not always easy to understand. The youngsters, combining the Hebrew initials of his first and middle names, dubbed him "Shai" Agnon and spoke of him with great affection.

Although he was brought up in a home where religious observance was traditional, Agnon for a short time in his life abandoned all Jewish traditions during a period of personal anguish, as a form of protest against what he considered to be the evils that permeated the world. However, this period did not last long, and he became again, and remained, an observant Jew, convinced that the only way the Jewish people could survive and flourish was through a total commitment to their ancient faith.

The Israel Prize for Literature was bestowed on him twice, once in 1954 and again in 1958. Agnon was not the kind of author who sought the limelight, and day in and day out, for a period of many years prior to the establishment of Israel and afterwards, in the difficult days of the fighting of 1948–49, 1956, and 1967, he remained at his desk in his book-lined study in Jerusalem, putting words to paper, creating a world that had existed once in central Europe and another that had flourished in the early years of Palestine, seeking to explain the motivations, the hopes, the frustrations of those bygone days. Many of his stories retain a dreamlike quality, and although he was struck by the sense of alienation that many people in the first half of the twentieth century experienced, he was equally convinced that people could achieve a genuine sense of serenity and inner peace if they remained faithful to the basic truths they had been taught that evolved from long centuries of suffering and travail.

Throughout his work Agnon demonstrated that there was an unbreakable kinship between the Jewish people and their ancient homeland. He wrote once about the Western Wall, the only remaining structure from the Holy Temple erected in Jerusalem:

> Now the Western Wall is all that we have left of our beloved Temple since ancient times. It has been left by the Holy One, blessed be He, by reason of his great pity for us, and is twelve times as tall as a man, corresponding to the Twelve Tribes, in order that each man in Israel should devote his heart and will to prayer in accordance with his height and his prayer. It is built of great stones, each stone being five ells by six, and their like is not to be found in any building in the world. They stand without pitch or mortar or lime between them, in spite of which they are as firmly united as if they were one stone, like the Assembly of Israel which has not even the slightest sovereign power to hold it together, yet is, nonetheless, one unit throughout the world.

When Agnon spoke at the banquet in Stockholm at which he received the Nobel Prize, he said that although he knew it was not so, he nonetheless felt that he had been born in Jerusalem. He said he could trace his ancestry to the ancient Levites, who were the singers and poets of Temple days, and he carried on all his work in that same ancient tradition—writing words that were in effect songs of praise to God.

Reading the works of Agnon requires concentration as well as imagination, for although he himself lived in the twentieth century, he often wrote as though his contemporaries were King David or Maimonides or Judah the Prince. His writing took little notice of historical facts and sought instead to unite the whole of Jewish history and experience into one tapestry of timelessness.

Many of Israel's younger writers have paid tribute to Agnon for showing them a way to reveal their innermost sentiments, and in that sense one can say that Agnon has laid the groundwork for an exciting new Israeli literature which is only now beginning to be recognized.

CHARLES STEINMETZ

Electric Power for the People

HE WAS GNOMELIKE IN SIZE and a hunchback. Some people said he was half angel and half child because he had a generous spirit and yet loved to engage in pranks with children of his own height. When he first arrived in the United States, a refugee from Europe, the immigration authorities wanted to keep him out and almost succeeded in doing so. Yet this brilliant scientist helped make life more enjoyable for tens of millions of people.

Charles Steinmetz was born in Germany in 1865, the son of a poor railroad clerk, also a hunchback. As a child he was a brilliant student, and he excelled in all the natural sciences as well as in the study of languages (German, Polish, Hebrew, French, Latin, Greek) and most especially in algebra, astronomy, and geometry. He came to accept his physical appearance and compensated for it by developing an outgoing way, joking with young and old, putting people at ease in his presence.

Like many other young people at the time, he became involved with a socialist movement that wanted to see better working and living conditions for the poor. Steinmetz was opposed however to any violent action that would lead to a new regime— he carried his gentle way into politics too.

The German police were not so lenient, however, and Steinmetz received a warning that he had better leave the country if he did not want to be imprisoned. He fled across the border to Switzerland, entered the technical institute in Zurich, and struck up a friendship with a young student who had been to America. The new friend, Oscar Asmussen, was deeply impressed by Steinmetz's mind and suggested that the two of them leave for America. Steinmetz had no funds, but when Oscar received a first-class ticket from a relative in the United States, he changed it into a pair of steerage tickets, and the two of them set sail.

When the U.S. immigration people looked at Steinmetz, they were unimpressed. When he confessed that he had no money, no friends or relatives in America, and hardly spoke any English, they were determined to send him back—until his friend intervened, explaining that young Steinmetz was a scientific genius who would do great things for America. The officials reluctantly let Steinmetz enter the United States—and two years later, when he was still only twenty-six, he was already carrying out an experiment in Brooklyn to replace a team of horses by an electrical engine. The experiment did not work perfectly, but for Steinmetz it was a first step toward a whole chain of inventions that would make life easier and more comfortable for practically everyone.

When the factory he worked for in Yonkers was bought out by the newly formed General Electric Company in 1892, he accepted a position working in GE's large laboratory in Lynn, Massachusetts, not because he wanted to make more money (he never cared about mundane things like money and, in fact, all his life refused to accept more than a very modest salary) but because he was convinced that he would be able to create important new inventions in a large, well-equipped lab. He quickly impressed his co-workers by his amazing mathematical wizardry, and taught them how to accept his odd appearance by continuing his practice of playing pranks and harmless practical jokes on them.

During his first few years in America Steinmetz had succeeded in solving the problem of electrical seepage, known as hysteresis. Now, in Lynn, in response to the challenge of "taming" alternating current—which was far more potent than the conventional direct current—he produced a manuscript crammed with complicated equations and titled *Theory and Calculation of Alternating Current Phenomena*. It required three thick volumes to print what was later acclaimed as a classic of scientific literature.

Before he was thirty years old, Steinmetz had harnessed the power of alternating current, which ushered in a whole new era in electrical energy.

The president of General Electric told his board that "Steinmetz was not cut out to be a maker of mechanical devices but an interpreter of scientific laws, a thinker in a class with Isaac Newton." When GE moved to Schenectady, New York, Steinmetz went along and was told that he could do anything he wanted. "Sit and dream all day, if you wish—we'll pay you for your dreaming."

In time Steinmetz developed a new type of street light, using magnetite as a filament. The crowds in Schenectady cheered when the light came on, for at that moment theirs was the brightest corner on earth illumined by artificial light. He was honored by a number of learned societies, by Harvard University, and by Union College in Schenectady.

He built a home in Schenectady and stocked it with scores of animals—a passion he had developed in recent years. Neighborhood children delighted in visiting the Steinmetz "zoo," but it was hardly a zoo in the traditional sense since so few of the animals were caged. He also took an interest in botany, and was especially attracted to cactus plants, which he admitted he admired not for their beauty but for their determination to remain hardy and survive. He did not have to spell out the fact that in a sense he saw himself in those somber-looking plants.

He had a rare ability to make friends, and a fantastic capacity for work. In addition to his work at GE, and caring for his animals and plants at home, Steinmetz taught engineering courses to fellow engineers in the evenings and found time to teach electrical engineering at Union College. He became the most popular teacher on the campus, enabling his students to ignore his appearance (which was never improved by his worn, baggy clothes) and see the inner man in their professor. He also continued his lifelong preoccupation with practical jokes, delighting in seeing a pompous visitor jump into the air as a result of a prankish electrical charge.

He continued to develop numerous electrical gadgets and dreamed of developments that have not yet come to pass. For example, he thought of harnessing the power of Niagara Falls as a source of electrical power, but since that would require diverting the mighty stream, he said he would compromise and let it run from Monday through Saturday but un-divert it on Sundays for the benefit of honeymooning couples.

Steinmetz talked of a plan to widen the Bering Strait, which separates the Asian and North American continents, between Alaska and the outer reaches of Siberia. Such a step, he believed, would bring warm Pacific waters flowing into the northern waters, gradually defrosting places like upper Canada and Greenland and warming the United States.

He continued to take an interest in the development of society, and proposed that people should not have to work more than four hours a day at jobs they considered drudgery. He also helped develop adult-education classes for immigrants and for the retarded, and designed walls of glass for classrooms used by tubercular children to maximize their exposure to sunlight. He believed in electrical power as a great source of light for everyone and used to say, "Let us bring light into the lives of people, a light that does not destroy but only heals."

Steinmetz took a great interest in everything about him, and the small boy in him stayed as active as ever, even after he became a world-famous celebrity, meeting and conferring with Marconi, Edison, Einstein, and other great figures. One of his great joys was a visit to the popular actor Douglas Fairbanks and seeing how a typical Western film was made.

He once told a reporter, "Only men of little minds declare there is no God. The greater the mind, the greater the belief that each one of us is a part of a Supreme Mind."

When Steinmetz died in 1923, he left the world a better place than he had found it.

HANNAH SENESH

Parachutist with a Mission

ON NOVEMBER 7, 1944, a twenty-three-year-old girl by the name of Hannah Senesh was executed by a firing squad in a prison yard in Budapest, Hungary. Although her Hungarian captors claimed she was an enemy agent parachuted into their country to disrupt their pro-Nazi war efforts, she was a parachutist whose main objective had really been to help her fellow Jews caught up in the web of tyranny and murder that enclosed that hapless country.

Hannah Senesh came from a home that thought of itself as more Hungarian than Jewish. The family discounted the rising tide of anti-Semitic outbreaks in Germany and Austria, but Hannah, then only eighteen, felt that there was no future for Jews except in Palestine. In 1939, leaving her mother's home in Budapest (her father had died earlier), she went to Palestine, where she joined an agricultural settlement. She learned Hebrew, enjoyed the hard work of scrubbing floors and doing the laundry, and would have been happy had it not been for the steady news reports of Nazi victories in one European country after another. She felt especially worried about her mother, who now, like millions of other Jews, was trapped in Nazi-occupied Europe.

She was a shy girl given to writing poetry and filling her diary with her innermost thoughts, but in January of 1943, when she had already become an established settler, she was suddenly struck with one idea: She would somehow get to Hungary, help in

any way she could with the underground smuggling of Jews out of the country and into Palestine, and try to include her mother among those who would be brought out. She wrote in her diary about her idea: "It seems absurd, but it is necessary and perhaps possible."

As though by fate, a visitor from a nearby village came to her settlement, announcing that a group of volunteers who were ready to parachute into Europe was being formed. She signed up at once, but it was a whole year before she was finally sent to Egypt for training in a British military center. She passed her training with ease, and in fact found herself reassuring one of the newer recruits. "It is nothing," she said. "You go up in a plane and jump, and immediately you are on the ground again. You'll enjoy it."

She was the first woman volunteer in the parachutist group, and the British officers who were doing the rigorous training and the other young Jews who had volunteered for the dangerous mission were filled with admiration. Her comrades remembered her as tall, blue-eyed, with brown, curly hair flowing about her elongated face. She had seen her brother, Giora, reach haven in Palestine only a short time before she started her parachutist training.

The Palestinian parachutists had all been trained to radio back to British headquarters military information that could be helpful in defeating the Nazis. Their secondary mission was to bring comfort and aid to the beleaguered Jewish communities. On March 13, 1944, the volunteers took off from an Italian airfield and were dropped in Yugoslavia among friendly partisans. Soon after they had settled in with the anti-Nazi fighters, word came that the Nazis had completely taken over Hungary, making entry to that country more difficult than ever. For the next three months, the Palestinian volunteers lived and fought with the partisans in Yugoslavia, Hannah among them. But she counted every day that she was not in Hungary as a wasted day, feeling that if she and her comrades could get to that country, then somehow, perhaps they could do something to help the Jews.

Finally Hannah and two other Palestinians set out to cross the border. It took nearly a month of marching and hiding out in the woods. They crossed the border singly, planning to meet in Budapest, and then suddenly squads of German soldiers and Hungarian police surrounded them all. All were captured and shipped to Gestapo headquarters for questioning. The chief aim of the interrogators was to learn the secret radio code with which the parachutists had planned to help guide British bombers toward their objectives. None of the parachutists, including Hannah, would reveal the code, despite the beatings and various torture methods used by the Germans.

When it was discovered that Hannah was originally a Hungarian and that her mother still lived in Budapest, the police tried to get Hannah to disclose the details of the code by threatening to kill her mother before her eyes, but she could not be swayed. The mother and daughter were reunited briefly in the Budapest prison and fell on each other amid much crying and weeping. Hannah cried out to her mother, "Forgive me, Mother. I had to do it."

Hannah remained in prison for several months. When she was with other Jewish prisoners, she told them about Palestine, encouraging them and setting an example of courage for them. For two months she was confined to a solitary cell, but the jailers could not break her spirit.

Later Hannah's mother was arrested again and kept in the same prison and the two would see each other from a distance, and at times they could converse. Her mother once asked her if she thought her trip by parachute had been worthwhile. Hannah replied, "My time in prison has not been wasted—I have made many Zionists."

Toward the end of her stay in prison Hannah was put back into a large cell with other prisoners, including two small children who had never learned to read or write. She taught them how to do both, and as a reward for their good work made them paper dolls, fashioned from scraps. Her manner was always buoyant, and she undoubtedly helped many of the other prisoners withstand the ordeal of confinement in a Nazi jail.

As the fate of the Nazi war effort became clearer, the Hungarian authorities began to change their attitude toward their prisoners. Hannah's mother was freed, and the one thing she tried desperately to do for her daughter, at Hannah's request, was to obtain for her a Hebrew Bible. Mrs. Senesh scoured all the bookstores and asked dozens of people, but none was to be found. It did not really matter, for in a few days Hannah was transferred to another jail for trial.

Full details of the courtroom proceedings remain unknown, but it has been learned that Hannah stood before her judges and told them defiantly that the Nazis and all their collaborators were a gang of war criminals who would soon be punished for their deeds. The Hungarian judges delayed the verdict for a few days, deeply impressed by the twenty-three-year-old woman from Palestine, and perhaps hoping that the Allies would soon step up their bombing raids or that the Russian forces would soon arrive and put an end to the Nazi regime.

On the morning of November 7 Hannah Senesh stood before a firing squad. The order to shoot was given and her death was instantaneous. Some of the prisoners whispered the traditional Kaddish mourners' prayer for her after hearing the sound of shots. Others, who had come to revere the young woman, remained mute for days on end.

After the war ended, vessels carrying Jewish immigrants to Palestine, mostly survivors of the Nazi concentration camps, fought their way to the shores of the Promised Land, since the British authorities had banned further Jewish immigration. One of these vessels bore the name of Hannah Senesh. It has become, for Israel's young generation, a name synonymous with courage and self-sacrifice.

A gifted poet, Hannah Senesh once wrote:

Happy the match, consumed kindling a flame,
Happy the flame burning in the hidden depths of hearts.

MAIMONIDES

Rabbi, Scholar, Physician, Philosopher

Schools, synagogues, and hospitals in many parts of the world have been named for him. A portrait of his bearded, scholarly, turbaned face has been reproduced on postage stamps of a number of countries as well as on book covers and notebooks numbering in the millions used by Jewish school children. There is a traditional saying: "From Moses [the Lawgiver] to Moses [Moses ben Maimon, or Maimonides] there is no one like Moses" —that is, there has never been another such great Jewish figure.

Who was this man, renowned as scholar, philosopher, communal leader, and physician?

Born in Cordova, Spain, on Passover eve in 1135, young Moses was the scion of an illustrious family of scholars. Even as a small boy, he displayed an affinity for learning that marked him for a future of scholarly distinction. When he was thirteen, however, he and his family had to abandon their peaceful, pious lives and flee. From across the Mediterranean a group of Moslem fanatics overran much of Spain and killed any "infidels" they could find.

The family wandered through Spain and North Africa, and finally settled in Cairo, then a flourishing center of the known world. During the years of flight and wandering, members of the family were forced to save their lives by pretending to be Moslems, but when they struck roots in Cairo, they shed all pretense and lived fully and freely as Jews.

Young Moses was soon recognized as a brilliant scholar, rabbi, and communal leader, and the Cairo Jews named him as head of the community. He was reluctant, however, to earn his livelihood as a rabbi and chose instead to become a physician and continue without fee with his scholarly and communal work.

His reputation as a man of profound learning as well as a gifted physician spread at once, and soon he was named court physician to the Sultan Saladin. Some historians reported that during the Crusades, when King Richard of England lay wounded in Jerusalem, Maimonides was summoned to treat him.

Because of the great regard in which he was held by the leaders and people of Egypt, the lot of the Jewish community in Egypt during his lifetime was a happy one. From distant isolated Jewish communities, letters began to arrive soliciting Maimonides' advice on a wide variety of religious questions as well as on political affairs that affected individual settlements of Jews.

Maimonides answered all these inquiries, expounding on the Torah and Talmud, explaining the significance of various laws and practices, and always urging strict adherence to Jewish traditions, no matter how difficult the circumstances.

One of his most famous letters was a communication he sent to the Jews of Yemen, who had pitifully little contact with other Jewish communities. They had written that their Moslem neighbors were demanding that they convert to Islam or face death, and turned to him for guidance. They were also struggling under the burden of extra-heavy taxation that had been imposed on them, and were puzzled by talk of the Messiah's imminent arrival preached by a local Jew.

Maimonides wrote back that the preacher was unbalanced and should be ignored, promised to use his influence to have their taxes reduced, and urged them to remain true to their ancient faith. The letter was written in simple language so that everyone could understand it, and the result was that the Yemenite Jews took new heart and rejected the fierce efforts to convert them to Islam. Their lot was eased when Maimonides succeeded in having their heavy tax burden reduced.

The great scholar devoted many years to the preparation of texts that have remained invaluable commentaries on Jewish life and are studied avidly to this day. Among his most famous works are the *Guide for the Perplexed*, in which he sought in a rational manner to show that there is no essential conflict between Judaism and philosophy, and his massive commentary *Mishneh Torah*, a guide to the Mishnah intended for the general reader. He also wrote commentaries on the talmudic tractates. One of his most important contributions was to codify the religious laws, making their observance far easier than previously for great masses of Jews.

In his personal life Maimonides suffered a tragic blow when his beloved brother David was lost at sea, and with him all of the family's valuables. The burden of caring for David's family fell upon him, and it took him a long time to reconcile himself to the death of his brother.

Among the many works of Maimonides were his important thirteen Articles of Faith, enunciating his own profound belief in the Jewish code of life. Each of the articles begins with the words *Ani Maamin*, or "I believe," and one of these statements—expressing confidence in the advent of the Messiah—was often chanted by inmates of Nazi concentration camps as a sign of their abiding faith. The Articles of Faith were also, centuries later, transformed into a beautiful poem, beginning with the words *Yigdal Elohim*. This verse-prayer has been incorporated into the prayer book and is usually sung at the conclusion of the Friday evening service.

As a physician, Maimonides was a forerunner of modern medicine in that he preached the importance of preventive medicine, stressing always the interrelationship between a patient's physical and spiritual side in arriving at a proper diagnosis. He wrote that a physician must use not only his medical knowledge but also "art, logic, and intuition" in treating a patient.

Maimonides' basic approach to his patients can best be seen in his medical treatise *The Preservation of Youth*, in which he wrote:

> Physicians have commanded that we beware of emotional changes in the patient and keep him under constant surveillance. We must also guard against emotional experiences that hurt the morale of the patient. In this way, the health of a normal person will improve—especially if the disease afflicts organs like the stomach or brain, where emotional factors and melancholy play such a significant role.

Not only was Maimonides an early practitioner of the psychological treatment of disease, but he also keenly understood the influence that ecology and environment have in the prevention of disease. He wrote:

> The quality of urban air compared to desert or forest air is like polluted water compared to pure, filtered water. . . . If you have no choice and must live near the city, try at least to live in a northeastern suburb, so that the northern wind and sun can dispel the air pollution and filter it as best as possible.

Although astronomy was then in a very early stage of development, Maimonides was fascinated by this field of scientific endeavor and spent many years studying all the known data. He was, however, unalterably opposed to all forms of astrology, which he denounced as a false science.

The works of the great scholar-physician-philosopher have been translated into many languages and remain a key subject in all courses of Jewish study. He died before his seventieth birthday and was buried in the ancient city of Tiberias, where his tomb now attracts visitors from all parts of the world.

One might describe Maimonides as having successfully attempted to bridge the gap between religion and science, and having bequeathed a method of understanding Judaism for all time.

YIGAL ALLON

Leader of the Palmach

HE HAS REACHED THE PINNACLE of Israeli leadership, serving as his country's foreign minister, consulting with Presidents, Prime Ministers, and world leaders in various fields, and his name has been mentioned on a number of occasions as a possible Prime Minister. And yet Yigal Allon is probably most at home in the small farming community where he grew up, nestled at the foot of historic Mount Tabor, where, for his bar mitzvah, his father gave him a gun and said it was time he learned to use it.

He was the youngest of seven brothers, whose mother died when he was still a small child. His father, Reuben Peicovich, was a strong-willed man of the soil who never shrank from a fight although he much preferred the peaceful life of tilling his fields. He was a tough man, and the Arabs who thought they could steal from his farm learned very quickly that he did not hesitate to resist, with gunfire if necessary. In time he won the respect of his Arab neighbors, visited with them, invited them to his home, and tried throughout his lifetime to establish a mutually respectful relationship between his own Jewish community and that of the Arabs.

Yigal grew up on the farm and worked the soil with love and skill. He studied modern farming and applied what he learned, and shared his new knowledge with his friends and neighbors. It was a

lonely life, especially after his sister and brothers married and moved elsewhere, but he and his father persisted in the life they had chosen—to make the ancient land fruitful again and to help lay the groundwork for a return of the Jewish people to the homeland.

Like so many other young men in Palestine in the 1920s and 1930s, Yigal Allon became a member of the underground Haganah defense organization. He was sixteen at the time but had already shown traits of leadership, courage, dedication to the cause of Zionism, and expertise with firearms. The Haganah carried out secret training exercises for select young people, and soon Yigal was chosen to be trained for a role as a Haganah officer. He had earlier led a number of patrols against bands of Arab marauders who had been harassing Jewish settlements, and reports of his daring and coolness in action had been sent back to headquarters.

When he was twenty years old, after having been taught the rudiments of modern military tactics, Yigal Allon was given special officers instruction by the Haganah, and made his first contacts with a number of future leaders of Israel, including Moshe Dayan.

A year later, Allon himself became an instructor in a school set up by Haganah for noncommissioned officers. He introduced a concept into the training that has remained a standard exercise for the Israeli defense forces to this day—drills carried out with live ammunition. This, of course, increased the risk of fatalities or wounds, but it also made the young trainees extra vigorous in the course of their training. The Haganah leadership approved his system and soon came to realize that Allon was destined for ever greater responsibilities.

Allon never sent his young volunteers into difficult night forays unless he himself was with them. More than most Palestinian Jews at the time, he felt he understood the Arabs' mentality, and he created the night-attack concept which proved highly effective both in those early years when isolated Haganah units were forced to fight against much larger and better armed Arab units and later when Israel was forced to face Arab armies that outnumbered her men enormously.

When World War II was launched in September 1939 by the German invasion of Poland, thousands of Palestinian Jews—a great many of whom were secret Haganah members—volunteered for service in the British Army. Allon was among the first who wanted to sign up, but his Haganah commanders vetoed the idea. They felt there was a greater need for men of Allon's caliber to remain in Palestine—for one thing, to guard against the possibility of Arab assaults and, for another, to prepare a defense against the possible breakthrough of German troops, whose plan was to seize North Africa, cut through to Egypt, move north to Palestine, and then hold the entire Mediterranean basin in their grip.

Syria and Lebanon in the spring of 1941 actually became pro-Nazi bastions when officials of the Vichy French government took command of those countries. The Haganah leadership even prepared a plan whereby, if the Germans came into Palestine, the Jews would hold out on Mount Carmel in a fortified redoubt from which they would stage surprise sabotage attacks against the enemy.

The uncertainty of the war raging in Europe, North Africa, and the Pacific was so great at the time that the Haganah commanders decided that, in addition to the self-defense Haganah organization, they needed a mobile striking force that could be sent at an instant's notice to any site of Jewish settlement and carry out preemptive attacks in order to avert onslaughts on the Jewish community. Allon was asked to organize such a force, which was named Palmach.

He quickly recruited one hundred Haganah volunteers and, at a special training camp near the Sea of Galilee, set about training a tough, commando-type unit that would be the striking arm of the Jewish community in Palestine. The British knew of the Palmach program and approved. In fact, soon after its formation, Palmach was asked to make its way into Syria and Lebanon to find out the extent of a reported large build-up of pro-Vichy, pro-Nazi troops in the area.

Allon led one group of scouts on a daring operation that prevented a possible massacre of a larger group of Australian soldiers bringing up the rear. The Australian officer in charge was deeply appreciative of the help the Jewish troops had given his men and offered to pay each of the Palmach soldiers. His offer was made through an interpreter since Allon at the time did not understand English. Drawing himself up to his full height, Allon told the interpreter, "Explain that we are not Zulus—we are fighting for our homes, not for money. If we are needed again, we'll be glad to help. After all, we have a common enemy."

In a matter of weeks, the number of Palmach volunteers grew
tenfold. The training was tough and merciless. When the British
called for volunteers to parachute behind enemy lines into Europe,
many of these turned out to be Palmach recruits. They were a
very tough, very serious, and very dedicated group of men and
women. And the leadership that Allon continued to offer served
them as an example and an inspiration.

When the Second World War ended, Palmach soldiers played
decisive roles in helping to smuggle thousands of Jews out of
Europe to Palestine in the face of British restrictions on Jewish
immigration. When Israel was established in May 1948, Yigal
Allon was commander of the Palmach, which numbered some
seven thousand men. The special force was assigned the most
difficult and most dangerous tasks in the war that followed the
proclamation of independence, and came through with flying
colors.

When peace came, Allon undertook to make up for his lack
of formal education. He studied at the Hebrew University and at
Oxford, became interested in politics, was elected to the Knesset in
1954 (where he has remained to this day), became Deputy Prime
Minister in 1968 and later Foreign Minister.

Allon would like nothing better today than to be able to visit
in the home of his Arab neighbor just as he used to do when he
was a youngster, converse in Arabic, and cement true bonds of
friendship. As a diplomat with a strong military background, however, he is realistic enough to believe that until such a time comes
his nation must remain ever vigilant.

HAYM SALOMON

He Financed Early America

His name has been given to a United States naval vessel. Students of American history know him as an early Jewish settler, during the bleak days when Washington led his embattled American troops against the British, who helped turn the tide of victory by making available large sums of money that were desperately needed for military supplies. Thus Haym Salomon has come to be known as the man who helped finance the Revolutionary War—but that does not really tell the story of this remarkable man adequately.

He was born in Poland in 1740, received an excellent education which included mastery of several languages, and at an early age was already a well-established merchant and banker. Nevertheless, he was unhappy in Poland—he hated the oppressive atmosphere that permeated everything and was especially incensed by the unceasing economic, political, and social oppression of the Jewish community.

When he was about thirty years of age, he began to hear of a faraway country, then a colony of England, where the people proclaimed that they lived in a new world where everyone was free to follow the dictates of his own conscience. The reports of America struck a responsive chord in him, and, although he was a rather frail man and the journey to America was a long and arduous one, he decided that he too wanted to become part of the new country.

Without further ado he set sail for America and arrived in 1772. Despite the problems of any new immigrant to a strange land, Salomon knew at once that this was what he had been looking for—the very air seemed to breathe freedom, and he set about building a new life. He sought out fellow Jews, of whom there were only a small number at the time, and soon he considered himself an established newcomer on American shores. As a banker with a reputation for complete trustworthiness, he became involved with European banks and companies, handling large sums of money for exports and imports, and he found that he was quickly becoming a very rich man.

He was sitting perched high on his stool in his office one morning when a friend came to see him. The man asked Salomon if he wished to join a group of Americans who were planning to throw off the yoke of English rule, which he said was restricting the new country's people. "We are taxed heavily, and yet we have no voice in our government," he said. Salomon did not hesitate and joined the secret group immediately. He still remembered the oppressed life he had known in Poland, and was determined that America should be helped to become a free, liberty-loving country.

He participated in clandestine meetings of early American patriots, pledging his help in securing guns and ammunition. In 1776 the war began in earnest, and after the British were defeated and driven from Boston, they re-established their headquarters in New York. One of the first things they did was arrest everyone known to be in sympathy with the revolution, and Salomon was one of those detained.

The American prisoners were marched off to a large, old building that had been converted into a prison. There were no blankets, and at night the prisoners suffered from the cold. For Salomon, who did not have a robust constitution, it was a terrible ordeal. But the British soon learned that their Jewish prisoner was a linguist, and he was pressed into service as an interpreter to help communicate orders from the British officers to the German-speaking mercenary Hessian soldiers.

What the British did not know was that when they ordered

Salomon to translate a set of orders, he did not do so literally. Instead, he added to and expanded the instructions so that in effect he was saying to the Hessian troops, "Look, what are you doing here? This is a great, beautiful country that will soon be free. Why do you want to lose your lives in a fight that is not yours, and in which the Americans will triumph anyway? Take my advice, lay down your arms, forget about the old country, and start a new life in America."

Many of the Hessians followed his advice, and the British could not understand at the time why so many of the mercenaries were disappearing into the night, never to be seen again.

A group of patriots managed to arrange for Salomon's release, getting him out of the makeshift New York jail in the middle of the night and making good their escape to Philadelphia. Here Salomon was pressed into service as the official broker of the brand-new Office of Finance of the Continental Congress. His financial expertise was needed to help smoothe the transition of the revolutionaries into a stable government.

In his new role, he met a number of times with George Washington, Thomas Jefferson, James Madison, and James Monroe and saw to it that there would be no interruption in the war effort, and later in the peaceful era that followed, because of any shortage of funds. It meant transferring all of his own money into the still practically empty treasury of the new nation, but he did not hesitate to do so. He even paid the salaries of several of the national personalities of the new country because there was no one else to turn to—and soon enough his own family was virtually impoverished.

But Salomon never complained. The spirit of America had taken hold of him, and he was anxious to help in every way he could. When two of his old friends of Polish days, Thaddeus Kosciusko and Casimir Pulaski, came to America to help the new nation, he knew that he had been right in uprooting himself from the soil of Poland and resettling in America.

In all the years of the revolutionary period Salomon did not forget that he was a Jew, and he continued to support his coreligionists in any way he could. Undoubtedly he took a special pride in the fact that, although there were hardly two thousand Jews in America at the time, mostly refugees who had fled in earlier periods from the Inquisition in Spain and Portugal, a number of high officers in the American army were Jewish, and one of them commanded a company in battle.

By 1783 the concept of America as a free nation had come to be accepted in nearly every part of the world. The new nation was growing and prospering. And in that same year one of the most grateful and joyous participants in a ceremony marking the dedication of the new Mikveh Israel Synagogue in Philadelphia was Haym Salomon.

The governor of Pennsylvania had come to attend in person, and the rabbi, Gershom Mendes Seixas, sat in the first row alongside other dignitaries in a manner that said clearly that this was America, not Poland, where every person was accorded an equal right to freedom of worship. Salomon sat through the special Sabbath service, delighting in the beautiful new structure that he had helped build, confident that on American shores his coreligionists would be able to build a good life, as Jews and as Americans.

Although it was hardly more than a decade since he had first set foot on American soil, it had been such a lively, exciting, and productive time that sometimes Salomon felt he had been living in America all his life. The journey from Poland to Philadelphia seemed more like a trip from another planet to a virtual Garden of Eden.

When Salomon died two years later at the age of forty-five, he left a widow and children who were practically penniless. The United States owed him more than six hundred thousand dollars in loans that he had made available over a period of years. He never pressed for the money, content in the knowledge that he had helped achieve something far more important than money. To this day, there is still believed by some to be a debt owed by the U.S. government to Salomon's heirs. It will probably never be repaid—but it is a debt in name only, since Salomon was more than happy to know that in his own way he too helped shape the course of American history.

NELSON GLUECK

The Archaeologist-Rabbi

DR. NELSON GLUECK WAS THE PRESIDENT of Hebrew Union College–Jewish Institute of Religion in Cincinnati when he died in 1971 at the age of seventy. In that capacity, he was one of the foremost leaders of Reform Judaism in the world, but he will probably be best remembered as an archaeologist of the first rank, whose discoveries helped open up unknown layers of ancient Jewish and biblical history.

He was born and raised in Cincinnati, and earned a degree in Hebrew literature from Hebrew Union as well as a B.A. from the University of Cincinnati. At the age of twenty-three he was ordained a rabbi, but even then he was determined to devote his life to biblical and Palestinian scholarship rather than serve in a pulpit.

He proceeded at once to Europe, where he earned a doctorate from the University of Jena, in Germany, after taking time out to visit and study at the American School of Oriental Research in Jerusalem. At the school in Jerusalem he came under the influence of the greatest archaeologist of the Holy Land of the past fifty years, Professor William F. Albright.

After teaching for a time at his alma mater, Hebrew Union College, Glueck returned to Palestine, serving as director of the American School of Oriental Research for a number of years, and spent some time also as a lecturer in Bagdad, Iraq. At the same

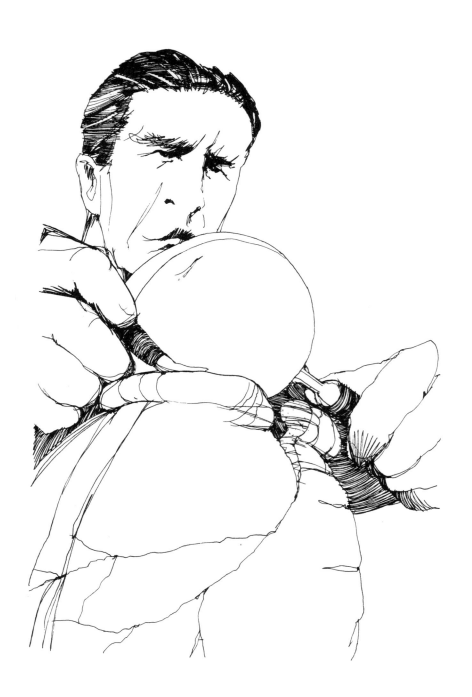

time, because of his growing scholarly reputation, he was named full professor of Bible and biblical archaeology at Hebrew Union College.

A tall, tanned, youthful-looking man all his life, Dr. Glueck searched every corner of the Holy Land, looking for archaeological finds. Using the Bible as his guidebook, he discovered more than a thousand ancient sites in Jordan and five hundred locations in the Negev region of Israel. He was able to date and pinpoint the exact location of King Solomon's ancient copper mines, and succeeded in delineating the precise boundary lines of the ancient biblical kingdoms of Edom, Moab, and Ammon. Thanks to his discoveries, an obscure people who inhabited the Negev, the Nabataeans, became known to modern historians and archaeologists.

During World War II the rabbi-archaeologist-scholar became an agent of the United States Office of Strategic Services (forerunner of the CIA), using his excellent contacts with Arabs in Jordan to obtain intelligence information helpful to the Allied war effort in the Middle East. He used the fact that he was an archaeologist as a cover.

In his extensive explorations of the Negev, which represents some three fifths of Israel's land area, he established that the vast region—long held to be an irreclaimable wasteland—had been inhabited successfully at various times in ancient days, including the period of Abraham and the era of the Judean kings. He was able to demonstrate through his digs that the Negev was home to both wandering and sedentary peoples as early as the fourth century B.C.E. He helped uncover the ancient system of irrigation methods that had made the purported wasteland bloom, encouraging the modern Israelis to attempt to turn the area into a verdant, productive region again.

Glueck roamed the Holy Land on foot, on horseback, and by car, making friends with all the people he encountered and winning the admiration of countless Arabs for his courage and endurance.

Thanks to his initiative, the Hebrew Union College established a branch in Jerusalem where rabbinical students must study for a year before attaining their ordination. He was elected president of the college in 1947, and was the recipient of a score of honorary degrees from universities around the world.

He was the author of numerous books, among which are *The River Jordan* and *Rivers in the Desert*. He was honored with an invitation to participate in the inauguration ceremonies of President John F. Kennedy, whom he blessed in the ancient biblical phrase "May the Lord be gracious unto thee," in Hebrew and in English.

When *Time* magazine featured Nelson Glueck on its cover, he was described as a paradoxical man—a rabbi who had never served a congregation but instead had spent his life roaming the ancient sites of the land of the Bible.

LEVI ESHKOL

Servant of His People

In Hebrew a person whom everybody considers an all-around capable man is called an *ish ha-eshkolot*—a "person of grape clusters." The meaning is that, like a cluster of grapes, he is good to the eye, good to the taste, and contains the sweet juice from which wine is made. Levi Eshkol, who served as a Prime Minister of Israel, was in every sense such a man, which led people to cite still another Hebrew adage, *Kishmo, ken hu*, or "A person is akin to his name."

Levi, whose original family name was Shkolnik, was born in Russia in 1895, the son of a poor schoolteacher who had made innovations in the teaching in Jewish religious schools, emphasizing the importance of modern Hebrew and striving to upgrade methods of teaching that had not been changed for centuries.

When he was still a very young man, Levi left his father's home to join the idealistic pioneers who were going to Palestine to fashion a new life on the soil of the ancient Jewish homeland. Like most other young people of the time, he went to work on the land, as farmer and road builder, and took turns standing guard against Arab marauders.

He was one of the early settlers of Degania Bet, and his fellow colonists soon recognized his abilities as a manager and executive. Although his kibbutz did not allow any members to own any property individually, the group's successful agricultural and industrial enterprises made it necessary for someone to take charge

of what amounted to big-business decisions in the buying of supplies and the sale of crops and products. Eshkol's skill in this area soon led to his being appointed head of the agriculture section of the Jewish Agency, which in effect made him "Minister of Agriculture" for the future Jewish state. When Israel was proclaimed an independent nation in 1948, Eshkol became Minister of Agriculture, and later he served as Minister of Finance, and finally as Prime Minister. He led Israel during the critical period prior to and during the Six Day War in 1967. He died in 1969, a greatly respected and deeply mourned leader of modern Israel.

Unlike David Ben-Gurion and Golda Meir, Eshkol was not the kind of leader who could stand up before large crowds and make speeches that would pull people to their feet cheering. He was a man who believed in hard work and in daily achievements. During his years of service as a leader of Israel, he liked to escort visitors personally to out-of-the-way settlements that had been established by idealistic pioneers, point out the buildings that had been erected, and listen carefully to the settlers' complaints and problems.

Eshkol had a down-to-earth manner that made it easy for all kinds of people to approach him and discuss their needs with him. He shunned all forms of pompousness, and his aides often addressed him on a first-name basis. Throughout his lifetime, his philosophy seemed to be: There is no time to waste; we are building a nation here; let us work hard and with imagination and put up homes and factories, and then people will come to Israel; they will work and enjoy their lives, and the country will continue to progress.

His directness carried over to meetings with heads of state, and during a visit to Washington to see President Lyndon Johnson, aides said that the two enjoyed one another's company enormously because they not only talked of affairs of state but were also able to speak from knowledge of cattle-raising, farm life as contrasted to city living, and the important role that teachers play in the life of society. (Johnson had started adult life as a schoolteacher, and Eshkol, the son of a teacher, often thought of himself as a teacher, with Israel his classroom.)

During the dark days of Hitlerism, Eshkol was sent by the Jewish Agency to Germany to help transfer Jewish communal property to Palestine. A member of the underground Haganah, he was responsible for the organization's finances, and remained an active Haganah figure all his life until the group was dissolved and became part of the regular Israel army. On a mission to Vienna in the 1920s to buy arms for the Haganah, Eshkol was arrested and spent a brief period in jail.

One of the great achievements that he was extremely proud of was the creation of the National Water Carrier project, which made it possible for large supplies of water to be brought from the northern part of Israel to the arid southern region.

From the time he arrived in Palestine in 1914 at the age of nineteen until his death at the age of seventy-four, Eshkol maintained a whirlwind pace of work in behalf of the development and defense of Israel. The concept of hobbies was completely foreign to him. Despite the fact that his family was steeped in traditional Jewish love for education, he found little time for study or reading, dedicating all his waking hours to what he perceived as the great tasks of building a country that had been neglected for nearly two thousand years. He spoke Hebrew, Russian, Yiddish, and a smattering of German, and when he found it necessary to know English, he took a crash course in a language that was very strange to him.

Even when he was Prime Minister, he remained essentially a self-effacing, modest man who hated to lose a minute from his lifelong schedule of work in behalf of Israel.

ROSALYN YALOW

Pioneer of Nuclear Medicine

THE NOBEL PRIZE IN MEDICINE for 1977 was bestowed on Dr. Rosalyn Yalow, as well as Dr. Roger Gueillemin and Dr. Andrew Schally. Dr. Yalow is one of the few women doctors or scientists ever to win the prestigious award.

Earlier Dr. Yalow had won the leading American award for medical research, the Lasker Prize. She is a most unusual woman, who combines a seventy-hour work week with the job of caring for her family, maintaining a kosher home, and somehow also managing to take an active part in community Jewish programs.

Born Rosalyn Sussman and raised in the Bronx, the daughter of a traditional family, she received her bachelor's degree from Hunter College in 1941 as that institution's first graduate with a major in physics. At the time few women were allowed to pursue a graduate education in physics; for a while, she had to work as a stenographer, but eventually she was accepted as a student at the University of Illinois and won her doctorate in physics. For more than a quarter of a century she has specialized in research work at the Veterans Administration Hospital in the Bronx. She is head of that institution's department of nuclear medicine and also teaches at the Mount Sinai School of Medicine.

The Nobel Prize was awarded to Dr. Yalow for having perfected a testing procedure that combines "immunology, isotope research, mathematics, and physics." The test is known as the RIA, for radioimmunoassay. It is so sensitive that it can detect the billionth part of a gram. As one member of the Nobel Prize com-

251

mittee explained it, the RIA is like finding a lump of sugar in a lake sixty-two miles wide, sixty-two miles long, and thirty feet deep.

Dr. Yalow is quick to pay tribute to her late colleague Dr. Solomon Berson for the successful conclusion of her work, described by the Nobel Prize authorities as being of major significance to practically every area of medicine. When the test that Drs. Yalow and Berson developed was described in a scientific paper, it was rejected by the editor of a leading medical journal, who subsequently had reason to regret his decision.

Doctors carrying out diagnoses of their patients are now able to detect what may seem like trivial changes in their patients' hormones, which can in turn produce radical effects on their health. The new method of testing and evaluation continues to lead to new discoveries and understanding of the nature of the human body.

The RIA is already in use by thousands of blood collection centers to prevent the inclusion of blood contaminated with hepatitis. Cancer research programs also are making extensive use of the new testing procedure.

During the many years that the testing procedures were developed, both Dr. Yalow and Dr. Berson made themselves available as guinea pigs, acting as volunteers for testing of the thyroid, blood, and albumin.

Dr. Yalow's husband, Aaron, whose father was a leading rabbi in Syracuse, New York, for many years, is a professor of physics. Their son, Ben, is a computer systems analyst, and their daughter, Elanna, is doing her doctoral work for a career in educational psychology.

At the Bronx VA hospital, Dr. Yalow is admired by her colleagues and by the young students who help her in her work. Sometimes she takes time out to prepare meals for her staff at the hospital, as well as doing the same for her family. She explains her ability to carry a full work load by the fact that she is thoroughly organized, and depends at home on a big freezer and a microwave oven.

Dr. Yalow was the first American woman ever to receive a Nobel Prize in science. Her vigorous and optimistic approach to her daily work routine make it seem likely that she will continue to develop important new advances in medical science.

RABBI AKIVA

Latecomer to Scholarship

HE WAS ONE OF THE GREATEST JEWISH SCHOLARS of all time—and yet he did not learn even the simplest Hebrew letters until he was forty years old. The story of Rabbi Akiva is one that has inspired many generations of Jews in every part of the world.

He was a poor shepherd, tending the flocks of his rich master, unhappy about the fact that he could not study. Years passed, and then one day the daughter of his master met him, and although he was older than she and a completely unsuitable match because of his lack of scholarship, she insisted on marrying him. Her father warned that if the two got married, he would disown his daughter and eject them both from his lands. And that is what happened. But Rachel—Akiva's wife—had come to believe that her husband was meant for greater things in life than tending sheep, and she urged him to leave her and go off to the schools and learn.

Akiva left his wife and stayed away, according to tradition, for twelve years, during which he was transformed from a virtual illiterate into a scholar of great promise. One day he returned home to see his wife and his small son, and—according to legend—he stood outside the modest home and heard his wife arguing with a neighbor. The woman had apparently bemoaned the fact that Akiva had been away for twelve years, leaving Rachel to support herself and their child entirely on her own.

"I don't care," Rachel is said to have shouted. "He can stay another twelve years, for he is studying and becoming a great scholar, and there is nothing more important!" At this point, the story goes, Akiva turned about and left for his studies, and did not return for another twelve years.

When he finally was reunited with his wife, he had become one of the great Jewish scholars of the day and was surrounded by hundreds of students who hung on his every word. The father-in-law was reconciled with him and his daughter and grandson, and everything should have been wonderful, except that this was the time when the Romans had taken the step that was eventually to lead to the exile of the Jews from their homeland. In the year 70 the Romans destroyed the Holy Temple in Jerusalem and dissolved the government of the Jews. It was a black, bitter period in Jewish history.

Although Rabbi Akiva was no longer a young man, he realized that the study of Torah was now more important than ever if the Jewish people were to remain united and the Jewish heritage was to be preserved. He traveled to exiled Jewish communities in Rome, Babylonia, and other centers, urging the Jews to remain loyal to their faith and to continue the tradition of Torah study. There were some in that bleak period who urged that the Jews launch a revolt against the Romans, but Akiva cautioned against it, insisting that it was bound to fail and would only result in large numbers of casualties.

The Romans at first permitted the Jews to obey their religious laws, and Akiva felt that this was ample and that patience was needed until a real change could come about. However, a Roman emperor, Hadrian, soon made his appearance and announced that the Holy Temple would be rebuilt, but as a center of worship for the pagan god Jupiter.

The elderly, peace-loving scholar became incensed and called for a revolt against the Romans. He supported the young Simeon ben Koziba, who became the leader of the Judaean forces organizing for a struggle to oust the Romans from the Jewish homeland. Rabbi Akiva was so impressed by Simeon that he called him Bar Kochba, or "son of a star," for he said he was the "star that has come forth from Jacob" to save the Jewish people.

The Jews recruited hundreds of thousands of volunteers, and

actually managed to capture Jerusalem and hold it against the Romans for two years. The far better trained Roman forces soon succeeded in crushing the revolt, and in doing so killed more than a half million Jewish soldiers. The Romans now issued stern orders: The Torah could no longer be taught; the Sabbath and holidays were not to be observed; any study of Jewish tradition or any following of Jewish ritual would be punishable by death.

Undaunted, the Jews now set about living as Jews in secret. Rabbi Akiva continued to inspire hope, and could be found in forests and faroff places teaching Torah, with guards posted nearby to warn of any approaching Roman soldiers. To those who urged him not to expose himself to possible Roman retribution, he replied, "Studying Torah is our life; and we may be in danger—but if we forsake the study of Torah, we will be in much greater danger!"

Rabbi Akiva was finally arrested for his secret teaching sessions. Despite his age—he was ninety—he was condemned to death. The action was carried out in public so that his death could serve as warning to all Jews who planned to continue to observe the Jewish laws in secret. He died with the words of the ancient *Shma Yisrael* prayer on his lips. After a time, the hated Roman laws were withdrawn and Judaism was permitted to be practiced. Rabbi Akiva's teaching and his willingness to fight for what he believed in helped to preserve the ancient Jewish faith and traditions to this day.

ALAN KING

Comic with a Heart

ALAN KING HAS MADE MILLIONS OF PEOPLE LAUGH—and he has also been very serious about raising millions of dollars to help schools and hospitals in Israel and in the United States. When he appears on stage, whether it is in a night club or theater, or before an audience of the Queen of England and members of the British aristocracy, he is able in a few minutes to establish a warm, one-to-one link between himself and the person in the audience—making people feel that he is talking about them, and directly to them. He is one of America's best-loved performers.

"The single, strongest motivation in my life," he says, "is my Jewishness. As a child I wasn't aware of it, since everyone I lived with in the old Williamsburgh section of Brooklyn was Jewish. When I went into the outside world, I realized that I had lived a very sheltered life, and I rejected it, thinking it was narrow and bigoted. What I used to think was ignorance, I now know is tradition.

"Later, when I matured and lived away from home, I understood I could not escape my heritage. By then I didn't want to—I decided consciously to accept it, to understand it, and to work at it. Being a Jew has given me a sense of identity and of being."

He was born Irwin Kniberg in 1927, the son of a poor immigrant from Poland who had a hard time earning a living as a factory worker, turning out ladies' handbags. The family was strictly Orthodox, and Alan was bar mitzvah in a traditional manner, with his grandfather, a rabbi who at times worked as a building superintendent, officiating.

He recalls that even in the worst of times, when his parents had to line up for welfare checks to keep the family going, there was always something to laugh at. Humor and charity, he says, are what have sustained the Jewish people through their long years of homelessness and troubles. Nevertheless, when he announced that he planned to enter show business professionally, his parents were appalled. "My mother said that the only people who worked at night were watchmen and burglars," he recalls.

He started out as a drummer in a band of which he soon became the leader. The teen-age musicians called themselves the Musical Knights, and for a while Alan called himself Earl Knight. While they were performing in the famous Catskill Mountains resort area, a hotel owner let Alan interrupt the music and tell stories—and that launched his career as an entertainer. He gave up the drums and turned comedian, and remembers that his weekly paycheck was for ten dollars.

Nowadays the boy from the poor neighborhood of Brooklyn who had to drop out of high school to help his family lives in a large mansion in an affluent suburban area, drives a Rolls-Royce, conducts a multifaceted show business career from a plush Fifth Avenue office, and devotes very large portions of his time to aiding those causes in which he believes deeply.

He has established and helped to provide funds for a major medical clinic in Jerusalem that bears his name. He has rallied people to buy Israel Bonds, contribute to the United Jewish Appeal, support local hospitals, and make funds available to send needy youngsters to school. When his mother, now living in Florida, was hospitalized in a Catholic hospital, he was so impressed by the treatment she received that he volunteered to act as master of ceremonies for a fund-raising dinner and raised $150,000 for the hospital.

He and his wife, Jeanette, have three adopted children, all of whom have received a traditional Jewish religious education, and he has taken them to Israel—which he visits often—on numerous occasions. He is a member of an Orthodox synagogue, explaining that he feels most comfortable in the same kind of worship service he knew as a youngster.

Once, he remembers, when he was at services, he complained gently to the rabbi that he felt embarrassed by his fellow congregants pointing him out. "If you'll come more often," the rabbi responded, "people will get used to you, and nobody will notice." Alan King laughs as he remembers the conversation: "I couldn't think of a suitable comeback."

HAROLD BROWN

Defender of the United States

He was born and raised in New York City and at an early age showed signs of his extraordinary intellectual capabilities. After graduating from the Bronx High School of Science at the age of fifteen (with a 99.5 per cent average), he enrolled at Columbia University, graduating at seventeen with a bachelor's degree in science; a year later he received his master's, and at the age of twenty-one earned a doctorate in nuclear physics.

During the years that John F. Kennedy and Lyndon Johnson were in the White House, Brown was one of a select team of nuclear-arms experts assigned to guiding the United States on immediate and long-range defense policies. He quickly got to be known as a whiz kid, and toward the latter part of the Johnson administration he was named Secretary of the Air Force.

For a decade Brown was president of the California Institute of Technology, one of the world's leading scientific-engineering educational and research centers. Under his leadership that institution expanded its medical and biology departments and significantly increased the number of its women students. He continued to retain a deep interest in world affairs, especially as they involved disarmament, and served as a member of the U.S. team in the delicate negotiations conducted by the United States and Soviet Union as they labored toward an agreement on limiting the production and use of strategic arms.

In 1977 President Jimmy Carter appointed Brown to his cabinet, to the post of Secretary of Defense, making him the first Jew ever to serve in that sensitive position. Thus, the United States has serving at its defense helm a man who is not only a nuclear physicist of the first rank but who, when applying for admission to Columbia University during World War II wrote, "I intend to let all my actions be dictated by the answer to this question—'Will this step, more than any other action, help in winning the war against fascism and in winning the peace that will follow?'"

The son of a lawyer whose parents had immigrated to America from central Europe, Secretary Brown is profoundly aware of the awesome responsibility he carries as the chief military planner and administrator of the United States. A clue to his thinking may be found in the comment he made with regard to America's intervention in the Vietnam fighting. Admitting that as chief of the U. S. Air Force he made mistakes when he advocated increased bombing of enemy forces and bases in that war, Brown now says, "A lesson we learned from Viet Nam is that we should be very cautious about intervening in any place where there's a poor political base for our presence."

Although he is not active in any organized Jewish group, Brown allowed himself to become a test case in applying for membership in a California club that had always been closed to Jews and other minority groups. He was gratified when the California club accepted him as a full-fledged member, contending that by this action he had helped in a small way to break down a traditional wall of prejudice. He also joined with fellow Jewish and non-Jewish scientists in appealing to the Soviet government to allow the emigration of Benjamin Levich, one of Russia's leading physicists, who had sought permission to resettle in Israel.

Dr. Brown has received several honorary doctorates, Columbia's Medal of Excellence, and other awards. A man fiercely dedicated to hard work and concentrated study, he has learned to relax between his arduous duties by becoming an excellent swimmer and tennis player.

SHALOM ALEICHEM

The Jewish Mark Twain

TENS OF MILLIONS OF PEOPLE throughout the world have seen and enjoyed a musical play and film called *Fiddler on the Roof,* which depicts the life of Jews in eastern Europe about a century ago with deep understanding. The show is based on the writings of Shalom Aleichem, the pen name of Solomon Rabinowitz, a Jewish literary genius whose talent came to be appreciated mostly after his death in the Bronx, New York, in 1916.

He was born in a small town in Russia, similar to the famous village of Kasrilevke depicted in *Fiddler on the Roof.* From his earliest days he showed a special talent for writing (and also acting) in a humorous vein, and he sensed that humor could cover up, at least temporarily, pain and suffering. Unlike most Jewish youths in Russia at the time, he received a good general as well as Jewish education, and for a while he served as a tutor and even a rabbi. He was a prolific writer, and because he enjoyed writing for large numbers of people, he turned to the Yiddish language in order to reach the largest possible number of Jewish readers. His father was a lover of Hebrew, and to avoid being harassed for writing in Yiddish, the young man adopted the pen name of Shalom Aleichem—an expression literally meaning "Peace be unto you," used as a common greeting rather like "How do you do?"

His literary efforts attracted a large and growing audience, and people used to refer to Shalom Aleichem as a jester who un-

derstood their everyday needs and problems. Earning money was always a problem for him, and it was not until after his father-in-law's death, when he inherited a sizable estate, that he was able to live comfortably, at least for a while.

Shalom Aleichem has been called "the Jewish Mark Twain," and he too, like the great American humorist, was a poor businessman and lost large sums of money in unsound investments. Twain (who once referred to himself as "the American Shalom Aleichem") learned how easy it was to reduce his financial worth through investing in a mechanical typesetting machine, while Shalom Aleichem thought of himself as a sharp speculator on the stock exchange who could make a fortune by clever investments. At one point, things got so bad that Shalom Aleichem had to flee his home in Russia, hiding out from creditors until all his debts were paid off by his mother-in-law.

Nonetheless, he remained an eternal optimist and saw life through lenses ground from humor. He continued to write steadily —novels, plays, stories, essays—and his work appeared in Yiddish newspapers in Russia, Poland, America, and elsewhere, and everywhere readers loved him, for he brought smiles and tears of joy to their otherwise drab and often difficult lives. His financial difficulties however were with him most of his life. When he died in New York, his funeral procession was accompanied by hundreds of thousands of Jewish factory workers who took time off from their jobs to pay him their last respects, but he died virtually a pauper.

Shalom Aleichem created a lovable character, Mottele, the cantor's son, who—like Mark Twain's unforgettable hero Huckleberry Finn—becomes an orphan and has to find his own way in life. Mottele's milieu was the small village of the East European Jews, which he described with love and wonder, notwithstanding the poverty and the ceaseless struggle to maintain some kind of order and dignity in an abysmal world.

Shalom Aleichem, in all his work, seemed to hold up a mirror to the hundreds of thousands of Jews of eastern Europe in which he showed them that, despite their difficulties, they had much to be grateful for and that their lives could be more bearable if they approached their problems with a smile and a laugh. To paraphrase the old Yiddish expression, he helped to make his readers laugh through their own tears.

In recent years a whole new generation of readers has begun to appreciate what a kind, understanding, and keen writer Shalom Aleichem really was. His works have been translated into Hebrew, Russian, English, and many other languages. A literary center in Tel Aviv bears his name.

In the latter years of his life, Shalom Aleichem allied himself with the Zionist movement and even attended one of the World Zionist Congress meetings as an official delegate. Still writing tirelessly, he also expended much time and energy traveling to communities all over Russia and Poland before World War I, giving readings of his works in order to increase his earnings. The travels he was forced to engage in eventually undermined his health, and he contracted tuberculosis.

He died at the age of fifty-seven, leaving the world a richer place for his wise and loving understanding of the Jewish people he loved so profoundly.

YIGAEL YADIN

He'd Rather Dig Than Fight

YIGAEL YADIN IS A RELUCTANT MILITARY LEADER. He much prefers to devote his time to his primary vocation and avocation—archaeology. He is one of the world's foremost figures in this field, certainly the leading archaeologist of Israel.

He was born in Jerusalem in 1917, the son of a famous professor of archaeology, Eliezer Sukenik. At the age of fifteen he became a scout for the Haganah, the secret underground army of the Jewish community in Palestine, then governed by the British. He knew that sooner or later a Jewish state would be created in Palestine, and he was anxious to participate fully in realizing the age-old dream of the Jewish people.

He rose in the ranks of the organization and by 1947 was named operations officer. When Israel proclaimed its independence in 1948, the then Chief of Staff, Yaacov Dori, who had been the head of Haganah, was confined to a hospital and Yadin became Chief of Staff, working closely with David Ben-Gurion, the Prime Minister, to assure that the infant nation would not go under in the large-scale fighting that followed the attacks of neighboring Arab countries.

In 1952 Yadin, now a general, resigned from the Israel Defense Forces to devote himself to scholarship, especially in the field of archaeology. It was as though he personally wanted to be transformed, in the spirit of Isaiah, from a sword into a plowshare. One of his principal contributions to the security of Israel was the in-

troduction of the system of conscription and reserves, a system that has enabled Israel to withstand the far greater numbers of soldiers found in the Arab countries.

He resumed his studies at the Hebrew University and in 1955 received a doctorate for his work on explaining the origin, background, and significance of some of the Dead Sea Scrolls, manuscripts preserved intact for centuries hidden in an inaccessible cave near the Dead Sea. The following year he was awarded the Israel Prize for his work.

As an archaeologist, Yadin was anxious to link the ancient past of the Jewish people in Israel with the present. Employing thousands of volunteers, he directed an excavation of a once great city, Hazor, located north of the Sea of Galilee, over a period of five years. In antiquity Hazor had been a major center, inhabited at different times by the Israelites under Joshua and by Canaanites, Persians, Greeks, and other peoples. Strategically sited, it was always known as a fortress city.

Using the Bible as a guide, Yadin and his teams began to dig, gradually peeling back layer upon layer of ancient civilizations, excavating invaluable artifacts, and finally finding evidence of the great battle waged against Hazor by Joshua in the thirteenth century B.C.E. The diggers found courtyards, chariots, staircases, reservoirs, jugs, pots, letters, temples, and palaces. For an archaeologist like Yadin, these finds were a glorious adventure back into the long-forgotten past.

A few years later Yadin led an expedition to the cliffs of Ein Gedi, looking for hard evidence of the existence of Simeon Bar Kochba, who led a rebellion against the Romans after the Holy Temple had been destroyed in the year 70. To enter the caves in the area, it was necessary to fly army helicopters to hover directly above the narrow entrances, lower a volunteer from a rope, let him swing back and forth like a pendulum, and then hope he would succeed in throwing himself into the slit entrance of the ancient, foul-smelling cave. The operation worked, and, among other valuable finds, the archaeologists came upon fifteen letters from Bar Kochba to his lieutenants, issuing orders for the continued military campaign against the hated Romans. The announcement by Yadin of the discovery of the documents was made at the residence of the President of Israel, and electrified the world.

In 1964 Yadin turned his attention to the natural fortress of Masada, a flat-topped mountain south of the Dead Sea, shaped like a ship, with practically vertical sides. It is a breath-taking place to visit, and today future officers of the Israel Defense Forces are brought there to take their oath of loyalty to Israel.

Masada is best known in Jewish history for the courage of a group of fewer than a thousand men, women, and children who encamped there following the Roman victory over the Jews, determined to continue to offer resistance, no matter how high the cost. The Roman soldiers surrounding the fortress began to build a huge ramp from which they would be able to send their soldiers into the Jewish stronghold and crush the rebels. Day by day the Romans brought earth and packed it tight, and the ramp continued to grow higher and higher. The leader of the besieged Jews, Eleazar ben Yair, knew that it was only a matter of time before the Romans would overrun the Jewish encampment.

According to the ancient historian Josephus, Eleazar called his followers together and told them, "Let us die unenslaved by our enemies, and leave this world as free men, together with our wives and children."

He outlined a grisly plan: Ten men would act as executioners and would go about killing every man, woman, and child on Masada and then execute each other. The last man to remain alive would be instructed to inspect the bodies making sure that all were lifeless, and then to take his own life.

When the Roman soldiers finally broke into Masada, they were sickened by what they saw: With the exception of one old woman and five small children who had remained hidden in a water conduit, all were dead. The message of zealousness for freedom had been made painfully clear.

Under Yadin's leadership, teams of volunteers set about to uncover the whole historic tableau. They dug up an ancient palace built by King Herod, complete with the throne room, reception halls, servants' quarters, and workshops. Mosaic floors installed centuries ago had stood the test of time and were clearly visible.

The Masada zealots had burned down everything they could before carrying out their mass suicide, and apparently the ashes that remained had helped preserve the artifacts of the time. Yadin's teams found ancient coins, letters, arrows, and even the skeletons of the martyrs. Jars containing food were uncovered, as were the ancient baths, bedecked with beautiful frescoes.

In the living quarters, the diggers came upon various household utensils—stoves, basins, dishes. Here and there sandals lay scattered about. A *mikveh*, a ritual bath, and the remains of a synagogue were found, too.

In 1965 Masada was dedicated as a national shrine in Israel. The watchword "Masada shall not fall again" became a national slogan.

Yadin's work has been acclaimed throughout the world, for he succeeded in shedding light on what had been a lost chapter in Jewish history. At his initiative, a peculiarly shaped building known as the Shrine of the Book has been established near the Israel Museum in Jerusalem, in which are kept the fragments of the Dead Sea Scrolls, as well as some of the Bar Kochba letters and other ancient artifacts.

In 1977 Yadin, who earlier had formed a new political party in Israel, the Democratic Movement for Change, was named Deputy Prime Minister.

JACOB BRONOWSKI

Science with a Human Touch

MILLIONS OF TELEVISION VIEWERS throughout the world have watched with keen pleasure and great admiration a series of scientific programs designed for the nonscientist. Offered under the overall title of *The Ascent of Man*, these superb documentary presentations were conceived, prepared, and narrated by a soft-spoken Jewish scientist, Jacob Bronowski, whose explanations of the world around us made people feel that life is good and the world a beautiful and remarkable place.

Dr. Bronowski himself, who died in 1974, was a remarkable individual. He was a mathematician, a philosopher of science, and a profound thinker who sought to combine scientific pursuit with a sense of humanism. He was born in Poland and raised in a traditional Jewish household; his father was an ardent admirer of the Hasidic movement that extolled life and living.

Bronowski was educated in Germany and England, and taught mathematics at the University of Cambridge. He also taught at MIT, and was a Fellow at the Salk Institute for Biological Studies in California, always striving to link the achievements of science within the greater culture. For a number of years he directed the prestigious Council for Biology in Human Affairs, made up of some of the world's leading scientific figures, which has been trying to make scientists aware of the social and political consequences of their work.

During World War II Bronowski was sent to Washington by the British government to become a member of the Joint Target Group. He was also a member of the chiefs of staff mission that operated in Japan immediately after the end of the war. A man of wide interests, he was, in addition to his work in mathematics and in science as a whole, an authority on the poet William Blake.

Bronowski believed that science can advance only if scientists themselves are "imbued with the aspiration toward truth and understanding." He wrote that "religion has learned from science what means will contribute to the attainment of the goals it has set. . . . the interpretation of religion implies a dependence of science on the religious attitude, a relation which in our materialistic age is only too easily overlooked."

Dr. Bronowski, noting that a reviewer of his book *Science and Human Values* had said that the author expressed the "ethical enthusiasm of my rabbinic ancestors," said that this comment made him proud. "My concern with ethical values," he said, "seems to express a central theme in the Jewish way of life."

On another occasion Bronowski wrote:

In a time of intolerance and violence, being a scientist and being a Jew has meant to me seeking at the heart of ethics the human values which gives a sense of pride and meaning to every individual life. . . . Through the symbolic ceremony and ritual of Jewish holidays, the worshiper drains off destructive energy and transforms it into life-giving wafers of spiritual and ethical reconstruction. . . . Judaism is not Puritanical and there is nothing in the Bible to justify making a virtue of austerity. On the contrary, the religious tradition among Jews, particularly among Hassidim, is one of fulfillment and delight in life. . . . The physical benefits of science have opened a door which will give all men the chance to use mind and spirit.

EUGENE FERKAUF

New Concepts in Selling

SOMETIMES GREAT OPPORTUNITIES come someone's way through sheer accident and sometimes through a stroke of luck and at other times through what seems to be a simple idea but is in reality a very creative concept.

When Eugene Ferkauf was discharged from the U.S. army at the end of World War II, he was one of millions of former GIs trying to readapt to civilian life and to make up for the years they had lost in the war. He was the son of immigrant parents, who had struggled to keep the family together through the difficult years of the Depression period, and now he was back in his home community of Brooklyn, grateful to have escaped injury in the war and not really sure what he was going to do.

He had completed high school, and the government was offering returning veterans many opportunities to pursue their education; but at that stage in his life he simply was not ready to go back to a classroom. After having been overseas, seen battle, and come back in one piece, he wanted to marry, raise a family, and settle down to a pleasant life in Brooklyn—at the time the home of one of the world's largest concentrations of Jews.

Realizing that America's military industries would be converting to civilian products very quickly and that millions of people would be needing and buying home appliances, Ferkauf decided to open a retail appliance store. It was a big step for a young man, but he was ambitious and willing to work hard, and he felt a genuine

sense of confidence about the future. He soon learned, however, that it was difficult for a small retailer to compete with large chains of stores, and it was very difficult for him to obtain merchandise from manufacturers and suppliers.

All of his money and some of that of his family and friends had been sunk into the venture. He had to make it succeed! Then one evening after a long day in the store, with sales far from brisk, a thought occurred to him: Perhaps if he could offer his appliances at lower prices to customers, he would get their business rather than the big chains. But to lower prices, he would have to cut out some expenses. He thought the whole thing through with great care and made his decision: He would solicit customers' specific orders and then, instead of placing an order with a supplier, he would pick up the item at the factory and deliver it directly to the customer, saving the costs of delivery to the store, from the store to the customer, bookkeeping, and overhead.

He even revived a word that had almost been lost in the American business lexicon: discount. That was it—he would offer his customers discounts. Even if it was as little as 10 per cent, it would be meaningful on an appliance for the home that cost a few hundred dollars.

Often riding the truck himself, Ferkauf began to obtain orders, deliver merchandise, and discount the price. He began to build a name for himself as a source of quality merchandise at lower than established prices. The discount fire that he kindled took hold, and within a few years, working long hours and pressing for low prices for his customers, he opened one store after another, expanding their contents from appliances only to general merchandise. He called the chain store Korvettes, and almost overnight he was credited with having virtually established a new industry in America, discount retailing, which is now part and parcel of the American economy.

The poor boy from Brooklyn had grown into a very wealthy business executive. He was happy and gratified, and he amazed everyone with whom he came in contact by remaining a low-key, easygoing person despite the fact that he controlled a business empire that had sales in the tens of millions of dollars annually and that made him a millionaire many times over. And then one day, at the height of his glory in the new role of business tycoon, after his picture had appeared on the cover of *Time* magazine, he sold out all his interests in the company and began to devote himself to a whole series of educational programs that he felt keenly about.

Always a member of a synagogue, he began to study the great Jewish classics and became a collector of rare works of Judaica. Remembering how much his parents had admired Yeshiva University, he gave the school one million dollars to establish a school of social work. (Refusing to pose for pictures handing over the money, he sent a check in the mail with a simple, hand-written note.) He was deeply concerned about the progress of Israel and volunteered his services as head of a new American company to ease the import and sale of Israel-made goods, working at this project for a number of years until he felt it was on its feet and then retiring for a while to devote more time to study and reading. He also established special schools and buildings at universities in Israel, and became a generous donor to the United Jewish Appeal.

Still boyish in manner, he has in more recent years begun to play the role of a "business doctor," advising ailing firms on how they can transform their losses into gains. In all his efforts for American companies and educational organizations in the United States, he believes that the "cause uppermost in my mind is the advancement of higher education—only through education can we hope to train the future leaders of our nation, the young men and women to serve this wonderful country of ours."

The man who almost singlehandedly started the discount industry in America today busies himself with doing good works for the benefit of all.

JOSEPH TRUMPELDOR

One-armed Hero of Israel

HE WAS A PACIFIST, and yet he died with a gun in his hand. He was a farmer who loved the land and worked as productively as anyone else despite the fact that he had only one arm. He went to battle for the czarist Russian government to help show that the accusation of Jews being cowardly was false, but when he learned of the deeply ingrained anti-Semitism that was rampant throughout Russian society, he left the country in disgust.

Joseph Trumpeldor was a man like no other. Circumstances have changed radically in the world since he lived, and the chances of there being another Trumpeldor are very slight.

He was born in 1880 in a small town not far from a Russian farming commune that had been established by followers of Tolstoy. The idyllic scenes of the life he observed in that agricultural setting were to influence his later decision to settle in Palestine and work on a similar basis.

As a teen-ager he began to hear of the nascent Zionist movement, and it intrigued him. He was persuaded to complete his studies before getting too involved with the new movement, and when he passed his examinations as a dentist, war had broken out between Russia and Japan and he was drafted.

To his surprise, he found that he enjoyed military life. For one thing, it gave him a chance to show conclusively that charges

of Jewish cowardice and draft-evasion were canards. For another, he had to admit to himself that going into battle for the glory of the country he loved was a marvelous experience.

He asked for duty at the front, at the time concentrated in Port Arthur, and during a shelling attack his left arm was shattered by fragments and had to be amputated. After recuperating, he asked for a gun and a sword and permission to remain at the front. His action startled the military authorities, and he was awarded a medal and named an officer.

When he returned home after the fighting, he discovered that the "Mother Russia" he had been fighting for was an illusion. On all sides, Jews and other groups were being brutally oppressed, and the freedom that he believed in and had fought for now appeared to him as a hallucination. In 1912 he left Russia and settled in Palestine, determined to help build a society based on the principles of equality and liberty that he believed in passionately.

When the First World War began, he (together with Vladimir Jabotinsky) led in the formation of a corps of Jewish soldiers attached to the British forces, which later became the nucleus of the Jewish Legion. He became second in command of the Zion Mule Corps, which saw action in the Gallipoli campaigns against the Turks. Wherever he went in recruiting for the Jewish unit, he preached the need for young Jews to settle in Palestine and help build a new nation.

When the war ended, he returned to his small farming community, Kfar Giladi, one of a tiny number of agricultural settlements isolated from the bulk of Jews in Palestine at the time. They were located in the Upper Galilee, in a border area that was disputed at the time, being fought over by the French and the British. To gain the upper hand, each side incited Arab bands to attack the nationals of the other in order to establish their own hegemony over the region. In a very real sense, the handful of Jewish settlements were caught in the middle.

For a while a number of the settlers seriously considered abandoning the sites and moving south to be closer to their fellow Jews, but this was never done. Notwithstanding enormous dangers that they encountered almost daily, they chose to stay on—encouraged in no small measure by Trumpeldor, whom they looked to for guidance.

When the day's farm chores were completed, Trumpeldor would teach the men and women in the villages, of practically all ages, how to handle guns and rifles. Almost nobody ever realized after a while that their instructor was a one-armed man.

As the tempo of Arab attacks increased, Trumpeldor kept sending letters to officials of the Jewish community and the kibbutz and moshav movements in Tel Aviv to organize squads of volunteers to help defend the ring of settlements. In a typical caustic note, he once wrote, "A new generation of free sons of the land of Israel stand ready on the border, prepared to give their lives in its defense—and there, in the interior of the country, they keep negotiating interminably whether to approve the budget or reject it, in other words, whether to help the defenders of the homeland or not." Eventually volunteers did come north to help man the isolated Jewish outposts, but the Arab attacks began to expand in number and intensity at the same time.

One day, while Trumpeldor was breakfasting in his own Kfar Giladi colony, word came that the settlers of nearby Tel Hai were being attacked. Trumpeldor grabbed a weapon and led a group of men to help in the defense. When they reached Tel Hai, they saw that the settlers were holed up in the largest house, sandbags blocking the windows and rifles visible at various positions in the building. Trumpeldor ignored the sporadic shots that Arabs were directing toward the building and led his men inside, successfully dodging bullets that seemed to come from all sides. Inside the house he took charge and made sure that all doors and windows were securely locked and protected. He urged the colonists to hold their fire until they could see the attackers clearly, and then to shoot for all they were worth.

Peering out of one of the peepholes he suddenly became alarmed. "The gate is open!" he shouted, "you have forgotten to lock the gate—they'll come right in!" Before anyone realized what was happening, he had thrown open the front door and dashed toward the gate, intent on closing it. Shots rang out the moment he showed his face, and in a matter of minutes he was hit twice.

The attack continued, but after a while the Arabs retreated, giving the settlers a chance to bring Trumpeldor into the building. A doctor was brought from an adjoining village, but it was obvious he was too late.

Never one to complain, Trumpeldor in his last moments said, "Never mind, it is good to die for our country." His name lives on in Tel Yosef, an Israeli settlement, and in Brith Trumpeldor (known as Betar for short), a youth movement that stresses militancy. A monument still stands on his gravesite in Tel Hai.

Joseph Trumpeldor died a hero's death in 1920, a forty-year-old Jew who has come to symbolize for young Israelis the highest possible form of patriotism.

HAVIVA REIK

"*A Flame in All Our Hearts*"

HAVIVA REIK KNEW TERRIBLE POVERTY as a small child growing up in an assimilated family in Czechoslovakia. At one time she
and her parents and five other children were forced to live for
months on end in a single room. When she was still a small girl, an
older brother hired himself out as a gooseherd for the daily wage
of a glass of fresh milk, which he brought her every evening.

She was born at the time that World War I began and
throughout her formative years knew what it meant to be hungry
and deprived. While still in her teens, she found work as a secretary and roamed the Slovakian countryside on a motorcycle as
part of her job, since her employer was a manufacturer of agricultural machinery. In the middle 1930s, after reading a book on Zionism, she became convinced that the re-establishment of a Jewish
homeland was the only solution possible for the oppressed Jews she
saw all around her. She joined a Zionist youth movement, became
an active leader, and by the time World War II broke out in 1939,
she had already reached Palestine, determined to start a new life.

The kibbutz to which she was assigned was young and ex-
periencing many difficulties. Haviva joined the men in the
toughest jobs, including quarrying, and with the passage of time
her dreams of a secure agricultural settlement began to be realized.
But she was far from being a happy woman—for with each passing
month additional news reports of the fate of European Jewry at
the hands of the Nazis reached Palestine, and she found herself
anxious to return to Europe to do whatever she could to help.

She volunteered, like Hannah Senesh, to become a British parachutist who would be trained to jump into German-occupied Slovakia on a double mission—to comfort and help the remaining Jews, and to provide information to the Allied war effort. In 1944 Haviva was almost thirty years old, much older than most of the volunteer parachutists, but she pressed her officers to speed up her training. One day, after she had made three jumps from different altitudes, she was stopped by a British officer, who expressed his admiration for her feat.

"I must hurry," she told him. "I must be swift. The fires are burning all over Europe."

In a letter to her kibbutz friends shortly before she took off for her mission to Slovakia, in the center of Nazi-dominated Europe, she wrote, "In a few days I will be thirty, and it is hard for me to say that I feel my age. The years go by quickly, I have no feeling of not having exploited the years for myself. This has been a war within me: private happiness versus the filling of duty. . . . I too wanted a quiet life, a family life. To give up having a child is not easy, but my optimism says it is never too late. Perhaps I too will fulfill that duty, surely the greatest for a woman."

A few hours before Haviva took off on her mission, she scribbled a note to her comrades in the kibbutz: "Is man made for war? Is a Jew made to kill? Is a woman meant to wage battle? I will return to my settlement, I will have a family, children. I think of you and that strengthens me. I am quiet and look with clear eyes to the future. We will meet soon."

Haviva's confidence was short-lived. She reached her destination in Slovakia only to find that the names and addresses of possible contacts were outdated. For several days she hid out in the woods and then joined a group of Jewish resistance fighters. Almost immediately afterwards, German patrols captured the partisans, including Haviva, and executed them all. Her mission to save lives ended abruptly with the loss of her own life on the soil she had left only a few years earlier.

When the war ended and the story of Haviva's unsuccessful rescue effort became known, a group of young kibbutz members held a bonfire rally in the mountains of Israel, building a huge flame to her memory and vowing to remember the young woman "who kindled a flame in all our hearts."

CHAIM MOSHE KATZ

Godfather of Israeli Pilots

THE PILOTS who fly Israel's incredibly swift and supersophis-
ticated planes—the country's first line of defense—are considered
among the world's finest. Nevertheless, the whole concept of Jews
flying in the air space above Israel is very new and came about to a
large extent because of an odd set of circumstances and because of
the vision of one man—Chaim Moshe Katz, a retired manufacturer
of clothing from New York.

Born in Russia, Katz came to New York at the turn of the
century, went into the clothing business, and prospered. He married, raised a family, loved America—and yet felt that something
essential was missing in his life. He had been a confirmed Zionist as
far back as anyone could remember, and he yearned to live in the
ancient homeland of the Jewish people.

A man of action, Katz sold his clothing business (for three
million dollars) and in 1926 left for Palestine with his family, establishing himself on a sizable tract of land between the growing
new city of Tel Aviv and the older settlement of Petah Tikvah.
He built a large, comfortable home, and soon enough the area was
named for him, Pardes Katz, or "Katz's orchard."

To help the country's economy and to keep himself occupied
productively, he rented an office and entered the citrus-export
business, shipping oranges to European customers. Life was good

despite the fact that the Jewish community in Palestine suffered periodic waves of unemployment and was subject to outbreaks of Arab rioting. But Katz and his family were living in the Holy Land, which was very slowly beginning to take on the semblance of a Jewish state-to-be.

Katz's reputation as an able, dependable businessman spread, and one day a young American flier came to see him. He was Eddie Lyons, and he explained that he and his wife and child were stranded in Palestine, without a steady job, and his only real asset was a small, single-engine plane. He proposed an idea: He would like to establish a flying school, the first in the country, and he asked for Katz's help.

As the young American flier talked, Katz thought: Young Palestinian Jews were already receiving naval training in Italy, and Zionist-minded Polish Jews were being trained in ground fighting in rural areas not far from Warsaw. Anyone with vision could see that a future Jewish state would need a modern army, and it was obvious that modern airplanes would become an important part of it.

Katz's son, Fred, was at the time in England studying flying. Everything seemed to come together: Katz helped his son and Lyons establish the Palestine Flying Service. He bought two additional planes, and with Lyons' original single-engine aircraft the school was in business.

The first class consisted of ten young men. They would meet in Tel Aviv, drive out to the Lydda airfield (now known as Ben-Gurion Airport), often ducking shots aimed at them from Arab villages and sometimes having to avoid shots directed at them when they were in the air.

The Palestine Flying Service operated for a year and a half, during which time thirty-eight young Palestinian Jews were trained as pilots. The British authorities then shut it down, but the thirty-eight pilots were to form the nucleus of Israel's future flying service. Many of them helped save the day when they used their skills in the 1948 fighting that followed the creation of Israel, flying small, patched-up, makeshift planes. Through the flying school the concept of air defense became an integral part of Israel's strategy, and has remained a key element in all military planning to this day.

When World War II broke out, Fred Katz, a seasoned pilot, returned to the United States, where he was assigned to a naval flying squad. He was severely wounded when his plane took off on a mission, and remained hospitalized for more than two and a half years. He lives today in New York. Eddie Lyons also returned to the United States, served as a pilot during World War II, and is now the co-owner of an airfield on Long Island.

Chaim Moshe Katz died at the age of ninety-three, having witnessed the establishment of Israel and the emergence of air power as a key element in Israel's defense. His home and lands were left for Israel, the former now transformed into a hospital. Among the superbly trained young Israeli pilots who maneuver the country's faster-than-sound aircraft through the skies, the name of Chaim Moshe Katz is recalled as the godfather of Jewish aviation.

HILLEL

The Gentle Rabbi-Scholar

ON THE CAMPUSES of colleges and universities in all parts of the United States there are student centers of Jewish learning known as Hillel houses. They are there to provide a place of worship and study for hundreds of thousands of Jewish college students. The fact that these important educational bases carry the name of Hillel indicates the great reverence that the Jewish people have always held for a teacher of ancient times, whose influence remains strong even today.

Hillel was born about two thousand years ago, in Babylonia, where there was a large Jewish community. He studied the Torah until he felt that he could learn more only by returning to Palestine, where great teachers were expounding on the meaning of the laws and commandments of the Bible. While he was a poor student, he worked as a woodchopper to earn enough money to devote as much time as possible to study.

In those days, long before the art of printing, the commentaries and interpretations of the Torah were passed down from generation to generation by oral instruction. Soon there was a great deal of Torah commentary, which came to be known as the Oral Law. Eventually it was written down and forms the bulk of the Talmud as we know it today.

That period in Jewish history was a time of great challenge for all thoughtful scholars. Every word, every sentence, every law in the Torah, sometimes known as the Five Books of Moses, re-

quired explanation and adaptation to the conditions of life then existing among the Jewish people. The Torah commanded, for example, that Jews should rest and enjoy the Sabbath day but did not specify how this was to be done. The commentators and interpreters, including Hillel, began to expand the Torah's words so that they became practical laws and traditions. Thus, for example, the Sabbath was ordered to be a day when prayers and study should predominate, when Jews should dress in their best clothes, and when the custom of candle-lighting and the recitation of the *kiddush* on wine should be followed. Observance of these additional laws helped to make the Sabbath day a day of rest and delight.

And so it was for every passage of the Torah. Interpreters are only human, however, and it became obvious that every law could be explained one way or another, sternly or compassionately. What distinguished Hillel's lifetime of study and commentary on the Torah was that he was always on the side of the gentle, more lenient commentators.

There is the story, for example, of how he and Shammai, a great scholar famed for his severity, responded to a student's question concerning a forthcoming wedding feast. The student said that, as was well known, it was customary for guests at a wedding party to sing the bride's praises just prior to the wedding ceremony.

"But," he asked, "what can one do if the bride is truly homely? What shall one say?"

Shammai's swift rejoinder was, "Speak the exact truth—describe the bride as she is."

Hillel, on the other hand, said, "You may always say the bride is lovely and good."

Another often-cited story tells of a pagan who wanted to become a Jew and challenged Hillel to explain Judaism to him while he remained standing on one foot. "What is hateful to you," Hillel responded, "do not do to your neighbor. The rest of the Law is commentary. And now go and study!" The pagan is said to have been sufficiently impressed to have himself converted to Judaism.

Hillel was admired by all but remained a humble person all his life. He saw his mission in life as teaching the essentials of Judaism, with patience, gentleness, and understanding. The school that he established at Yavneh made Johanan ben Zakkai the greatest Jewish scholar of his generation—and he always attributed this to his years of study with the gentle Hillel. Gamaliel, Hillel's great-grandson, became the head of the Sanhedrin, the great legislature of Jewish law.

Hillel, by his own example and by his teaching, taught that the chief purposes of Jewish law were to encourage love of neighbors and to strengthen justice for all. Nevertheless, he explained that, in order to be a good Jew, one had to follow certain basic rules every single day.

Many of Hillel's famous sayings have come down to us to this day, and are worthy of study. For example, Hillel said:

"If I am not for myself, who will be for me? And if I am for myself only, what am I? And if not now, when?"

"Leave it to the people. If they are not prophets, they are the sons of prophets."

"A fool cannot keep from sinning, and an ignorant man cannot be a saint. A shy person cannot learn, and an impatient man cannot teach. He who spends all his time on business will not become wise."

"In a place where there are no men, try to be a man."

"Do not separate yourself from the community."

SELMAN A. WAKSMAN

Quest for Microbes

NOT MANY OF THE WORLD'S PATIENTS ill with certain forms of pneumonia, whooping cough, meningitis, dysentery, typhoid, and other diseases know that the antibiotic streptomycin and a whole series of other antibiotics which can effectively cure these infections were produced in the modest New Jersey laboratory of a microbiologist by the name of Selman Abraham Waksman. However, the award of the Nobel Prize in physiology and medicine to Dr. Waksman in 1952 made it amply clear that the world's leading scientists and medical practitioners appreciated his great work.

Selman Waksman did not arrive in the United States from his native Russia until he was twenty-two. He was born in a small Ukrainian town in 1888, the son of a small-town merchant who wanted young Selman to study industrial chemistry, but even as a youngster he was far more interested in the world of microbes. After graduating from the college-type Gymnasium school in Odessa, Waksman immigrated to the United States, planning to study microbiology at a medical school.

Five years later, in 1915, he received a degree from the College of Agriculture of Rutgers University and in that same year became a naturalized citizen. He went on to earn his master's and Ph.D. degrees, concentrating on experimental work in microbiology and teaching soil microbiology at Rutgers, first as a lecturer and later as a full professor.

From very early years one thought obsessed Waksman: He was convinced that there were micro-organisms in the soil that could be transformed into helpers of humanity. He was determined first to find them and then to guide them to that objective. He wrote once that there are "more different kinds of tiny plants and animals in the soil than there are on top of it," and he insisted that these minute and countless micro-organisms were constantly at war with each other. His theory was that the battling micro-organisms created chemical killers in their struggle for survival, and that these same chemical weapons could be used to fight the micro-organisms that afflicted people.

For nearly thirty years, in his cluttered laboratory in New Brunswick, he experimented, convinced that his theory was correct. He found various micro-organisms but discarded them: Either they did not do anything to cure a diseased patient, or else they proved to be injurious rather than helpful. The Rutgers University officials allowed him to continue his research, although at one time it was proposed that Waksman be dismissed for reasons of economy and because, one official said, there was no possible future to Waksman's work.

And then one day in 1943 Waksman studied a culture taken from the throat of a sick chicken. He and his team experimented with a new culture and produced the first strains of an effective disease-killer, which succeeded against tuberculosis where penicillin had failed. The tests were carried out among animals, and the time had come for experimenting on people.

The new culture, named streptomycin, was shipped to the Mayo Clinic for use on desperately ill tuberculosis patients. The reaction was instantaneous, and a cure had been found for a disease that had plagued mankind for a great many years. Many other diseases were subjected to dosages of streptomycin, and almost all collapsed in the face of this new wonder drug.

Three years later Waksman's miracle cure was being used by physicians throughout the world to help cure a wide variety of diseases. But Dr. Waksman did not desist in his laboratory work. He now continued to produce a whole new series of additional antibiotics which attacked other infections immune to streptomycin. A grateful world blessed his name.

In 1949 he became the first head of the newly formed Institute of Microbiology at Rutgers, and in the course of the next few years he was given not only the Nobel Prize but also awards from France, Italy, Japan, Denmark, Holland, and of course the United States. In addition to a great many scientific papers and more than a dozen texts in the field of microbiology, Waksman wrote an autobiography, *My Life with Microbes,* which became a nationwide bestseller.

He became deeply interested in scientific research in Israel soon after the establishment of the new nation in 1948, and an institute devoted to industrial microbiology was established in his name at the Technion–Israel Institute of Technology in Haifa with the long-term goal of utilizing microbes in industrial experimentation and development.

Waksman retained his Russian-Yiddish accent throughout his life, but that never seemed to bother either his students or the large audiences that turned out to hear his scientific lectures. In his latter years he spent long periods of time addressing various scientific groups in Israel, urging the young researchers there to press forward with their work and not become discouraged, just as he had not given up for a period of nearly thirty years.

I. I. RABI

Nuclear Energy for Peace

HE HAS SERVED AS CHAIRMAN of the Science Advisory Committee under President Dwight Eisenhower. In 1944 he was awarded the Nobel Prize in physics for his discovery of the resonance method of determining the magnetic properties of the atomic nucleus. For a number of years he led the advisory committee of the Atomic Energy Commission, and he is today one of the most respected men of science in the world.

Isidore Isaac Rabi, usually known by the initials of his first and middle names, was brought to the United States as a small child and grew up in a poor home. His father was a grocer and had worked for a time in a dress factory. After graduating from a New York high school, young Rabi was awarded a scholarship at Cornell University and earned a degree in chemistry in three years. For the next few years he worked at a variety of jobs, trying to decide exactly what to do, and then he resumed his graduate work, first at Cornell and later at Columbia, in physics, supporting himself as a tutor at City College.

He had switched from chemistry to physics, and his special expertise in this area won him a chance to travel to Europe to work and study with some of the great physicists of the time—Bohr, Stern, Heisenberg, and Pauli. He became fascinated by the new field of molecular beams, especially as it was related to the measurements of atomic magnetism.

He joined the Columbia physics faculty, and has been part of the famous university's innovative physics department since 1927. In 1977 he was honored for a half century of teaching physics at Columbia, which has turned out one quarter of all the American Nobel laureates in physics.

Like many immigrants to the United States, Rabi has always had a deep attachment to his new country. He became interested in helping in the defense of the United States at about the same time that the Nazis rose to power in Germany. Soon after war broke out in Europe, he divided his time between his teaching duties at Columbia and a project being carried out secretly at MIT in Cambridge, Massachusetts, that led to the development of military radar. Simultaneously he was also involved in the top-secret Manhattan Project, which led to the creation of the first atomic bomb.

When the Nobel Prize was awarded to Rabi in 1944, the war was still raging and he did not deliver the traditional lecture in Stockholm. He was too involved with the work he was doing for the U.S. military at the time anyway; a few years later the defense department awarded him the Medal of Merit, honoring him for "exceptional meritorious conduct in the performance of outstanding service to the United States, from November 1940 to December 1945, as consultant to many key defense organizations, [and for maintaining] the highest level of inspirational initiative in the application of scientific techniques to military problems."

The distinguished scientist also took a deep interest in the development of a number of important scientific institutions in Israel, especially the Technion–Israel Institute of Technology and the Weizmann Institute of Science. He loaned his name to a number of organizations that were working in behalf of Israel, and visited that country a number of times, offering his services as a mentor in various phases of scientific development.

A decade after the first atomic bomb was dropped on Hiroshima, Rabi was one of the principal figures in a worldwide Atoms for Peace Conference convened in Geneva under United Nations auspices. Like other distinguished nuclear scientists, he was fearful of the misuse of atomic energy and tried to use his influence to reducing its easy accessibility and potential for destruction.

Although he has received the highest honors and accolades

that can be given, Rabi has remained an essentially modest man, anxious to learn and teach, trying to see the bright side of things, hoping that the world's entrance into the atomic age will bring with it an era of peace and prosperity but mindful that there are very real dangers of unscrupulous individuals or governments appropriating the new force for their own, diabolical ends.

Of the first detonation of the atomic bomb in the New Mexico desert, Rabi has written:

> The atomic age came at about five-thirty in the morning of July 16, 1945. It was a sight which I have attempted from time to time to describe. I never felt successful in doing it. One has to go back to the Bible, to witnesses of the ancient miracles, to get some impression of the tremendous emotional experience it produced. . . . Many things can be done which were quite impossible up to now. Very important developments in chemistry, particularly in biological chemistry and medicine, will be brought about. We will be able to learn things which we could not find out before. We have a real revolution ahead of us through the use of [radioactive] materials.

The diversion of nuclear energy to peaceful, helpful, life-saving goals has become the primary objective of the distinguished Nobel laureate in physics.

ELIEZER BEN-YEHUDA

Father of Modern Hebrew

PEOPLE USED TO CALL HIM A FANATIC, but that didn't trouble him. He was a man obsessed with a dream unlike any other dream or any other man: He believed that the future of the Jewish people would be immeasurably strengthened if there were once again one common language, the ancient biblical language of Hebrew, that bound Jews together, and he set about to turn his dream into reality. Amazingly, he succeeded. Ben-Yehuda is believed to be the only man in history who ever revived a language of ancient times and made it again a living, spoken tongue.

He was born in 1858 in Lithuania, and his family name was originally Perelmann. He changed it to reflect the ancient method of using one's father's first name as a family name when he left for Palestine in 1881. When he and his young bride, Devorah, set foot on the soil of the ancient Jewish homeland, then under the control of harsh Turkish authorities, he told her from that moment on they would never again speak anything but Hebrew—and he was true to his word.

Their son, Itamar, was raised in the first Hebrew-speaking home of modern times, and because the other children of the Jewish community, made up largely of Orthodox Jewish families, spoke only Yiddish, reserving the use of Hebrew for prayer and study of the Bible and Talmud, the youngster had a hard time making friends.

Ben-Yehuda ignored all of his opponents who said the idea of reviving Hebrew was a wild scheme. The ultra-Orthodox Jews claimed it was blasphemous to use a holy tongue like Hebrew for

everyday needs, while even some of the Zionist leaders expressed grave doubts that the idea could ever possibly work. Jews at the time spoke Yiddish, Russian, German, and in the case of Sephardic Jews, Ladino. True, they all knew Hebrew from their prayers and Bible study, but nobody actually spoke or wrote the language.

Nevertheless, Ben-Yehuda persisted. He said that sooner or later Jews would leave the Diaspora because of violent or non-violent anti-Semitism or because of the threat of assimilation into the mainstream of their respective lands of exile, and they would need a common language to help form a united people. Reviving Hebrew, he insisted, not only would give them that language but also would serve as a bridge between the days of the Temple—some two thousand years past—and the present time, buttressing their right to return to the ancient Jewish homeland.

When he first arrived in Jerusalem, Ben-Yehuda found that most of the Jews there were ultra-Orthodox, who knew Hebrew well from their daily prayers and Bible study. He decided to try to win them over to transforming Hebrew into a daily, spoken language, and to accomplish this, he began to act the role of an Orthodox Jew.

He grew a beard and sidecurls and persuaded his wife to wear a *sheitel*, a wig worn by Orthodox women. The subterfuge did not work, however, when the Orthodox Jews saw that Ben-Yehuda was trying to turn Hebrew from a purely holy tongue into one of mundane use. They soon turned against him, and he subsequently became a lifelong opponent of religious fanaticism.

He took a job as a teacher in a Jerusalem school run by the Alliance Israélite Universelle and succeeded in introducing the teaching of Hebrew, at least for courses in Judaica. It was a beginning, and soon thereafter he launched a Hebrew-language weekly newspaper, which struggled with each issue to introduce new words to describe developments and objects that could not even have been imagined in biblical times. He always sought to coin new words that had their origin in ancient Hebrew words or roots, although at times he was forced to adopt terms from foreign languages.

His wife died in 1891, and he married her younger sister, Hemda, who was destined to spend a lifetime raising funds for his magnum opus—a Hebrew dictionary that would encompass all words from the ancient past to the present day. Ben-Yehuda devoted all his time to inculcating his concept of a revived Hebrew language among all sectors of the nascent Zionist movement, as well as to his dictionary and his newspaper.

At one time Ben-Yehuda was imprisoned for allegedly having written an editorial in his newspaper calling for a revolt against the Turkish authorities. The utterly false accusation had been instigated by a number of the older Jerusalemite Jews who were bitterly opposed to his "heretical" ways. His jailing actually helped his work, since most segments of the younger Jewish community came to realize that his cause was just and rallied to his defense, in effect aligning themselves with his efforts on behalf of Hebrew.

A critical situation developed for Ben-Yehuda in the early 1920s, when "the war of the languages" broke out. Influential and wealthy German Jews had decided to establish a technical school in Haifa and insisted that the language of instruction be German. A number of the teachers in the new school and early leaders of the Zionist movement then living in Palestine urged Ben-Yehuda to rally a campaign against the use of German. It became a cause célèbre, with student and teacher strikes, popular petitions, and appeals to influential Jewish leaders in Europe. Eventually, the conflict was resolved, and Hebrew won out as the language of instruction in the new technical school (originally called the Technikum and later Hebraized to Technion). The linguistic victory became the watershed that led to a growing use of Hebrew in all schools in the country.

Ben-Yehuda took no time out for victory celebrations, always mindful of the dictionary project he was working on. He traveled with his wife to London and other European capitals, where he immersed himself in scholarly libraries, seeking clues to long-forgotten Hebrew terms, while his wife met with local philanthropists and Zionist supporters, seeking financial aid for the dictionary her husband was preparing.

When the first volumes appeared, they created a sensation in the philological and scholarly worlds. There, in black and white, Ben-Yehuda had succeeded in listing words and idioms that had been all but buried in the Bible, the Talmud, and other religious and legal works dating back many centuries. The dictionary was thick with Jewish history and geography, and Ben-Yehuda's achievement was immediately hailed by scholars.

A Language Academy was formed in Jerusalem, in which scholars began to contribute their own words—sometimes coined, sometimes rediscovered from ancient sources—to the growing old-new language. Ben-Yehuda was deeply involved with that, too.

The massive multivolume dictionary was not completed at the time of his death in 1922, but Ben-Yehuda lived to hear Hebrew beginning to be spoken on all sides of him as the size of the Jewish community in Palestine continued to grow. His son, Ehud, carried on his father's dictionary project, and in 1959 the entire seventeen-volume work appeared, a vast and vital contribution to Hebrew learning and lexicography.

Hebrew today is spoken not only by the more than three million Jewish citizens of Israel but also by scores of thousands of non-Jews living in the country. A major part of the curriculum of Jewish religious schools in all parts of the world includes the teaching of Hebrew, not only for prayers but also for use as a language of everyday life. In the United States, England, Canada, and a number of other countries Hebrew is offered as a full-fledged foreign language on college campuses as well as in some high schools. There are even Hebrew-speaking summer camps in various parts of the United States. Conversely, the study of Hebrew is banned in the Soviet Union, a prohibition that has led many thousands of Soviet Jews to study the language from secretly home-produced texts.

Although Hebrew has not become as widespread or popular as English or French, a great joy was felt among all lovers of the language when the Israeli author S. Y. Agnon, who wrote in Hebrew, was awarded the Nobel Prize in literature.

The Hebrew language, like all modern tongues, is a living, organic entity, and the Language Academy is still busy coining new words, seeking wherever possible to base these on ancient terms.

Ben-Yehuda's dream of a reborn Hebrew language to help unite the Jews returning to Israel has been realized. Jewish immigrants from Rumania, England, North Africa, Latin America, and many other countries—where both Yiddish and Ladino have been on the wane—now study Hebrew in intensive courses and can meet each other on the common ground of a common language, thanks to Ben-Yehuda's vision and determination.

RUTH KLUGER

Rescue Mission in Rumania

VERY FEW PEOPLE TOOK SERIOUSLY the threats of Adolf Hitler, who seized power in Germany in 1933, when he openly declared that his government would obliterate the Jews from the face of the earth. Although small numbers of Jewish refugees began to leave various European countries in the years before the war erupted, notably from Germany and Austria, the then small but militant Jewish community of Palestine took the Nazis at their word. They began to plan to bring as many Jews as possible out of Europe to Palestine. The work had to be carried out secretly since the British government, which was at the time the Mandatory Power in control of Palestine, had sharply restricted the number of Jews who could enter the country.

One of the people who became involved in this rescue effort was a young woman named Ruth Kluger, who had been raised in Rumania and settled in Palestine at the age of twenty. A few months before the Nazis invaded Poland in September 1939, launching the Second World War, she said good-bye to her husband in Tel Aviv and made her way to Rumania. Her mission was clear: to persuade and to help as many Jews as possible in that country to leave their homes, board "illegal" and in most cases hardly seaworthy vessels, and sail to Palestine, before the Nazis reached that part of eastern Europe and organized programs for their total destruction.

She was in Rumania secretly when the German armies swarmed over Poland, imprisoning Jews in ghettos, concentration camps, and slave labor camps, and she found herself arguing with her Rumanian coreligionists that they should not wait but make every effort to flee immediately. Most of the Rumanian Jews, she recalls, were "stunned by the ghastly reports that had begun to come out of Poland, but they remained where they were, unwilling to believe that the same fate awaited them, too."

Gradually a small exodus of Jews began to develop. Through the efforts of Ruth Kluger and her colleagues in the underground organization they had set up, Jews boarded vessels that claimed as their destinations countries in the Western hemisphere but that were really setting course for the shores of Palestine, where the local Jewish community had made preparations to absorb the illegal immigrants into various settlements and villages. Although only a small number of Rumanian Jews were rescued, there is little doubt that had Ruth Kluger and her compatriots not worked feverishly to bring them out of Rumania, they too would have suffered the same fate as awaited the overwhelming majority of European Jews.

When the Nazis expanded their dominion over eastern Europe, including Rumania, Ruth had to flee for her life, and she made her way to neutral Turkey. She continued her work in behalf of the secret organization that kept on pressing for the rescue of as many European Jews as possible throughout the war years. In all, some 200,000 Jews were smuggled out of Europe to Palestine, and even though the number of those rescued is small contrasted to the six million who perished, Ruth Kluger and those who worked alongside her can take a measure of comfort from the ancient Talmudic comment that he "who rescues even one person, it is as though he has saved the world."

Ruth Kluger, who changed her last name to Aliav at the suggestion of the late Prime Minister of Israel David Ben-Gurion to mark her work for *Aliyah*, or immigration to Israel, lives today in Tel Aviv, where she had been honored on several occasions for her wartime rescue efforts. She occasionally lectures at Israeli universities and is an active leader of the Israel branch of the International Federation of Business and Professional Women. Her book *The*

Last Escape describes the awesome period she lived through in Rumania from 1939 to 1941.

In 1938, she recalls, a conference of thirty-eight countries took place in Switzerland to discuss the problems of rescuing European Jewry. Each of the nations in attendance "politely and diplomatically declined" to open its doors to admit large numbers of Jewish refugees, an action that could have precluded the Nazis from carrying out their plans for the Holocaust.

The great sage Hillel taught, "If I am not for myself, who will be for me? And if not now, then when?" Throughout history, Jewish communities have demonstrated an extraordinary concern for helping one another in times of distress. During the Nazi era, in spite of enormous, nearly insurmountable obstacles, the Jewish communities of Palestine and the United States in particular exerted heroic efforts to aid their coreligionists. These efforts were directed first at rescue and later at rehabilitation and transfer to places of refuge, notably Israel.

When the Nazis surrendered to the Allies in the spring of 1945, Ruth Kluger was the first Palestinian Jew to enter the concentration camps and to carry on the work she had begun years earlier—to bring the surviving Jews out of an inferno to a new life of hope and a future.

IRVING S. SHAPIRO

Chemical Supplier to the World

ONE OF THE WORLD'S LARGEST COMPANIES is the Du Pont
Company, of Delaware. It is approaching its two-hundredth birthday and has links with practically every country in the world. It
employs huge numbers of people, directly and indirectly, and
plays a major role in the economic structure of the Western world.
A few years ago it named Irving S. Shapiro, the son of immigrant
parents from Lithuania, as chairman of the board and chief executive officer.

Irving Shapiro was born in 1916 in Minneapolis. He and his
two brothers received a traditional Jewish religious education. The
expanding field of science attracted young Shapiro, and when he
was twenty-three he earned a bachelor of science degree from the
University of Minnesota. He knew himself well enough, however,
to understand that a career devoted to science alone was not quite
right for his analytical mind, and two years later he earned a law
degree, also from the University of Minnesota, and began a career
as a lawyer with a rich background in science.

He and his wife, Charlotte, moved to Washington, where
Shapiro went to work for the Department of Justice, appearing
frequently before the Supreme Court. For nearly two years he
worked for the wartime Office of Price Administration, and
helped to set up a rationing program that went into effect when
America entered World War II.

In 1951 Shapiro joined the legal department of Du Pont, the world's largest chemical company. He was actively involved in antitrust litigation as well as in legal aspects of a wide range of manufacturing problems. By 1965 he had risen to the position of assistant general counsel of the giant corporation, and seven years later he was named a senior vice-president. A year later he was appointed vice-chairman of the board, and in less than a year he was elected chairman and chief executive officer—the thirteenth chief executive officer of the firm, and the only one who came from a background in law, all the others having been primarily scientists, engineers, or financiers.

In addition to serving on the boards of several large companies, Shapiro has remained an active member of his local Jewish community and has begun to play an important role in national Jewish affairs. He is a director of the Jewish Federation of Delaware and of the Kutz Home for the Aged, a well-known Wilmington Jewish institution. He is also a member of the board of governors of the Jerusalem Institute of Management in Israel.

Shapiro in recent years has been consulted on national economic problems confronting the United States by various sections of the legislative and executive branches of the federal government. He is keenly aware of the fact that his lofty position in industry affords him a special opportunity to attempt to bring about a rapprochement between Israel and her Arab neighbors, and he has been working in that direction without fanfare or publicity for a number of years.

In 1978 Yeshiva University, America's oldest rabbinical seminary, conferred an honorary degree on him for his exemplary service to the community as a whole and to the Jewish people in particular.

DAVID BEN-GURION

Architect of Israel

HE WAS ACKNOWLEDGED AS THE ARCHITECT and principal
founder of the State of Israel and served the new nation as Prime
Minister and Minister of Defense. He could be charming and
tough; he read the Bible assiduously and could quote at random
lengthy passages, particularly from the book of Isaiah; and because
he admired the early Greek philosophers and was not satisfied to
read them in translation, taught himself ancient Greek and studied
the works of Plato, Socrates, and Aristotle in the original.

He was born in 1886 in Plonsk, at the time in Russian-held
Poland, the son of an ardent Zionist whose family name was Gruen
(Ben-Gurion later Hebraized his surname). His mother died when
he was eleven, and young David received a relatively modern Hebrew and secular education, much of it from private tutors. When
he was fourteen he was already involved with an early Zionist
group and began to travel around Poland, calling for adherence to
a Zionist answer to the problems of the Jewish community. In
1905 the authorities arrested him, but his father managed to obtain
his release, and the next year Ben-Gurion left for Palestine.

He earned a living picking oranges in Petah Tikvah and
working in the wine cellars of Rishon le-Zion. Palestine at the time
was part of the Ottoman Empire and Ben-Gurion and his lifelong

friend Yitzhak Ben-Zvi, who later became Israel's second President, decided to enroll in Turkish universities to study law and try to establish better relations between the small Jewish community then in Palestine and the Turkish leaders. The two young students were arrested instead and deported to Egypt; within a year they set sail for the United States to help expand the Zionist movement there.

In 1917 Ben-Gurion met and married a New York nurse, Paula Munweis, herself an ardent labor Zionist. In the same year the British government issued the Balfour Declaration, expressing its support for the establishment of a Jewish homeland in Palestine, and the next year a Jewish Legion was formed to help defeat the German and Turkish forces. Ben-Gurion was one of the early volunteers for the Legion, and arrived in Egypt in May, as part of a contingent attached to the British army.

When the war ended, he proceeded to Palestine and threw himself into the political work that he hoped would lay the groundwork for a Jewish state based on socialist principles, especially on the credo of the kibbutz movement. For a decade he was an active leader of the Histadrut, and in the early 1930s he became more closely identified with the official Zionist movement. He became chairman of the Jewish Agency executive in 1935, in effect sharing the leadership of the worldwide Zionist movement with its president, Chaim Weizmann.

In 1939 the British government announced a sharp curtailment of Jewish immigration to Palestine, despite the deteriorating situation of European Jewry in a continent in which the forces of Hitlerism were on the upsurge. Ben-Gurion led the Jewish community's denunciation of the new policy and called for resistance to it as well as expansion of so-called illegal immigration of Jews to Palestine.

At the conclusion of World War II he visited the displaced persons camps where scores of thousands of former inmates of Nazi camps and ghettos were waiting for an opportunity to emigrate from blood-soaked Europe. In his fiery manner, he told the Jewish survivors of Nazism, "We shall not rest until every one of you who so desires joins us in the land of Israel in building a Jewish state." He directed all-out efforts to help bring as many of the refugees to Palestine as possible, even it meant using unseaworthy vessels. At the same time, he ordered the leaders of Haganah, the Jewish defense organization, to start acquiring arms, for he felt that sooner or later the Arabs surrounding the Jewish community in Palestine would mount a full-fledged attack.

In November 1947 the United Nations voted to establish a Jewish and an Arab state in Palestine. A month later, armed Arab attacks against Jewish settlements began, which were escalated when the State of Israel was proclaimed on May 14, 1948. Although he had able military people around him—including the American volunteer Colonel David ("Mickey") Marcus—in essence Ben-Gurion in his role as Defense Minister directed the war effort, in the same manner and spirit as Churchill had done in England a few years earlier.

The proclamation of independence was not something desired by all of the Jewish leaders at the time. Some felt Israel was too weak; others said waiting for a more propitious moment would be more practical. Ben-Gurion overruled all objections, saying that the Jews had waited nearly two thousand years to re-establish the Jewish homeland, and after the bitter years of the Hitler era and the postwar sufferings of the survivors of the Holocaust, the time had come for such a step.

On a Friday afternoon, in great secrecy, the leaders of the Jewish community of Palestine gathered in Tel Aviv and solemnly pronounced the establishment of the State of Israel. Ben-Gurion was named the first Prime Minister, and within a few minutes of the announcement, transmitted worldwide by radio, the United States became the first country to recognize the new state.

In the proclamation of Israel's independence, the country was described as the

> land where the Jewish people came into being. In this land was shaped their spiritual, religious and national character. Here they created a culture of national and universal import and gave to the world the eternal Book of Books. . . . The State of Israel will be open to Jewish immigration and the in-gathering of the exiles.

While crowds of exuberant men, women, and children cheered and danced in the streets of Tel Aviv and Jerusalem, Arab armies proceeded to try to crush the new state in its very infancy. For the next few years, Ben-Gurion labored mightily, supervising first the defense of the country and then the task of integrating the huge shiploads and planeloads of Jews who began to stream into Israel. He served in his dual capacity as Prime Minister and Defense Minister for five years, and then after a hiatus of two years, resumed his old job for a stint of eight more years.

In 1963 he left government service and retired to a spartan life on a kibbutz in the Negev, hoping no doubt that his example of settling in a remote corner of Israel would be emulated by others. He devoted himself to writing a history of the rebirth of Israel and to pursuing his own prodigious reading and study.

During the period that he helped fashion Israel, the country's Jewish population rose from less than three quarters of a million at the time of the proclamation of independence to more than two and a half million when he stepped down from office (it is today more than three million). Agriculture, industry, education, defense, housing—virtually all areas of the life of a modern nation—grew during his tenure of office. He visited with the leaders of several west European countries to cement better ties between Israel and the older, more established democracies. He conferred with President John Kennedy, and often spoke to Jewish fundraising meetings in America. One of his most dramatic tours of the United States took place when he flew around the country in a chartered plane, helping to launch the Israel Bonds program.

When he died in 1973, Jews throughout the world felt that *the* founding father of Israel was no more.

JANUS KORCZAK

Physician of the Children

At first glance, his is not even a "Jewish" name. And then, it seems hardly pronounceable. Yet, so long as men and women continue to admire moral courage and a heart brimming with kindness, the name of this remarkable man—pronounced *ya'noosh kor'chak*—will live on. If Jews had a system of saints, he would certainly be high on the list of candidates for canonization.

His real name was Henryk Goldszmidt, but he was so well known as an author of books for children and a writer on children for educators and parents under the name of Korczak that that is how he is best remembered today.

The exact date of his birth is not certain, although it was probably 1878. The family into which he was born was wealthy and assimilationist, and if you were to ask its members, all of them ardent patriots of Poland, if they were Jews or Poles, the immediate response would be the latter.

Young Henryk grew up in comfortable circumstances and chose to become a physician. The terrible condition of the poor, especially the orphans, of Poland in the early years of this century moved him to help them improve their lot. First, the young doctor volunteered his services as a social worker—physician in a summer camp for underprivileged children, and later he was named director of a Jewish orphanage in Warsaw.

In those days, orphanages were large, impersonal, often cruel institutions run by apathetic people who were not really interested in the children's welfare. Discipline was tight, and boys and girls would line up with their spoons and bowls into which hot food was ladled—like some scene out of a Dickens novel—and that would be a major part of the care extended.

The idealistic, compassionate young doctor saw that the system was all wrong, and set about changing it. He introduced a method whereby the children themselves were given responsibility for running the orphanage, feeling that they would then not have to be reminded about such prosaic subjects as cleanliness, manners, and decorum. His innovations were then unique, and he began to write about them in the hope they would be emulated by other orphanage directors for the benefit of the parentless children.

The young charges in Korczak's care realized very quickly that this was no ordinary man who had come to run the institution but a sympathetic, warm human being who really had their best interests at heart. Unfailingly he dealt with each child as though he were indeed his or her father, sometimes teaching, sometimes scolding gently, always encouraging the youngsters to understand that they had an opportunity to improve their station in life through serious study, genuine interest in other people, and a code of high moral standards.

To say that the orphans in his care loved him and he loved them in turn would be an understatement. In the wee hours of the night he would sit and write imaginative stories for children, about a world in which the government was run by children—children who knew no guile and who practiced what was right and just without reference to "practical" considerations. His stories were of a mythical kingdom, but they expressed his strong belief that boys and girls were basically pure of heart and if given a chance could do a better job of running the world than the adults had been doing for as long as people could remember.

Typical of the books that he wrote for educators and parents, long before similar approaches began to be taken by modern innovators in pedagogy, were *How to Love a Child* and *The Child's Right to Respect*.

From 1911 until the beginning of the Nazi invasion of Poland in 1939, Korczak ran his orphanage, through which passed thousands of children during that span of almost three decades. His pioneering, far-sighted methods won him a wide reputation, and social workers and others came to visit and observe his institution from many parts of the world.

The strong Jewish identity he had missed in his own youth had gradually taken hold of him as he dealt on a daily basis with the youngsters in his care. He became interested in the kibbutz movement in Palestine and went there to observe and study, expressing his admiration for the way the children of the kibbutz were being treated and raised. The Jewish leaders of Palestine, sensing no doubt that here was a rare man who could help them fashion an even better system for caring for their youngsters, urged him to stay on in Palestine, but he declined, explaining that he was needed in the orphanage in Warsaw. He returned to Poland, although the Nazi war clouds were already visible.

Korczak never married, and thus devoted all of his time to the children in his care. If anything, his gentleness and patience seemed to grow with each passing year. In 1942, after the total collapse of Polish resistance to the German invaders, he and his two hundred young orphans were forcibly removed from the building they occupied and herded into a section of the Warsaw ghetto, where they lived among an estimated 300,000 other imprisoned Jews. Like so many other Jews in the ghetto, Korczak heard rumors of what the Germans were doing to the Jews trapped in Nazi-dominated territory but refused, at first at least, to believe these incredible reports.

Conditions in the Warsaw ghetto gradually grew worse. Hunger and disease were everywhere, and in the winter months there was no fuel for heating or cooking.

And then one day one of the Jewish policemen employed by the Nazis, a member of a hated group who sought to save themselves by helping the Germans, knocked on the door of Korczak's apartment. His eyes were bleary and red-rimmed, betraying his drunkenness. Tears in his eyes, he told the director of the orphanage that he had learned that Korczak's orphans were scheduled to be deported the next day. Taking a deep swallow from a flask in his hand, the informer begged Korczak not to reveal that he had been notified in advance.

By now Korczak was convinced that the reports of the deliberate extermination of the Jews caught in the Nazi trap were true. He did not know what to do, where to turn. Should he tell his young wards that in a matter of days or weeks or months they would all be dead? Dared he panic them, frighten them more than they were already frightened? Should he try to help them somehow to escape, or put up some resistance in the hope that at least some of them would evade the fate that now seemed so clear to him awaited them all? Or should he perhaps try to make their last hours on earth as enjoyable as possible, by an act of deceit?

The dilemma tormented him until he finally decided what he must do. With a forced smile on his lips, he summoned the children and announced that the next day they would all go on a picnic. He told them to put on their best Sabbath clothes and get a good rest that night. The children were delighted.

The next morning, the informer's tip was proven right. All the people on the block, including the two hundred orphans, were rounded up and taken in sealed trucks to a railway station outside the walls. Korczak assured the children that all was well, that they were merely getting a train ride out into the country.

At the station, before the Jews were ordered into the cattle cars that would transport them to the Treblinka death camp, one of the Nazi officials, aware of Korczak's worldwide reputation as an educator, offered to release him, but the doctor refused.

Wearing their best clothes, the whole group, led by Korczak carrying a very small child in his arms, entered the train. They were never seen again.

The governments of both Israel and Poland have issued postage stamps bearing the saddest expression ever seen on a man's face —that of Janus Korczak, who loved all children and who lived to see a world in which fellow human beings deliberately exterminated his beloved children because they were Jewish. The look on his face will eternally haunt humanity.

MIRIAM BEN-PORAT

A Woman on the Supreme Court

SHE IS THE ONLY WOMAN MEMBER of a Supreme Court in the world. A lawyer and then a professor of law, a public prosecutor, and a district judge, she was named a justice of the Israel Supreme Court in 1976. Miriam Ben-Porat has come a long way from the time she arrived in Israel from Lithuania, as a teen-age immigrant.

She was born in 1918 and immigrated to what was then Palestine in 1936, three years prior to the outbreak of World War II. A graduate of the Hebrew Gymnasium in Kovno, Lithuania (the equivalent of a junior college), she earned a law degree at the Hebrew University. She was a local judge for eighteen years before being named a member of the Israel Supreme Court. She also continues to teach law at the Hebrew University.

Justice Ben-Porat believes that because of women's special biological role, "those with careers and families actually have dual roles, and must prove that they are capable of doing both." She remembers the first time that she had to preside as a judge, when she was only thirty years old: "I was unsure, even a little shy, but I was determined to do my best. Gradually, I began to develop the self-confidence that a judge must possess, plus of course the stamina to prepare myself for each and every case with as much care as possible."

From the very beginning of her judicial career, Justice Ben-Porat has remained aloof from all political involvements, deter-

327

mined to remain as objective and fair as possible about every case brought before her. During the many years that she sat on the bench before her appointment to the Supreme Court, which sits in Jerusalem, she tried cases involving homicide, morals, economics, and politics.

One of the most celebrated cases she presided over was the trial of a Greek Orthodox clergyman, Father Capucci, who was found guilty of smuggling arms from Lebanon to Palestinian terrorists stationed inside Israel. She also sat on a case in which a group of fanatical Israeli Jewish youths tried to carry out a religious service on the ancient site of the Temple Mount, now a holy site for Moslems and still revered by Jews as the location of the Holy Temple. In that case, she overruled a lower court's decision that exoneratd the youths for their action, explaining that "in view of the sensitive and dangerous situation prevailing against the intercommunal background, the exercise of the Jewish right of prayer on the Temple Mount is charged with grave dangers to public order as long as no regulations are adopted."

Justice Ben-Porat has consistently emphasized that a judge's duty is to interpret the law in the most just way possible. There is no jury system in Israel, but this is as it should be, she believes, because in so small a country it is "nearly impossible to find a dozen people who don't know each other or who do not have a prior opinion of a case before the courts."

Unlike other countries, where there are large bodies of written laws, Israel law must deal with new cases on a basis of daily improvisations. Justice Ben-Porat believes Jewish religious laws exist for the country's religious courts but the civil court system must fall back on the "realities of the day" set against a background of fundamental legislation that is common to most Western countries, she says.

Justice Ben-Porat's husband is a retired industrialist who watches with pride as his wife pursues her judicial career. From the very beginning, they both explain, he encouraged her to pursue a career and run a household, an innovative approach even in a country as progressive as Israel.

Justice Ben-Porat defines the task of women in the latter part of the twentieth century: "I believe most women need legal protection, despite the current view that a woman's career is her own business—if she wants to work day and night to fulfill herself, it is a matter of her own choice. Laws governing the minimum marriage age, tax exemptions for working mothers—all these are essential. We need protective legislation for them, since many elements of our population groups still bear a tradition of discrimination against women. After all, women comprise at least half of the population, and discriminatory practices against them would only result in delaying the building up of our country."

Justice Ben-Porat was raised in a family where education was the watchword; six of her seven brothers and sisters received a higher education. "Mother used to bake bread and we all wore hand-me-down clothes so that there would be enough money for tuition fees," she says.

For relaxation she listens to music, plays the piano, and reads serious books on a wide variety of subjects. "Sometimes, when I am tired and need relaxation, I read something light and enjoyable, even rubbish," she adds.

ELI COHEN

A Spy Who Died for Israel

THE WORD "SPY" has a sinister connotation. One thinks of shadowy figures lurking in the dark, doing things that are not legal in order to serve their respective countries. Eli Cohen was a spy in the service of Israel, but he was anything but a sinister person. He grew up in Egypt, and from his early youth he dreamed of being able to emigrate to Israel and join his coreligionists in building a Jewish state that would be an example of a modern, progressive, democratic nation steeped in the ancient biblical teachings of the prophets.

He was born in 1924, but it was not until 1957, when he was thirty-three years old, that he managed to make his way to Israel. He was now married and had a family, and he felt that he was being given a second chance in life, for he found that he loved every aspect of Israel even more than he had dared dream when he was a youngster.

One day he was approached by a representative of the Israeli military intelligence service. The man said that Israel desperately needed to know what was going on in some of the Arab countries, so that there would be no chance of any sudden, sneak attacks. He explained to Cohen that the intelligence service knew that he was a loyal Jew, deeply devoted to Israel, that he spoke and knew Arabic fluently, that he could pass for an Arab. He was asked to consider taking on a very dangerous job—to serve Israel as a spy in an Arab country.

The agent explained to Cohen further that his family would be well taken care of and that, if he agreed to take on the job, he should understand that his principal reward would be in knowing that he was carrying out a mission for Israel that could help save hundreds, perhaps even thousands, of Israeli lives.

He was advised to think it over, and under no circumstances to discuss the conversation with anyone. The agent also stated very clearly to Cohen that the risks of being a spy were great and that, if he were caught, the chances of his being executed were very high.

Eli Cohen did not take very much time to consider the offer. He let the agent know that he was prepared to undertake the assignment. It was decided that his wife should be told that he was being sent abroad to carry out important business missions for Israel and that these trips made it difficult to communicate regularly. She acknowledged the explanation, although it is conceivable that in her heart of hearts she suspected that her husband was undertaking a secret, dangerous mission for Israel. She knew how much he loved his new country.

For the next several months, Eli Cohen lived undercover somewhere in Israel and was taught how to operate a secret radio transmitter, how to code and decipher messages, what kinds of military information to look for. His assignment was Syria, which at the time was in control of the Golan Heights overlooking Israel's Galilee region, from which there was an almost never-ending barrage of artillery fire, as well as terrorist attacks on isolated settlements. The Israelis felt they had to know much more about the military situation in that area in case there should be an outbreak of fighting, as most of their intelligence people suspected would happen sooner or later.

Eli Cohen was shipped off to Argentina, which has a large Arab community, and began to live a double life. He posed as an Arab businessman, made friends with the military attaché of the Syrian Embassy, and generally let it be known that he was a successful young executive who also enjoyed the pleasures of life. He was a free spender, inviting his new friends to dinners and parties, and soon became well known and well liked. He was known now as Kamal Tabas.

Some time later he returned to the Middle East, specifically to

Damascus, Syria's capital, which is relatively close to Israel. He rented an expensive apartment, installed his secret radio transmitter, and began to broaden his circle of friends and acquaintances in the ruling circles of the country, especially the military.

His lavish home became a center for parties where Syrian military and government officials found a warm host whose bar seemed constantly well stocked, where they could meet attractive, exciting people from the world of the theater and art, and they always seemed to have a very good time. Of course, only Eli Cohen / Kamal Tabas knew that in the ceiling of the apartment, only a few feet from where the parties took place, there was concealed a secret radio transmitter which the Israeli agent used almost daily to provide information that he hoped would eventually enable the Israeli military intelligence to know in depth and in detail the exact strength of various units of the Syrian armed forces, their locations and capabilities, and their tactical and strategic plans.

For long stretches of time, Eli Cohen did not communicate directly with his family, and left it to his superiors to explain his absence as best they could. During the time that he carried out his assignment—a matter of years—there can be little doubt that he was terribly lonesome for his wife and children, and for Israel itself. The constant threat of exposure and execution must surely have kept him in a state of high tension; but throughout the time he was a spy, he never let it show, not to his friends in Syria nor to his superiors in Israel. It seems that he had been almost born to the job.

He learned how to pretend to be a heavy drinker, and listened carefully when guests in his home who had been drinking too much began to talk of military information. He remembered every detail, and when his guests finally left, he would spring into action, first making notes and then transcribing the information into code, and finally broadcasting it to Tel Aviv, at a specific time on a special radio band. He felt that every bit of information he passed to Israel was another powerful weapon in helping to defend the country.

After a while top Syrian military officials began to invite him to their Damascus headquarters, where they actually let him look at classified documents, trusting him implicitly. At one time,

Cohen / Tabas was even invited to broadcast a special radio program from Syria to the Arab community in South America, relaying official government propaganda—which he proceeded to do, urging his "Arab brothers" over the seas to support the Syrian government.

In all, he remained in Syria for three years, and during that time managed to visit Israel and his family for brief periods, doing so through circuitous routes and disguises. One of the early pieces of information he brought with him to Israel was specific planning on Syria's part to divert the essential waters of the Baniyas River so as to dry up Israel's chief water source, the Sea of Galilee and the Jordan River. Efforts by the Syrians to implement the plan were blocked by the Israelis' accurate artillery fire that pinpointed and then destroyed their efforts.

He became a frequent visitor to the Syrian-Israeli border, at the invitation of high Syrian military officials, and would look, observe carefully, and soon transmit everything that he had seen. The information that was thus assembled helped the Israelis immeasurably when the 1967 Six Day War erupted and the Syrians were driven back from their positions on the Golan Heights.

In 1964 Cohen's radio signals were found to be interfering with official transmitters located in the Syrian military compound nearby. His transmitter was traced, and his true identity was discovered. The black moment that Cohen had undoubtedly always feared had indeed arrived. The Syrian counterintelligence people who now crowded into Cohen's apartment, where his secret radio was discovered, at first assumed that he was an Arab traitor. When the truth emerged that he was a Jew from Israel, they could not bring themselves to believe it.

On the day of his capture Cohen was forced to transmit a false message to Tel Aviv to confuse the Israelis. However, he sent the message at a slower speed than was normal, which was the signal to his superiors in Israel that he had been apprehended, and they discarded the incorrect message sent—and realized that the time for tears for their man in Syria would soon arrive.

For a while, when it became known that an Israeli spy had been captured in Damascus, panic swept over the city. Hundreds of people were arrested on suspicion of collaboration, but eventually things quieted down, and a trial took place in February 1965.

No foreign newsmen were allowed into the courtroom, but at one point General Al-Hafez, who had questioned Cohen, said of the spy, "He conducted himself in a very brave and honorable fashion during a most trying experience."

At the trial, when he was asked to identify himself, Cohen said, "I am Eli Cohen, Israeli soldier."

He was sentenced to hang, and the execution took place after midnight. His body was left dangling in the public square, wrapped in a large sheet of paper on which was scrawled, "Eli Cohen was sentenced to death in the name of the Arab people of Syria after being found guilty of delivering secret information to the enemy." Thousands of people who could not come to the square saw the dangling body on Syrian television.

The request of Eli Cohen's family that his body be returned to Israel for burial was refused. In Israel tens of thousands of Jews mourned the loss of a man who had given up his life willingly to help defend the country he loved.

In Jerusalem, Israel's capital, a street has been named for him. His story has become a glowing chapter in the history of the young nation.

MARK SPITZ

Olympic Champion

WHEN HE WAS ONLY TEN YEARS OLD, Mark Spitz won his first award for swimming. He knew from that moment on that he would attempt to become one of the great swimmers of the world.

He was born in California in 1950, but when he was only two his parents moved to Hawaii, a swimmers' paradise. He spent many days at the famed Waikiki Beach, dashing into the water without fear, seeming to find himself in his true element. A few years later the family returned to California, and Mark continued his swimming practice and began to study swimming from professional instructors.

He attended religious school and was bar mitzvah. By the time Mark was fourteen, the great swimming coach George Haines predicted that he would become one of the greatest swimmers of all time. People used to line up at indoor and outdoor pools to watch him flit by in the water at unbelievable speeds.

In 1967 the magazine *Swimming World* named him the Swimmer of the Year. That was the year that he had broken three American and five world records, and had also won five gold medals in the Pan-American games held in Canada.

The next year he entered the Olympics, held in Mexico. He was superbly confident of his skill and was sure he would win six gold medals, but only managed to capture two. The next year he went to Israel, where he entered the Maccabiah, the sporting event held every four years for Jewish athletes from all parts of the world. He walked off with four gold medals.

When the 1972 Olympics were announced in Munich, he was a leading entry, although he knew that overconfidence could cost him dearly. A seasoned, experienced swimmer by now and a wiser contestant, he said little and made up his mind to do his best.

The first race he entered was a tough one: the 200-meter butterfly contest, which called for strenuous strokes; he won his first gold medal at Munich. The next day there was a 400-meter freestyle relay race, and again he walked off with a gold medal. The next day he won yet another gold medal; in three days, he had already accumulated five gold medals at the Olympics, and still there remained two more races to enter. In quick succession, as though he were more a creature of the sea than a human being, he completed both races successfully, winning two more gold medals, for a total of seven—a record that has not been beaten.

His achievement was incredible: He was not only the first person in Olympics history to win seven gold medals in swimming but the first person to win seven gold medals in any sporting event in the Olympics. He was honored by all lovers of sports the world over, and was named Male Athlete of the Year by the Associated Press.

The victory at Munich was marred for Spitz, however, by the murder of a group of Israeli athletes by Arab terrorists. People throughout the world were shocked and grieved by the attack, but Mark Spitz was especially stirred.

After his return home to California and the first few weeks and months of basking in the limelight of worldwide publicity for his stunning achievements, he seemed to take a new and more serious attitude toward his Jewish background. He loved swimming, of course, but it seemed as though he suddenly came to the realization that zooming through the water at breakneck speeds was not the only worthwhile thing he wanted to do with his life.

Mark Spitz decided that he would use his new fame to help causes and programs that he felt keenly about, and for the past number of years he could be found delivering speeches to groups of Jewish students and to various organizational meetings, urging that they support the needs of Israel and take a deeper interest in their own Jewish heritage and background.

Only time will tell if anyone will ever again match or top the incredible successes that he piled up at the Olympics in Munich.

SHAUL EISENBERG

To Jerusalem by Way of Japan

His name is commonplace among hundreds of Jewish families—Eisenberg. All his life he has shunned personal publicity, preferring the ancient motto as his guiding light *Lo hamedrash, elah hamaaseh*—"Deeds, not words, count." Among those who know him or know of his multifaceted activities, he is almost a living legend. In Israel especially, where he has made his home for many years, people often nod their heads knowingly and repeat with amazement, even awe, "Shaul Eisenberg? Oh, yes, of course . . ."

His story begins soon after the rise of Hitlerism in 1933. The Jewish community of Germany, some 600,000 strong, began to make plans to leave what they felt would soon become a very bad situation. Shaul at the time was about fifteen. He had been reared in a strictly Orthodox home, had been an average student, and like many other teen-agers, his interests were still being crystallized. The Eisenberg family—Shaul, his mother, brothers, and a sister—emigrated from Germany and made their way to far-off Shanghai, at the time a free port city with a growing number of Jewish refugees, all of them waiting to use their planned interim stay in the Chinese metropolis as a stepping stone to a permanent, new home.

It is not clear exactly how, but around 1940—a year after the outbreak of World War II in Europe—Shaul made his way to the great Japanese port city of Kobe, leaving his family in Shanghai. There was at the time a Jewish community of some two hundred people in Kobe, and each person felt responsible for the welfare of the other. Shaul had divested himself of some of the more rigid rules of the Jewish religion, but he remained a strongly motivated traditional Jew, intent at the time on one goal—survival, for himself and for his family.

He always had an entrepreneurial turn of mind, and began to be active in business and to learn Japanese. One day he met a Eurasian girl, the daughter of an Austrian art expert and a Japanese mother. Her father had come to Japan many years earlier to help the Japanese set up a modern art academy. He had fallen in love not only with a Japanese girl but with the country as a whole, and now made Japan his home.

Shaul and the girl soon realized that they were in love, and Shaul persuaded the half-Oriental, half-Christian girl to convert formally to Judaism. She readily agreed and underwent conversion under the guidance of a local rabbi. She changed her name to Leah, and the two lived as a Jewish family in Tokyo, aware that they and their fellow Jews constituted a tiny islet in a huge sea of Japanese who at the time were conducting an all-out war against the United States and other Western powers, in collaboration with their Nazi allies. Surprisingly, the Jews in Japan (and those in Shanghai, which had by then fallen under the rule of the Japanese) did not fear for their personal safety.

When the war ended in the defeat of Japan by the United States, the leading Japanese industrialists and businessmen were not allowed by the occupation forces to resume their former business interests. Many of the most influential Japanese industrialists and importers had gotten to know Shaul Eisenberg through his father-in-law, whose home was a cultural and artistic center for the country. Gradually, first one and then another and finally many of these Japanese businessmen asked Eisenberg to become their representative and to act as an intermediary with the large American firms with which they had done business for many years.

Eisenberg very soon emerged as a key business figure, helping the Japanese economy to recover, and expanding various major American companies' interests not only in Japan but also throughout southeast Asia. He quickly became a very rich man, and although the news of what had happened to the Jews of Europe filled him with anguish, he was grateful to know that his own family had survived in Shanghai, and, as soon as it was possible, he arranged for his mother and siblings to leave for the newly established State of Israel. Two of his brothers, who had remained strictly observant Jews throughout the ordeal of their enforced exile, soon became the heads of *yeshivot*, or religious academies.

Meanwhile, Eisenberg and his wife were expanding their own immediate family—six children were born to them, and all the children were taught the rudiments of the Jewish faith and were reared as Jews. Eisenberg himself now plunged into his expanding business empire, determined to enlarge his business interests. He was constantly on the go, traveling to India, Burma, Korea, Indonesia, setting up companies of various types, and watching with satisfaction, and perhaps with some measure of incredulity, as his business grew almost beyond measure.

In the late spring of 1967 Israel was threatened with an all-out attack by her Arab neighbors. A huge array of tanks and artillery surrounded the small nation, and the feeble efforts of a number of Western countries to help resolve the crisis frightened virtually every Jew into believing that another Holocaust was imminent. When, six days after the fighting erupted, Israel miraculously succeeded in defeating the combined forces of Egypt, Jordan, and Syria, a feeling of euphoria and relief swept through the Jewish communities of the world. Eisenberg, whose children were now growing up, made up his mind that his place was in Israel, and soon he and his family purchased an estate there and became permanent residents of the Jewish state.

Officials of the Israel government soon became aware of this man in their midst—a former German Jew, married to a half-Japanese woman, whose brothers were religious-school principals, who seemed to have worldwide business ties, and who was reported to be a paragon of charity: Whenever he was approached to help a needy family, a school, or a hospital, he never said no, insisting only on anonymity. From time to time, the hard-pressed Israel government officials borrowed funds from him to help tide them over a difficult time. The sums involved were always in the millions of dollars. Eisenberg watched with joy as over the years the country grew and developed into a viable, productive modern state.

Eisenberg's children entered the Israel armed forces, enrolled in local universities, and have become full-fledged citizens. All of them married Jewish partners. Eisenberg himself continues to direct his far-flung business empire and to provide vital support to religious, health, and educational institutions in Israel and to some extent in the United States. A recommendation he made to the Israel government has been turned into a law, often called the Eisenberg Law, which is credited with helping to attract major investors to the Jewish state.

Evenings, when the sun has dropped into the Mediterranean and the air has cooled, Eisenberg can be seen in the garden of his home, pondering the strange fate of a former yeshiva student in Germany, caught up in the maelstrom of war, who has established himself in Israel with his Eurasian wife, who joins him regularly on their frequent visits to the local synagogue.

His principal objective today is to utilize his vast fortune and his worldwide business links to aid Israel achieve a viable economy so that its foundations will be strengthened. Sometimes he wonders, in a moment of mystical fantasy, if his enormous business success is really part of a divine master plan that brought him to Israel so that he could help the old-new state achieve economic security.

BESS MYERSON

The First Jewish Miss America

IN 1945 SHE BECAME THE FIRST—and to date the only—Jewish girl to win the Miss America contest. The event transformed her life. It also made the American Jewish community extremely proud of the five-foot ten-inch brunette who explained to the pageant judges that she had entered the contest in order to win the five-thousand-dollar scholarship—to enable her to continue her musical education.

Bess Myerson was born in the Bronx, one of three daughters of a struggling immigrant house painter who felt that music was the key to success in America and provided musical training for each of his daughters. Bess studied the flute as a youngster and later took up the piano too.

As she never tires of telling audiences, life was difficult when she was growing up. She often had to earn extra money as a babysitter and as a camp counselor.

After winning the Miss America contest, Bess did complete her musical studies and then made her formal debut at Carnegie Hall. The critics, however, were lukewarm, and Bess decided that life as a concert pianist was not really what she wanted anyway.

She launched a career as a television personality and soon became a popular star on various quiz programs, appearing at times as a hostess and at other times as a panelist. She also became a commentator for special programs, including a stint as a Miss America hostess. For a while she broadcast the leading spectaculars, including the annual Rose Bowl pageant.

She gradually began to take an interest in politics and in Jewish affairs. When the then mayor of New York, John Lindsay, named her Commissioner of Consumer Affairs, a whole new career opened up for her. For a number of years she directed a vigorous campaign against dishonest business practices which victimized thousands of New Yorkers.

When she left her job for the city, she began to write a popular column for the New York *Daily News*, guiding consumers on a wide range of subjects on how to avoid being taken advantage of by unscrupulous businessmen. She also gave courses in political science at Hunter College. Her popularity was so high that she was urged to become a candidate for the Senate on the Democratic ticket against the incumbent Republican senator, Jacob K. Javits, but she declined. She took an active part in the campaign to elect Edward Koch as mayor of New York, and many people felt that her support helped him win the election.

Her interest in Israel and other Jewish affairs developed gradually, and today she is one of the leading campaigners for the United Jewish Appeal, Israel Bonds, and other similar drives. In one of her early appearances, she was introduced to Golda Meir, later to become Israel's Prime Minister but at the time Foreign Minister. Mrs. Meir's name had been Meyerson before she Hebraized it to Meir. Embracing the former Miss America, Mrs. Meir quipped, "So you're the famous Myerson girl I've been hearing so much about!"

Bess Myerson is today a leading and unique personality on the American scene. She is active in politics, consumerism, and Jewish affairs and has a loyal following of many tens of thousands of people who accept her endorsements and recommendations as coming from an informed, knowledgeable, and reliable public personality. Compared to other beautiful young women who have won the Miss America contest, she has emerged as the best known and the most influential. She has grown and matured, with the full support of the public at large, into a thoughtful, attractive, and persuasive individual who has given people the feeling that a beautiful woman can become an effective public personality.

WALDEMAR HAFFKINE

Conqueror of Cholera

ONE OF THE GREAT MEDICAL MEN OF THIS ERA, Waldemar Haffkine helped save the lives of hundreds of thousands, perhaps even millions, of people, and yet he is all but forgotten. His is the story of a brilliant man with a strong commitment to healing the sick, who at the same time did not veer from his Jewish religious convictions even one iota.

The saga of Dr. Haffkine begins in 1860, in Russia, where he was born. At a very early age it was evident that he was a gifted bacteriologist, and soon he was working closely in Odessa with the Nobel Prize-winner Elie Metchnikoff. The Russian authorities offered him a permanent academic post in Odessa, where he would be able to continue his research, but only if he renounced Judaism and became a convert to the Russian Orthodox Church. He refused and left Russia, settled in Paris, worked for a while as librarian at the Pasteur Institute, and later became assistant to the director.

In 1892, when the dread disease cholera had swept through southeast Asia, as it had engulfed other places in previous centuries, Haffkine developed an effective vaccine against the killer plague. The vaccine had to be tested, and the following year Dr. Haffkine traveled up and down the villages of India, inoculating volunteers against cholera. Less than three years later, when chol-

349

era struck India, all those who had been inoculated by Dr. Haffkine remained immune to the disease—and medical leaders throughout the world hailed him for his achievement.

Requests for the vaccine flooded into his laboratory in Paris, and scientists from China, various European countries, and the Western hemisphere went to the French capital to learn from Haffkine how to produce the vaccine and to inoculate the citizens of their own countries. Queen Victoria, at the time the leader of the vast British Empire, named him a Companion of the Order of the Indian Empire and granted him British citizenship.

In 1902 another epidemic raced through the Punjab region of India, and tens of thousands of Indians were inoculated, of whom nineteen died. Charges were hurled that Haffkine had sent impure vaccine, and he was dismissed from his post in disgrace. It was not until four years later, after a careful investigation by the London *Times* that the charges were found to be without foundation and Dr. Haffkine was exonerated. He spent the following years in India, carrying out additional research, returning later to Paris, where he became active in the early efforts to establish a Jewish state in Palestine.

The Indian government honored him by issuing a postage stamp bearing his photograph, and the Plague Research Laboratory he had established and directed in Bombay for many years was renamed the Haffkine Laboratory.

Throughout his life, even when he was living in remote areas of India, Dr. Haffkine continued to be an observant Jew. A year before he died, he bequeathed his fortune, estimated at half a million dollars, to provide religious, vocational, and scientific education to the scores of thousands of yeshiva students in various parts of eastern Europe.

In an essay he wrote about the Torah he said:

> For any community of people to remain Jewish, they must be brought up from their earliest childhood to regard the Torah as the title deed of their birthright, which they must hand down unaltered from generation to generation. Is there a Jewish community anywhere, however safely ensconced, that has relinquished the Torah for even one generation and has survived that separation?

Those who forsake the Torah, bringing it into disrepute and weakening the hold it has on us, are working at the destruction of the brotherhood that cradled and sheltered their fathers and forefathers through all the vicissitudes of bygone ages, to whom they owe their own life and presence on earth. The Torah is a fountain of life. In it is protection greater than in fortresses.

JAN PEERCE

Lower East Side to the Met

Jacob Pincus Perelmuth, better known as the world-acclaimed operatic tenor Jan Peerce, was born in 1904 in a cold-water apartment on the Lower East Side of New York. His early years were very difficult, and he never forgot them. He has evolved into a compassionate friend of all people in need.

As a young student, the field of medicine appealed to him, but then he discovered that music was even more important to him than the art of healing. He learned to play the violin, and played for many years with a dance orchestra. Occasionally he would sing; gradually it dawned on him that he was blessed with a remarkable voice, and he concentrated on a singing career.

The late great conductor Arturo Toscanini heard him sing at Radio City Music Hall and signed him to a long-term contract as soloist with the new NBC Symphony Orchestra. A few years later Jan Peerce made his debut as an opera singer, and by 1941 he was the leading tenor in the Metropolitan Opera's production of *La Traviata*.

Peerce never shies away from letting his audiences know that he was once an impoverished Jewish boy brought up in the tenements of New York. He has delighted concert and opera audiences throughout the world, and through television has come to be known and admired by millions of people for his sensitive interpretations of classical operatic works.

353

One of the roles that he played with special effectiveness was that of Tevye in the highly successful *Fiddler on the Roof*. Peerce is an observant, committed Jew, who delights in singing cantorial works, Hebrew and Yiddish songs, and the role of the poor but wise milkman in the Shalom Aleichem classic seemed almost custom-made for him.

He has performed in Israel many times, frequently donating his fees to various welfare institutions. When he travels, he often takes along canned fish and other preserved food since he is meticulous about the observance of *kashrut*. He likes to tell the story of the time he was visiting in Moscow, where he was scheduled to sing. He was in his hotel room early in the morning and had put on his *tefillin*, when the Russian maid entered the room, saw him preparing to place a large *tallit* or prayer shawl around his shoulders, and went screaming from the room. She was convinced that something demonic was about to take place.

When his late brother-in-law, Richard Tucker, the noted Metropolitan star, was alive, the two would often harmonize, enjoying especially renditions of nostalgic old Yiddish folk songs. In 1977 the America-Israel Cultural Foundation presented him with its Tarbut–Culture Medal, for his "outstanding, diversified and continuing contribution to the cultural life of all people."

In his autobiography, *The Bluebird of Happiness*, Peerce continued to express his wonder at the fact that a youngster from the slums of New York could rise to become one of the world's best-loved and acclaimed performers.

ABRAHAM ISAAC KOOK

The Compassionate Rabbi

BORN IN LATVIA IN 1865, Abraham Isaac Kook (sometimes spelled Kuk) was recognized as a prodigy at an early age. He immersed himself in the study of Talmud and also delved deeply into Jewish mysticism. Despite a virtual communal ban on secular studies then in force, young Abraham also studied philosophy, science, and history.

In 1904 he arrived in Jaffa, then part of the Ottoman Empire, and served as rabbi to the growing Jewish community there. When World War I broke out, he was in Europe, attempting to persuade religious Jewish leaders to support the still fledgling Zionist movement. He was unable to return home until the war ended, and took a temporary position as rabbi of a London congregation, dedicating much of his time to spreading the Zionist philosophy among British Jews. When he returned to Palestine in 1921, he was named the first Ashkenazi Chief Rabbi and used his position to try to bridge the gap between the religious and irreligious Jews of Palestine.

Rabbi Kook took an extremely tolerant view of even the most irreligious Jews, maintaining that the very act of rebuilding the ancient Jewish homeland was itself a religious act. He fought all his life to inculcate the principle of *ahavat Yisrael*—love of Israel—among all Jews, preaching that the Holy Temple had been destroyed and the Jews exiled because of *sinat hinam*, or groundless hatred among Jews. He established a world-famous yeshiva,

355

known as Merkaz Ha-Rav, in Jerusalem, whose students carry on this same philosophy and which includes in its curriculum secular as well as traditional Jewish religious studies.

Rabbi Kook taught that the return of the Jews to Israel was the beginning of "divine redemption" but that the Zionist movement was incomplete because it concentrated on the material needs of the Jewish people, omitting the spiritual side. Many extremist rabbis were critical of him because of his outspoken support for Zionism, which they opposed because they felt that it was necessary for Jews to wait for the Messiah, who would bring them a new life.

In all his teachings, Rabbi Kook stressed the need for love and harmony. Once a group of religious leaders came to him, asking that he condemn a group of left-wing farming pioneers who continued to work even on the holiest day of the Jewish year, Yom Kippur. He refused to do so, explaining that he viewed these irreligious Jews as identical with those workers who erected the Holy Temple and who were themselves not necessarily observant of religious law and tradition. What they are doing is religious, Rabbi Kook said, and in time this spirit of observance will reach them, too.

What did make him profoundly sad was the realization that the influence of religion, including Judaism, had been on the decline for a number of generations, and he sought all his life to identify the meaning and thrust of religion in modern society. He used to say that the many young Jews who had abandoned traditional Judaism to fight for justice and equality for all mankind were acting in a true biblical spirit which permeated all Jews' lives, even those who had cast off the outer trappings of religious observance.

Rabbi Kook explained that he viewed life as a ladder, with the lower rungs being the need for material possessions and comforts, and the higher rungs—attained only through religious observance and study—reserved for a higher, spiritual fulfillment. He was utterly opposed to people's lifelong pursuit of material goals and pointed out that the Bible had established a Jubilee year, when all efforts to acquire possessions had to be suspended. This should be, he explained, a "year of quiet and peace, without oppressor or master, a year of equality and tranquillity, without any particular private property or any special privilege."

Rabbi Kook also refused to draw a sharp line between what is holy and what is profane. He preached that whatever is important for human beings is basically holy. All scientific advances were part of mankind's intellectual development, he explained, and did not in any way undermine or contradict religion, but rather religion was at fault for not having maintained the same pace of growth.

On the other hand, he was opposed to pure science that ignored the ultimate needs of people. Scientific research, he said, can explain things that exist all around us but cannot show us their significance in relationship to mankind's inner needs. He interpreted the story of Adam and Eve in the Bible as follows: "We must recognize that man, even after he has risen high, can lose everything by wickedness, and may harm himself and generations to come. This is the meaning of the story of Adam in paradise."

Although he believed that the world as a whole was gradually moving to an era when universal brotherhood would reign, he said that the Jews had the right to retain their individual national identity because they had been chosen to "work with the utmost devotion" to advance the divine goal of human perfection and universalism. Jewish nationality, he said, was not based on geography or history or socioeconomic foundations but on divine decree: to make the Jewish people and the Land of Israel a shining example for all peoples.

At his death, Rabbi Kook was mourned by thousands of Jerusalemites, religious and irreligious alike, for his rare blend of compassion and understanding with commitment to Zionism.

HERBERT H. LEHMAN

Conscience of the Senate

HE WAS BORN WITH THE PROVERBIAL SILVER SPOON IN HIS MOUTH but from an early age displayed a sincere, deep interest in the welfare of people less fortunate than himself. When he died, he was mourned by all Americans, for he had brought to his role as a public servant a rare combination of compassion and toughness.

Herbert Lehman was born in New York in 1878, the son of a wealthy German Jewish immigrant who had established a major investment house and who had been one of the founders of the Cotton Exchange in New York. After graduating from college, young Lehman would travel from his family's comfortable home in the upper part of New York to the Lower East Side to work as a volunteer with the Henry Street Settlement, where he personally ministered to the needs of the poor and the ill. He never said it in words, but it was clear to all those who worked alongside him that he enjoyed performing these acts of kindness.

At a later date he was persuaded to enter the family's banking and textile businesses, but after serving on a commission to revise the existing banking laws, he realized that he could be more effective in aiding the needy through politics than through banking, and in 1928 he was elected lieutenant governor of New York, serving alongside the governor, Franklin D. Roosevelt. When Roosevelt became President in 1932, Lehman became governor

and was re-elected four times. His record as a devoted executive profoundly interested in the welfare of all the people made him one of the most popular governors in the country. Other states began to copy the models of labor reform, protection of the aged and the young, and the laws against religious and social discrimination that he instituted and carried out.

President Roosevelt, even before the Second World War ended in 1945, designated him to lead a special worldwide relief and rehabilitation organization that was established to ameliorate the suffering of millions of people in war-ravaged countries. The agency eventually became the UNRRA, attached to the United Nations, and Lehman ran it with exemplary success and outstanding results.

In the period immediately after the end of the war, Lehman devoted considerable time and effort to aiding the United Jewish Appeal amass the many millions of dollars needed to aid the Jews who had survived the Holocaust and to help in the plans for creating a Jewish homeland. He had been one of the leaders of the Joint Distribution Committee for many years, which was set up after the end of the First World War to aid the uprooted and impoverished Jewish communities.

In 1949 Lehman was elected to the United States Senate, where he soon became known as the "conscience of the Senate." He led in strong support for the State of Israel, and was a leader of the small progressive body of liberal senators who battled against the era of McCarthyism that had overtaken the country. He remained an influential leader in the Democratic party after he left the Senate, and died in 1963, assured that he had made the world a little better than when he had first entered it.

TZIVIA LUBETKIN

Mother of the Warsaw Ghetto

ONE OF THE MOST INCREDIBLE BATTLES OF ALL TIME, described by some as the bravest battle in history, was the uprising of the entrapped Jews in the Warsaw ghetto against their Nazi captors. It was a battle that the Jews knew they could never hope to win but one they felt they had to wage nevertheless—to avenge the murder of hundreds of thousands of fellow Jews, to go to their deaths in honor and dignity, and to alert the world to the true character of the Nazi menace.

Outside the walls of the ghetto there were large divisions of German and co-operating Ukrainian troops, equipped with tanks, artillery, grenades, and an unlimited supply of smaller weapons and ammunition. The Germans could, if they wished, call in the Nazi air force to bomb the Jews into submission. Inside the walls, the Jews who had survived the years of imprisonment despite the spread of disease, inadequate supplies of food and medicines, and the lack of virtually any support from the outside world had managed to obtain a pitifully limited quantity of small arms. They had also learned how to fashion home-made bombs, known as Molotov cocktails. Above all, they were determined to resist the never-ending deportation by the Nazis of thousands of Jews almost every day to the death camps awaiting them in remote parts of Poland.

The leader of the fighting force in the ghetto was Mordecai Anilewicz, who perished in the fighting. One of the few women leaders in the revolt was Tzivia Lubetkin, who miraculously survived. She lived for many years in Israel, in the settlement set up by survivors of the wartime ghettos, a living symbol of courage for all people.

When the revolt in the Warsaw ghetto broke out in 1943, Tzivia Lubetkin was barely thirty years old, but she already had become something of a legend to the tens of thousands of ghetto inmates. She could have escaped to Palestine when the war began but chose instead to send as many of her fellow Jews to safety as she could, and remained behind to help, to lead, to keep up the spirits of the Jewish community in Poland suddenly imprisoned by the Nazi armed might. For her daily acts of kindness in the ghetto, she came to be known and loved as the "Mother of the Ghetto."

She had been an active member of the Zionist organization in her youth and in the summer months before the outbreak of World War II had been sent by her group in Poland to attend the World Zionist Congress in Basel, Switzerland. In the early months of 1943, when she and her husband, Yitzhak Zukierman, were confined to the Warsaw ghetto, they realized that the diabolical plan of the Nazis to deliberately annihilate all Jews was no empty threat. They learned that hundreds of thousands of their coreligionists had already been executed in the death camps, and joined the other leaders in the ghetto in deciding to stage a revolt. Some of them hoped that somehow a measure of help would come their way— from the Polish partisans, from the Russians in the east, or from the Anglo-American forces in the west.

During the Jerusalem trial of Adolf Eichmann, the notorious Nazi murderer who was kidnapped from his hiding place in Argentina and brought to Israel to face charges of mass murder, Tzivia Lubetkin was one of the principal witnesses. She said in her testimony:

> I was standing in an attic on 33 Nalewski Street, when suddenly I saw thousands of Germans armed with machine guns surrounding the Ghetto. Suddenly they entered, thousands, armed, and we, some twenty young men and women, had a revolver, a few grenades, some bombs, home-made ones, that had to be lit by matches. It must have been strange to see us. Twenty Jewish men and women happily standing against the heavily armed enemy, happy because we knew they would

pay heavily for our lives. . . . When the Germans approached, and we threw our hand grenades and bombs, it was a joy for the Jewish fighters to behold the wonder of these German heroes, retreating, terrified by the home-made bombs and grenades of the Jews. . . . Although we knew we would be killed, we were satisfied to know that we had taken revenge for the death of our brothers.

When the Germans crushed all Jewish resistance on May 8, 1943, a small number of the fighters made their way to safety through the sewers of the ghetto. Tzivia told the Jerusalem tribunal:

We descended into the sewer with heavy hearts. It was an abyss of darkness. I felt the water splash around me as I jumped in; I was overcome by a dreadful nausea. I felt nothing, not even freedom, was worth this. Sixty people crawled through the narrow sewer, bent almost in half, the filthy water reaching up to their knees. Each of us held a candle. We half-walked, half-crawled like this for twenty hours, one behind the other, without stopping, without food or water, in that horrible cavern. All of us were poisoned by the thought: how shall we explain? why did we not remain behind? why are we alive at all? More than once, one of us would fall and beg to be left lying there, but no one in all that journey was abandoned.

When the nightmare was over, the Warsaw ghetto survivors escaped to the deep Polish forests, and Tzivia Lubetkin joined the local partisan fighters, serving until the war ended in 1945. She helped organize Jewish units among the partisans who carried out numerous actions against the Nazi enemy.

She and her husband settled in Palestine after the end of the war and took part in the War of Independence in 1948 that accompanied the establishment of Israel. For thirty years Tzivia Lubetkin was active as a leader in the kibbutz movement in Israel, the memories of the Warsaw ghetto never far from her daily thoughts. She died in 1978, a heroine of her people.

DAVID DE LEON

The Fighting Doctor

HE WAS BORN IN SOUTH CAROLINA less than half a century after the establishment of the United States. Practically all the men in the family had been physicians, and David de Leon chose to follow the same path. His ancestors had been Jews, and when the Inquisition came to power in Spain, many of them became Marranos —secret Jews, people who pretended in public to be Catholics but continued to follow the basic practices and customs of Judaism in private.

When the family arrived in the United States, one of the first things they did was abandon the secrecy and proclaim themselves to be Jews openly and proudly. One of the strong motivating forces that led them to abandon their homes in Spain was the promise of freedom that was offered in America.

The de Leon family settled in Charleston, and David's father became a successful importer. When David was old enough to decide on a career for himself, he chose medicine, sensing that the new country would need a doctor more than another businessman. Epidemics were common in those days, and many Americans often needed medical care since there were frequent battles with local Indian tribes.

David de Leon went to Philadelphia, attended medical school, and returned to Charleston a doctor at the age of twenty-three.

367

Medical training in those days was far from what it is today; David knew that he would obtain his most important education in the day-to-day practice of the art of healing. Because his youthful appearance did not fit what people thought a doctor should look like, he grew a beard and moustache. He began to build up a practice and soon enough became a respected and successful physician. He was happy in his chosen calling and grateful that he and his fellow Jews could live as Jews without fear or threat. He developed an intense love for the new American nation and was determined to help it prosper.

At the time, the American settlers were gradually expanding the frontiers of the new country westward. Attacks against the pioneering settlers by Indians, particularly the Seminoles, had increased, and when the United States issued an appeal for doctors to join its army's medical corps, Dr. de Leon enlisted.

He was appointed an assistant surgeon in the army and very soon established himself as a competent, compassionate physician, not only with the American soldiers but with the Indians too, for he never hesitated to tend the wounds of the Indians hurt in battle.

One night in front of a group of tents on the battlefield that served a unit as a mobile hospital, while the young doctor was taking a short walk before returning to his duties, an Indian stole up behind him, his tomahawk raised, ready to deal Dr. de Leon a death blow, when a soldier shot the attacker from close range. The Indian was near death, but Dr. de Leon performed emergency surgery on him and pulled him through. After his recovery, the Indian approached the doctor and swore that he would serve him the rest of his life. He was named the doctor's orderly and served him faithfully.

Some time later, the Indian turned orderly overheard a group of Seminoles plotting to kidnap the doctor and warned him in time. The would-be kidnappers were seized, and Dr. de Leon was saved.

Dr. de Leon began to think of returning home to South Carolina, but again the United States appealed for physicians to serve the army that now had to turn its attention southward to Mexico, from which bands of invaders had begun to harass and massacre isolated American colonies. During a crucial battle in 1846 at Chapultepec the commander of the Americans was killed in battle.

The American troops were disheartened and, without a leader, were unsure as to what to do. Dr. de Leon temporarily put aside his medical role and appealed to the soldiers to defeat the Mexican bandits and adventurers who had killed men and women in the United States cruelly and wantonly. The men responded that they would continue the attack if he, Dr. de Leon, would lead them, and without a moment's hesitation he did. On two different occasions he led cavalry charges against the Mexicans, with the Americans emerging victorious both times. His heroism was cited in Congress, and there were some who said that he had helped win the war in Mexico. He became known as "the fighting doctor."

When the Civil War broke out between the North and South, Dr. de Leon, as a Southerner, fought on the side of the Confederacy even though he was personally strongly opposed to the idea of the South seceding from the Union. He organized the medical department of the Confederate army and was later named its first surgeon-general.

AHARON SHEAR-YASHUV

From Convert to Rabbi

Most Jews are born into the Jewish community. But some become Jews, abandoning their original religious persuasion, out of the conviction that Judaism offers them a more rewarding, meaningful way of life.

Traditionally, Judaism has been opposed to seeking converts, but when a person from another faith has shown a genuine desire to be part of the Jewish community and has conformed to the rules governing such a conversion, he has been accepted wholly and fully as a Jew with equal rights and obligations with all other Jews. One of the most famous converts, of course, is the biblical Ruth, great-grandmother of King David. Scattered through the United States, Israel, and other countries today are several thousands of recent converts, who have chosen to become part and parcel of the Jewish people.

One of the most unusual and remarkable such converts is a rabbi now living in Haifa, Israel. His new name is Aharon Shear-Yashuv, and to look at him one would never guess that he was once a German Christian. The *yarmulke* never leaves his head, a full beard girdles his face, and as the rabbi-in-residence of an Israeli university he is kept busy advising students, teaching, leading services, and supervising and conducting marriages, circumcisions, bar mitzvah ceremonies, and other events.

The story begins in Germany soon after the end of World War II, when he was a small child. All around him there was gloom and depression as the German people sought to reconstruct their lives after the black years of the Nazi era and their defeat by the Allies in one of the cruelest wars in history. The young man's father was believed to have been sympathetic to the Nazi movement, but at that time there was no talk of this.

He grew up in a small town, was a good student, and decided to become a lawyer. Once in the university, however, he found himself drawn to studies of philosophy and religion, and soon he began to take as many courses as he could in theology. He took a special interest in Judaism, and one of his professors recommended that he continue his studies at the Hebrew Union College in Cincinnati, a rabbinical seminary for Reform rabbis which offered nonrabbinical students an opportunity to study Judaism on a graduate level.

At the Cincinnati campus, the young German student involved himself deeply in his studies. He learned Hebrew, Talmud, Jewish mysticism, and history, and gradually it dawned on him that he was moving toward conversion to Judaism. He met frequently with his academic advisors and with various scholars, and finally decided that, as much as he liked the Cincinnati institution, he had a feeling that he was learning a watered-down version of Judaism since it was Reform-oriented. He made up his mind that the only place for him to learn the authentic forms of Judaism was in Jerusalem, and in an Orthodox school.

He proceeded to Jerusalem and was enrolled in a yeshiva of higher learning. He had by this time mastered Hebrew and Aramaic well enough to be able to study Talmud in the original. He was a model student, often surpassing many of the Jewish students in his zeal and comprehension. The aura of Jerusalem, and of Israel itself, had a great influence over him. From time to time he would visit the Yad Vashem, an imposing memorial for the Jews who perished in the Holocaust.

Finally he announced that he planned to become a Jew, and after he was examined, challenged, and interviewed, he was accepted and underwent all the rituals of formal conversion. His mother and sister in Germany accepted his decision, but his father broke off all contact with him. After years of intensive study and training, he was ordained a rabbi in Jerusalem, and later was appointed as rabbi of the Technion–Israel Institute of Technology in Haifa, which has a student body of about nine thousand.

Rabbi Aharon Shear-Yashuv married a *sabra* (native-born Israeli) girl and they have three children. Students and visitors to the Technion campus who attend services at the institute's synagogue enjoy his sermons, as well as the classes he teaches to students and faculty members. They come to him for counseling as they would to any rabbi.

Occasionally Rabbi Shear-Yashuv visits his family in Germany, and he especially likes staying at his sister's home because it is within walking distance of a small traditional synagogue. One of the tasks he feels most keenly about is introducing recently arrived Soviet Jewish students to the fundamentals of Judaism. With barely a smile, he explains, "They were cut off from our heritage for more than half a century, and it is a *mitzvah* of the highest priority to reintroduce them to the fountains of our tradition."

HENRIETTA SZOLD

Savior of the Children

A SMALL, WHITE-HAIRED WOMAN of eighty-five died in Jerusalem a few years before the establishment of Israel, and a whole generation of Jews mourned for her. She had devoted her life to the welfare of her people, saving thousands, encouraging tens of thousands, and inspiring hundreds of thousands. Her name was Henrietta Szold.

The daughter of a rabbi and scholar, she was born in Baltimore in 1860, and although few girls in those days received more than a nominal Jewish education, Henrietta was an exception—her father taught her Hebrew, Bible, Talmud, Jewish history, and the great texts of Jewish literature. She became a teacher in a Baltimore girls' school and also taught religious classes in the synagogue school.

In the 1880s, following an outbreak of pogroms in czarist Russia, Jewish refugees began to stream into Baltimore, and she decided she wanted to help them personally. She conceived the idea of a night school where adults could study English and the rudiments of American life, and before long her idea became a reality and she became one of the teachers of the newcomers. The plight of the refugees, the problems they encountered of adjusting to a totally new life, and the knowledge that there remained in far-off Europe many hundreds of thousands of other Jews still living miserable lives under the domination of despotic governments made her decide that she would devote herself to helping her fellow Jews.

One area she felt was vital was the lack of English-language translations of the great Jewish classics, and so she set about translating a number of works, including the multivolume *Legends of the Jews* by Louis Ginsberg. To further this end, she went to work for the Jewish Publication Society in Philadelphia, seeking to open up the great Jewish literary treasures to a largely English-speaking Jewish community in America.

Soon after the turn of the century, at the age of forty-three, she moved to New York and enrolled as a student at the Jewish Theological Seminary, the only woman in an all-male rabbinical seminary. She explained that she was driven by a desire to learn and to share that learning with all who were interested. A few years later, having adopted the Zionist program launched by Theodor Herzl in Europe, she set sail for Palestine to see for herself that strip of land that she knew only from reading. When she returned to New York, a woman already in her fifties, she was determined that something had to be done to provide medical help for the Jews and the Arabs in Palestine: She had seen the ravages of malaria and trachoma and the absence of elementary hygiene standards, and she sensed that this was the challenge that had been awaiting her all her life.

On Purim, the festival that celebrates the victory of Queen Esther over the wicked Haman, who planned to murder all the Jews in the ancient Persian Empire, Henrietta Szold told a group of women in a Jewish study circle, "If we are Zionists, as we say we are, what is the good of meeting and talking and drinking tea? Let us do something real and practical—let us organize the Jewish women of America and send nurses and doctors to Palestine." The suggestion caught fire, and then and there a new organization was born, Hadassah, which is the Hebrew name for Queen Esther.

Henrietta Szold became the first president of the group, and the first step planned was to send two nurses to Jerusalem to heal the sick and to teach the fundamental laws of health. Six years later, when World War I was ended, a whole medical unit organized by Hadassah set sail for Palestine, consisting of forty-four people, including physicians, nurses, and public health specialists, and equipment for a fifty-bed hospital. Since that time, Hadassah has grown into an organization of 350,000 women who have provided vast amounts of medical care for hundreds of thousands of Jewish and non-Jewish patients alike, first in Palestine and now in Israel. The Hadassah Medical Center in Jerusalem is considered one of the greatest lifesaving institutions in the world.

Like many other people, Miss Szold, who settled in Palestine in the 1920s, had believed that the year 1918 marked the end of all wars, but of course the rise of Nazism changed her thinking. Early in the 1930s, soon after the persecution of the Jews in Germany began, she and others set up a massive rescue program for young people whose parents were unable to leave Germany. The program, called Youth Aliyah, eventually brought tens of thousands of German (and later Austrian) Jewish youths to Palestine.

Whenever a ship bringing a new contingent of these Youth Aliyah immigrants arrived at Haifa, Henrietta Szold was on the dock, waiting to greet them and help them in their first difficult months of adjustment to a new life—just as she had done so many years ago as a young woman in her native Baltimore. She wrote once that as the years of World War II progressed, the children reaching Palestine as Youth Aliyah wards seemed to change: "They seemed to become more sick, more bitter, without hope for the future. . . . It took months of patient effort for our social workers and nurses and doctors to restore their self-confidence, and to give them back their hope in the future."

Although in her earlier years she had translated more than ten books from German and Hebrew and had been an active collaborator in the publication of the *Jewish Encyclopedia*, which appeared in 1905, she was now no longer interested in anything except the saving of lives.

She also saw in Hadassah's major medical and health programs in Palestine an opportunity to build a bridge between the Jews and the Arabs. In a letter to her sister, Bertha, prior to the establishment of Israel in 1948, she wrote:

> You know the Arabs are using violence and terror to stop us. They even killed two Hadassah nurses on their way to take care of Arab patients. . . . I warned our young people to use self-control whenever there is a clash between Jews and

Arabs. . . . We hope for friendship with our Arab neighbors, we want to develop the country for the good of both the Jews and the Arabs. . . . We do not know what the future will bring but we pray and work for healing and peace.

Tens of thousands of young Israelis are still receiving help from the Youth Aliyah organization, only now they are not being rescued from Nazi Germany but are being taken from environments which have turned them into criminals and delinquents and are being given a chance to rehabilitate themselves. Tens of thousands of middle-aged Israelis who reached the shores of Palestine in the years before the outbreak of World War II in 1939 look upon Miss Szold as a true guardian angel.

And in America, in the same spirit of resolve and dedication, vast numbers of Hadassah members and their families press forward in the work of healing and rescue that Henrietta Szold first conceived when she saw the victims of czarist tyranny arrive in Baltimore in the latter part of the nineteenth century.

Is it any wonder that Henrietta Szold, who herself never married, has nevertheless been called a veritable matriarch of Israel in our own time?

SAMUEL GOMPERS

Father of Labor Unions

NOWADAYS NEARLY ALL WORKERS are members of labor unions that afford them protection against unjust exploitation. Men and women who work for a living in factories, offices, and schools, on ships and on farms are united in the organized labor movement that has helped raise the living standards and working conditions of American workers and has set a standard for workers in many other parts of the world. But labor unions as we know them and working conditions now prevalent practically throughout the United States did not always exist. They are the direct result of the lifetime efforts of one determined man, a Jewish idealist who knew from bitter personal experience that a life full of harsh working conditions was all too often a cruel, frustrating journey from the cradle to the grave, and he was determined to rectify the situation.

Samuel Gompers was born in London's East End, a neighborhood similar to the impoverished Lower East Side of New York. His parents, he, and five brothers and sisters lived in one room in a tenement, depending for a living on his father's meager earnings as a cigar maker. During the day the room was a workplace, and at night a curtain was hung up and the Gompers parents entered their "bedroom." One large bed was shared by three or four brothers.

Samuel entered the Jewish Free School in London at the age of six, where he studied Hebrew and Talmud as well as reading, writing, and arithmetic. When he was ten, conditions at home were so difficult that Samuel left school and became an apprentice shoemaker, his slim earnings helping to feed the family. Later he joined his father at the trade of cigar making, and although his workday was never less than twelve hours, six days a week, he managed to continue his education by attending a makeshift night school. In 1863, after a journey that took nearly two months, the family arrived in the United States, hopeful that their life would be easier in the new country.

Both Samuel and his father found jobs making cigars, and conditions for the Gompers family improved somewhat, but Samuel felt that the workers were nevertheless being exploited. At the age of fourteen he began to talk to his fellow workers about organizing a union, with its first goal being to reduce the number of hours the workers had to work each day. A year later there was a cigar makers' union, and Samuel was named its first president even though he was barely sixteen years old.

One of the workers in the factory where Samuel worked had poor eyesight, and the foreman deliberately had him work in a dark area, away from the window and the light. Samuel protested, the foreman mocked him, and within minutes the young man led his fellow workers out of the factory, announcing that they would return to work when the worker with the poor vision was given his old place again. The foreman relented, the workers returned, and suddenly Samuel and his colleagues realized that they had a powerful weapon at their disposal to help them right the many wrongs they saw all around them—the strike, a labor weapon that has been used many times in the past century.

Working conditions did not improve overnight. The eight-hour working day was achieved only after many years of struggle. Gradually workers in other industries began to organize, and eventually they formed an umbrella organization of all labor unions and called it the American Federation of Labor. Gompers became its first president and was re-elected as its head every year until his death in 1924.

Whenever there was a strike by any of the labor unions, Samuel Gompers was there to encourage the workers and to negotiate a settlement. When police clubbed the strikers and arrested them, Gompers suffered the same fate. It took him many years to teach the American public, and the workers themselves, that they had the right to work under humane conditions, to earn a decent wage, and to spend their day working in clean, safe surroundings—things that are taken for granted today but that had to be fought for over a long period of years.

There are many monuments honoring the memory of Samuel Gompers, but perhaps the greatest of them all is the fact that American working people are now able to spend their working days in pleasant surroundings, earning a fair compensation for their labors, and able to look forward to a period of retirement, with a degree of financial security, when they are older—achievements that an idealistic young immigrant from England devoted his life to realizing.

DAVID ''MICKEY'' MARCUS

West Point to Jerusalem

HE WAS BORN IN 1902 on the Lower East Side of New York, was appointed to West Point when he was eighteen, and graduated from the famous military academy in 1924. He became a lawyer, worked for a time in the United States Attorney General's office, and later became Commissioner of Correction in New York City.

When World War II broke out, he returned to the U.S. army, serving as a judge advocate with the rank of lieutenant colonel, and later trained the crack Rangers for combat in the Pacific and also was among the planners in the Pentagon. When the American forces prepared to invade Nazi-occupied Europe in 1944, he insisted on parachuting in with the advance forces, and did so, landing on the beach in Normandy. After the war he was a key officer in the military government and soon afterward was named head of the army's War Crimes Branch. In 1947 the athletic David Marcus resigned from the army with the rank of colonel, the holder of numerous American and British decorations, determined to return to private law practice.

He had seen the Nazi concentration camps and had met with the survivors, and although he had not been formally involved with any Jewish organizations, he felt a strong sense of identification with the remnants of European Jewry, and a deep anger at their persecution. He was first and foremost a man who was com-

mitted to justice, and anguished over the injustice that his fellow Jews had suffered.

In 1947, more than a year before the Jewish community in Palestine proclaimed its independence and established the State of Israel, the leaders of the nascent Jewish state realized that the day of the British Mandate over Palestine was drawing to an end and that the future nation would require a modern, organized army, in contrast to the brave but improvised defense force that it then possessed. They looked about for a senior military officer, preferably a Jew, who would teach them practically overnight how to transform their fighting force into a suitable armed organization, and soon enough they approached Colonel David Marcus and asked him to carry out what they said would be a historic task for the Jewish state. He was reluctant at first, having lived for years as a fighting officer and not willing to leave his wife, of whom he had seen very little over the years. However, he was even more reluctant to say no.

Assuming the false name of Mickey Stone, he went to Palestine, examined the existing structure of the Jews' military forces, and quickly realized that, although man for man the young Israelis were among the best fighters and the most committed soldiers he had ever seen, there was a serious lack of overall planning, management, and basic military structure.

He set about adapting the U.S. army's military manuals to the special needs of the Israelis, and was gratified to see how swiftly and efficiently his recommendations were transformed into a new code of military planning. The Israelis welcomed Marcus's contributions, for they felt that they had learned from him in a matter of months what might have taken years to learn from other sources. As a token of their esteem, soon after the State of Israel was proclaimed in May 1948, they designated Marcus the first *aluf* or brigadier general in modern times. It was as an *aluf* that he was soon thereafter appointed commander of the Jerusalem front, one of the most crucial areas in the fighting that erupted between the Jews and Arabs in May and June of 1948.

On June 11 a tragic event took place that cost Marcus his life. Unable to sleep because of the heat, he emerged from his tent, a sheet lightly wrapped around him, and wandered away from the camp, deep in thought. He knew almost no Hebrew, and when a sentry challenged him in the half-light before dawn and Marcus did not respond as expected, he was shot and killed. The broken-hearted young Israeli soldier later told a military court of inquiry that he thought the figure in the sheet was an Arab wearing a traditional Arab coverall.

Marcus was buried with full military honors at West Point, and the anniversary of his death is observed every year at his gravesite. An Israeli settlement, Mishmar David, is named for him. The modern, sophisticated army of Israel regards David Marcus as its spiritual father.

RECHA FREIER

The Stubborn Heroine

IN THE YEAR 1932, with the whole world in a state of economic depression and the Jews in Germany becoming more and more concerned about the growing Nazi movement, there was a rabbi's wife in Berlin, one Recha Freier, who sensed that a very bad time was just over the horizon for Germany's six hundred thousand Jews.

At the time there were many Jews, inside and outside Germany, who chose to ignore the expansion of Nazism and dismissed Hitler and his followers as a group of crackpots who would soon disappear. Many other Jews in Germany expressed confidence in the high cultural standards of Germany, reassuring one another that their country, world-renowned for its attainments in music, literature, and science, would soon overcome its economic and political problems and re-emerge as a free and prosperous society.

Recha Freier thought otherwise. She was a writer with an ability to project into the future. What she saw frightened her. Softly at first, and then with greater conviction, she expressed her fears to her Jewish friends, Zionists and non-Zionists alike, and almost everyone scoffed at her.

The gnawing feeling of a disaster soon to overtake Germany's Jewish community persisted with Recha Freier. And then one day, a year before the Nazis seized power in Germany, she conceived

387

of an idea: German Jewish boys and girls, preferably those in their teens, should be helped to proceed to Palestine. She argued that the young people would help build the agricultural settlements and become part of the growing Jewish community in the old-new homeland. They would be out of harm's way, she insisted, if something terrible were to happen to Jews in Germany.

Her first steps to implement her idea were dismal failures. The director of the Jewish Labor Exchange, himself an ardent Zionist, derided her fears when she came to him, soliciting support. The troubles in Germany, he explained, were only a reflection of the worldwide economic situation and would soon pass.

Undaunted, she turned to the women's organization WIZO (Women's International Zionist Organization) and tried to persuade its leaders to back her plan to spirit German Jewish youths out of Germany to Palestine, and once again she was met with scorn. Some of the women in the group actually laughed at her when they realized she was proposing a virtual Children's Crusade to Palestine.

But Recha Freier was a determined woman. Each day's fresh headlines convinced her that the majority of the world's Jewish leaders, including those in Germany itself, were engaging in self-delusion and that the Nazis were a real threat to world Jewry.

She approached a number of German-language Jewish periodicals, asking them to publish an article that she had written outlining the reasons for her program—and again she was rebuffed.

At first only one small Jewish organization agreed to cooperate. This was a Jewish agricultural society known as Ezra ("Help"). But then Mrs. Freier began to visit Jewish religious schools where there was a strong Zionist orientation. She propagandized her plan among the students themselves and was met with great enthusiasm. The children's support was what she had needed to keep her going, and she was galvanized into a spurt of new activity.

Gradually the Vaad Leumi in Palestine—the Jewish National Council, forerunner of what was to become the future Israel government—and the World Zionist Organization both agreed that there was merit to her plan. She was advised to contact Henrietta Szold, founder of Hadassah in the United States, and then living in Jerusalem, who was in charge of immigration for the Council.

But even that great lady was initially opposed to the idea. Living in Jerusalem, all she knew about the events in Germany was what she had read in the newspapers, which she was sure was vastly exaggerated. Besides, she felt strongly that there were insufficient facilities in Palestine to offer proper care for the youngsters, and that bringing the children to Palestine under those conditions would be counterproductive.

There were others, however, who saw the merit of the plan for Youth Aliyah, as the rescue organization was now called, and in October 1932 the first group of twelve boys left Germany for Palestine and a new lease on life. Although they did not know it at the time, they were the vanguard of a movement that brought several thousands from Germany to Palestine, until the outbreak of World War II, when conditions precluded any additional emigration.

It was really only after the Nazis had come to power in 1933 and had begun their systematic attacks on Jews that Mrs. Freier's program for rescue received support, grudgingly at first and then with increasing enthusiasm. One of the great backers of the program in the United States was the popular entertainer Eddie Cantor, who helped raise large sums of money for its implementation.

Henrietta Szold had to be convinced of the seriousness of the situation before she threw the full weight of her office and leadership into the battle, and this did not happen until she personally visited Berlin in 1933 and saw with her own eyes the shocking and incredible things taking place that she had first assumed were propaganda lies.

With her customary boldness, Miss Szold joined Recha Freier in accelerating and expanding the Youth Aliyah organization, enabling thousands of Jewish teen-agers to be plucked from what within a few years would become the inferno of Europe.

Mrs. Freier herself eventually reached haven in Palestine. For the remainder of her life she had a dichotomous reaction that would not leave her: On the one hand, she *had* succeeded in effecting the rescue of thousands of Jewish children, but on the other hand, could she have been more forceful, more persuasive, more dramatic, so that many thousands more could also have been spared the fate that was to befall one million Jewish children in Nazi Europe?

RASHI

Interpreter of the Bible

HIS REAL NAME WAS RABBI SOLOMON BEN ISAAC but everyone
knows him to this day as Rashi, which represents the first letters of
his Hebrew name. He was born and lived in the small French town
of Troyes, where he earned his living as a grape-grower and
devoted his entire life to producing a commentary on the Bible and
Talmud that has enabled hundreds of thousands of students during
the past thousand years to understand better the basic works of the
Jewish religion.

Rashi lived from 1040 to 1105, and during that time he wrote
by hand commentaries on every sentence in the Torah—commentaries that acted like a magic key, for his explanations unlocked
meanings and ideas that clarified and illuminated passage after passage. To this day, students of the Bible are accustomed to reading a
sentence or two and then looking at the accompanying commentary of Rashi to see what he says the passage really means and how
better to understand the full significance of the text.

At the time he worked on the commentary, printing had not
yet been invented. After a day's labor in the vineyards, Rashi
would return home, take down his copy of the Bible, and proceed
to read and explain, composing his sentences on paper with a quill
pen dipped in ink, which had to be dried with grains of sand.
Young students from Jewish communities in nearby countries

were always staying with him, listening to his comments, making their own notes on what he said, and returning to their own communities to share their new understanding of the Bible with fellow Jews.

Rashi did not think that working with his hands in the vineyards was anything to be ashamed of, and whenever a fellow rabbi or student would urge him to give up his work on the soil, he would scoff and remind them that in ancient times there were among the greatest of Jewish teachers men who earned a living as a woodcutter and shoemaker. He would comment to his non-Jewish fellow grape-growers that to "work is truly a blessing and certainly not a disgrace."

Rashi and his wife had three daughters, and although it was not customary in those days especially for girls to receive an education, he taught his daughters as though they were sons, and they often helped him in his lifelong study of the Torah. As they grew and began to read the Torah, they began to ask questions of certain phrases and comments, and these were the questions that Rashi felt most Jews would also ask during their study of the Torah, so that his commentary was in a very real sense a series of answers to his own daughters' queries. All three of his daughters married students who had come to study with Rashi, and two of his grandsons—Rabbi Shmuel ben Meir, known as the Rashbam, and Rabbi Jacob ben Meir, known as Rabbenu Tam—also became well-known and greatly beloved commentators on the Bible.

After the invention of printing, the first Hebrew book that was printed appeared in Italy in the year 1475. It consisted of the Bible with the commentary of Rashi. Visitors to Jewish day schools to this day can see young students poring over a text of the Bible alongside of which there appears, in small type and in a special script known as Rashi script, the famous commentary by the great master who lived nearly one thousand years ago.

Thousands of French words were used by Rashi to explain sections of the Bible, and scholars today refer to his commentary since it is a useful source of old French terms. His commentary was translated into Latin and helped make the Bible more understandable to Christian scholars over a period of many centuries.

Most of Rashi's explanations were intended to clarify the reader's understanding of the Bible's text, but there were a few

393

passages that even Rashi felt he could not understand, and so he merely wrote that these sections he could not explain.

The great commentator and scholar found time to establish a school of Jewish learning. Visitors to Troyes today are told by the townspeople that this community prides itself on being the birthplace of the great Rashi.

To understand how Rashi explained the text of the Bible, one can take as an example the phrase "And thou shalt love" that appears in the sentence "And thou shalt love the Lord thy God with all thy heart."

Rashi commented: "And thou shalt love" means that people should perform the commandments of God from a sense of love rather than from fear. When someone serves his master out of fear and the master becomes too oppressive, the servant will run away from him.

In the same vein, the Bible refers to "And these words that I command you this day." Rashi commented: These words should be seen not like an old law that has become obsolete and that people no longer obey but rather like a fresh, new law that everyone is anxious to follow.

In addition to his commentaries, Rashi was a scholar of Hebrew grammar and language, and his contributions to a scientific understanding of the biblical language are still considered to be of great value.

Toward the end of his life he was saddened to see the beginning of the Crusades, which swept through Europe en route to the Holy Land, leaving thousands dead in their wake. A legend says that he died at his desk, while writing the word *tam*, or "pure," in a new commentary.

DANIEL PERSKY

Love Affair with Hebrew

THE REVIVAL OF HEBREW and its modernization is truly one of the miracles of the Jewish people of the twentieth century. The name of Eliezer Ben-Yehudah, who struggled and fought against nearly incredible odds to re-establish the ancient language as the national tongue of reborn Israel, has become a household word there.

He was not, however, the only early Zionist dedicated to the Hebrew language. There were many such linguistic pioneers who realized that the return of the Jews to their ancient homeland from all parts of the world would be enhanced if they would readopt the ancient language, make it theirs, and use it to unify the many strands of Jewish life. Thus, a newly arrived Soviet Jew and a Yemenite Jew and an immigrant from Argentina can, and do, communicate together in their common tongue, Hebrew.

One of the most colorful and memorable people involved in the Hebrew language's rebirth was a man called Daniel Persky. A bachelor, a wit and humorist, a columnist for a Hebrew weekly for more than three decades, a teacher to more than two thousand students, he was a remarkable individual who was never forgotten by a single person who met him.

395

He lived alone in a shabby room just a few blocks from the Lower East Side of New York City when that area was a thriving Hebrew-Zionist-Yiddish-Jewish cultural center. His room was something to behold: Stacks of newspapers, in various languages, carefully piled atop each other, reached to the ceiling. Several times a year, just before the stacks actually touched the ceiling, Persky would bundle them, drag them to the post office, and ship them to the embryonic Hebrew national library in Jerusalem to be used as a source of basic information for scholars of the future.

And then, in the course of time, the newspaper stacks would begin to rise again.

He wrote a widely read column of satirical comments, dealing with events of the day. For this purpose he had a special orange pen, and he knew he had to fill exactly fourteen pages of precise Hebrew and deliver his copy on time. Over a period of years he also wrote a number of books dealing with the lighter side of the Jewish holidays.

The best time of the day for him was the evening, when he would stride down the old Yiddish newspaper block on East Broadway, where the presses of *The Day* and *The Forward* were busily spewing out thousands of copies of newspapers chronicling the early stages of the Zionist movement, and later somberly reporting the growing menace of Nazism abroad. He would enter a modest building on the corner which housed the Herzliah Hebrew High School and Teachers' Seminary.

He was a master teacher of Hebrew language, grammar, syntax, and style. He imbued all his students with an abiding love for the old-new language, and encouraged them to use it in their daily lives. He was an acknowledged philologist and welcomed all student efforts to test his knowledge. Studying Hebrew with Persky was a rewarding experience, for it merged the mastery of a language and a continuing, warm relationship with a rare human being.

Persky's appearance never seemed to change. His suits were worn until they shone, became spotted, and finally disintegrated. Then he would appear one day in a new suit, actually embarrassed since it was common knowledge that virtually every cent he earned went into one Hebrew-oriented project or another. His students delighted in ribbing him about his short-lived elegant appearance, to which he would reply, "Don't worry; it won't take long, and this suit too will soon look just like all the others." He was right of course.

He had cards printed up that read, "I am married to the Hebrew language." His greatest joy was to attend the weddings of his students, where he would put their parents at ease by conversing with them in Yiddish or English but reverted at once to Hebrew in addressing his students. The product of a large family himself, he encouraged his former students to rear as many Hebrew-speaking children as possible.

Whenever he had a student who showed an aptitude for Hebrew letters, he encouraged him to pursue a career that would include extensive usage of Hebrew. He made everyone he came into contact with feel that the most important thing in the world was the widespread use of the ancient language, the tongue of the Prophets and the Bible.

Why he never married, he never explained, although he unashamedly admitted he had an eye for pretty girls. By remaining in touch with his former students, seeking them out often in popular vacation resorts, he became a veritable godfather to hundreds of Hebrew-speaking couples and their offspring.

He hated pomposity and pedantic manners, and so long as a joke was told in Hebrew, he did not mind if he was the target. In all his dealing with people, he was unreservedly kind and humble—except when it came to Hebrew, when he was ready to take on the world.

He seldom read anything in English, and when the prestigious *New Yorker* magazine published a lengthy profile about him, he took it in his stride. Lauren Bacall, the actress, née Betty Persky, was his niece, but he seldom let on, indicating that he would have been prouder if she had devoted her talents to the study of Hebrew. His nephew Shimon Peres, a former Israel Minister of Defense and one of the country's top leaders, won him over because of his own excellent command of Hebrew.

Each person whose life he touched came away a little richer for the experience. When he died, he was mourned by thousands of people in all parts of the world, but especially in the United States and Israel, where many of his students had gone to live and to use the language that he had made them fall in love with.

HYMAN G. RICKOVER

Submarines for Security

THE FIRST ATOMIC-POWERED SUBMARINE in the United States navy was built because one man, a tough, dedicated naval captain from Chicago, believed it was in the best interests of the country to develop vessels powered with the newest form of energy. He had to overcome great obstacles placed in his way by tradition-oriented naval planners, and he had to fight against almost the entire navy establishment to bring the American navy up to what he considered the minimum requirement for the sake of American freedom of the seas. He is looked on today as a dedicated man with a mission. President Jimmy Carter, a former navy man who studied with him, has singled him out for high praise, calling him his tutor.

He was born in 1900 in Poland and came to the United States with his family when he was six. The family settled in Chicago, where young Rickover's father worked as a tailor, supporting his wife, son, and twin daughters. It was a meager living, but the family managed, although everyone practiced the strictest kind of frugality. From his earliest years, young Rickover displayed a penchant for spartan living, not only ignoring frills and luxuries but developing a lifelong dislike for such affectations.

In high school the young, slight student supplemented the family income by working eight hours every day after school as a Western Union messenger. He was never home before midnight but managed to do well in school nevertheless. He made few friends, never having time for extracurricular events, and even as a

child and later as a teen-ager he demonstrated a stubbornness that he was to retain all his life. He asked for little from others, and volunteered little. He was the quintessential lone wolf.

In 1916 he delivered a telegram to Warren Harding at the Republican National Convention, and a photo of him in the traditional Western Union uniform was published the next day in many papers. The temporary spot in the limelight helped him when a meeting was arranged by a family friend with Congressman Adolph Sabath, who agreed to sponsor the young man's appointment to Annapolis. Rickover was thrilled, because this meant that he would have an opportunity to obtain a college education, something his family could not otherwise afford.

First, however, he had to pass a series of tough entrance exams, and he applied to a prep school that specialized in such coaching, located near Annapolis, paying three hundred dollars in advance—his entire savings, earned from his messenger job. After a few weeks of study, however, he concluded that he was wasting his time at the school and decided to lock himself up in his room and cram on his own, forfeiting the tuition fee. He studied diligently in his room in a boarding house for two months, passed the exam, and entered the Naval Academy.

His basic traits never changed during his long naval career. He was not interested in dances, sports, or anything else that took him away from his work, first as a student and later as an officer, both at sea and on shore. He found that he preferred to spend his evenings studying, reading widely on any aspect of science or world developments that would affect the standing of the United States navy. Although at first he thought he would spend only the minimum number of years in the navy required after his education at Annapolis, and then would leave and find a better-paying job, he discovered to his own surprise that he genuinely liked navy life. He saw himself as a young child from Poland who had been snatched out of a poor life in Chicago and had been given a chance to rise in America—and he wanted to show his gratitude for the opportunity by serving the navy as best he could.

He has never spoken of his very early years in Poland, but it is conceivable that he has thought that if he had not been brought to America by his family, he might have remained a second-class citizen, a Jew in Poland, slated to lose his life during the Nazi era with the overwhelming majority of Polish Jewry.

His career was not spectacular at first, although he was credited with saving the lives of a number of enlisted men in the course of shipboard accidents. He was never afraid to say what he thought, even to the highest officers, earning for himself a reputation as a tough, frank navy captain who could be counted on to get things done.

By 1939, when war broke out in Europe, Rickover was convinced that the United States would be involved sooner or later, and he became a key person in Washington, moving the navy machinery forward into a better-equipped, more alert position for that time. He had picked up a master's degree in electrical engineering and had come to respect the thinking of a number of engineers inside and outside the navy, and he began to form them into a group to help transform the service into an up-to-date fighting force. As head of the electrical section of the Bureau of Ships, he led in the development of new designs for vital components for all naval vessels, teaching his subordinates how to cut through red tape and how to deal with what he considered to be barnacled naval tradition. His method of operation brought results, but he did not endear himself to many of the older career officers.

Rickover's greatest achievement came after the end of the war when he fought for the creation of an atomic-fueled submarine, which he considered of vital necessity to America's defense. There was considerable opposition from various quarters, and the fight was carried to the floor of the Congress, which also raised the question of why he had been passed over twice for a routine promotion to the rank of admiral.

In time, however, he prevailed, and the U.S.S. *Nautilus* became the first American nuclear submarine. The navy brass reluctantly gave him the rank of admiral, and although he could have retired long ago because of age, he chose to remain on active service, continuing to guide in the production of a modern naval defense for the United States.

Rickover has remained a committed, stubborn man about the ideas he believes in, and shrugs off any criticism of his ramrod methods of getting things done. Rickover's early love affair with the United States has not cooled, and he feels that all he is doing is helping to protect the greatest democracy that ever existed.

MARC CHAGALL

"Cows Cannot Be Painted Green!"

HE WAS BORN NEARLY A FULL CENTURY AGO in the small city of Vitebsk, located in the border area between Russia and Poland. As a child he loved to wander through the streets of his neighborhood, just looking—and what he saw was to register on his subconscious mind for use in sketches and paintings he would set to paper and canvas in later years. The small boy with the curly blond hair, the son of a hard-working father who earned his livelihood by pushing and heaving heavy barrels of salt herring in a local warehouse, was Marc Chagall, one of the great artists of the twentieth century.

Life in Vitebsk was hard for the Chagall family. There was usually just about enough food on the table to feed the family, but to a dreamy boy like Marc there were other sources of nourishment. He enjoyed visits in the country to his grandfather, a butcher, and he especially liked to accompany his uncle, who would take him along on day-long trips into the farming villages to buy cattle and then entertain the young boy by playing the violin far into the night. Marc was a small child, first learning to understand the life all around him, but he exuded an air of enthusiasm and joyfulness that quickly made him everyone's favorite.

Like all the other Jewish boys in the town, Marc attended the simple school in the community—known as a *heder*, or "room"—

where he studied Hebrew and the Bible, and the ancient figures in the Bible became living, breathing people to him. He also studied Talmud as he grew older, took violin lessons, and, because he had a pleasing voice, became a member of the synagogue choir, turning over the monies he earned to his hard-pressed mother.

One day—he could not have been more than twelve—he discovered in the local library a stack of illustrated Russian magazines. The pictures—of people, of city and rural scenes, of faraway places—fascinated him. With a stub of a pencil he began to copy them on a sheet of paper, improvising his own version of what he saw, adding a dreamy quality that was to become characteristic of his work, and gradually deciding what he wanted to become—an artist.

This was not an easy decision to reach in a community like Vitebsk, where young boys were urged to become clerks since very few of them had an opportunity to get an advanced education. Sometimes he thought he would like to become a cantor since he enjoyed standing up in the synagogue and enthralling the congregants with his beautiful singing. At other times he seriously thought of studying the violin. But as the number of his sketches continued to increase, he abandoned the other ideas for the goal of becoming an artist. When he drew a picture—and now he was sketching original portraits as well as copying from existing pictures—he seemed to be talking in a special language, one without words, a language of pictures that expressed his innermost dreamy qualities.

Becoming an artist in Vitebsk was not easy. For centuries Jews had traditionally frowned upon painting pictures because of the second of the Ten Commandments, which forbade the making of "graven images." The only picture that could be found in the homes of the town's Jews were portraits of famous religious leaders; there was no tradition of Jews devoting their time to painting, either as a full-time occupation or even as a hobby—at least none that Marc ever heard of.

He overcame his family's resistance and began to take art lessons from a local teacher, and quickly realized that his own paintings were markedly different from the cold, almost photographic quality of those of the older man. At the age of twenty, still a dreamy young man and rather shy, he set out for the big city, St.

Petersburg (now Leningrad), determined to study with the best teachers he could find and to find a place for himself in the world of art. Meanwhile, he continued to paint, gradually learning to master the various tools of the artist, sketching scenes from his childhood that he often did not even know he possessed. The portraits flowed through his nimble fingers as though they were guided onto paper by another person.

Life in the great Russian city was very difficult. Marc had little money and usually lived on one meal a day. For a long time he did not have a room of his own and was forced to share a bed with strangers, paying a few kopeks for the privilege. Occasionally he earned a little money by working as a photo retoucher, but he did as little as possible of this, not wanting to take away any time from his own creations. He studied at an art school for a while but left after a short time because he felt he was not learning enough from his teachers. He did sense a growing confidence in his own work, but this came mainly from his unceasing production, which he often dragged around, not quite knowing what to do with his "portfolio."

He tried his hand at becoming a sign painter, which would at least give him a chance to earn enough to live on. Although he tried hard, he failed the qualifying test. And then one day a lawyer named Goldberg, who was also a lover of art, saw some of his work and liked it. He arranged for the young man to become a servant in his home, a subterfuge necessary at the time since otherwise Marc would not have received permission to remain in the city permanently. Goldberg gave him a tiny corner in his comfortable home where he could sleep, and in effect said to him, "All right, now go ahead and paint, young man."

It was about this time that Marc Chagall met the beautiful girl Bella, who was later to become his wife. In 1910, when he was twenty-three, the young artist set out for Paris, the art capital of the world. He continued to study, to paint, and to form friendships with other artists, poets, and writers. This was an exciting new world for him, filled with art galleries, musical performances, creative people on all sides competing with each other, helping one another, and always ready to recognize and acclaim true talent. He worked furiously, producing new work all the time, exhibiting some, and gradually beginning to win a name for himself.

At night, asleep on a modest cot, he often dreamed of his old life in Vitebsk and worried about his family. There was a rumbling of war in the air, and he decided to return home to see his family—and to marry Bella, for whom he longed constantly.

In 1915 Chagall and Bella were married, and soon his works began to be exhibited in important galleries in Moscow and St. Petersburg. He became known as one of Russia's leading young artists. Two years later the country was rocked by revolution, and Jews hoped that the new government would be more kindly disposed toward them than had the czarist regime. The young Chagall joined in that hope, but it was not to last for long: Soon Communist officials were criticizing his work, complaining that "cows cannot be painted green."

In 1923 he and Bella went to Paris, and he devoted himself to art, many of his paintings being used as book illustrations. In 1930 he made a trip to Palestine to see the Holy Land for himself, for he was determined now to execute paintings with a biblical theme. The trip was one of the most inspirational of his life.

Chagall was brought out of Nazi-occupied France in 1941 to safety in America, where he continued to work, mostly for the New York Ballet Theater; later his works were displayed at the Museum of Modern Art. He came to love America but decided to return to France in 1948, where he has continued to paint.

Chagall's work now hangs in almost every major museum in the world. His depiction of the Twelve Tribes of Israel has become a masterpiece, and people come from faraway places to see the original stained glass windows in Jerusalem on which they appear. His murals hang in the Metropolitan Opera House in New York, and his tapestry in the Israeli parliament. At the age of ninety he was named a Distinguished Citizen of Jerusalem. The dreamy little boy from Vitebsk had gone a long, long way.

ABE KROTOSHINSKY

He Saved the Lost Battalion

THERE ARE FAMOUS PEOPLE who devote a whole lifetime to performing important work that benefits many people. There are also people who lead relatively ordinary lives but who, once during their lives, are confronted with a rare opportunity to display outstanding courage and who perform an act that makes them go down in history. Such a man was Abe Krotoshinsky.

Like many other poor immigrant Jews, he had arrived in New York's Lower East Side anxious for a new beginning. Life in the old country had been harsh, and although he had the barest of education and no skills to speak of, he was hopeful that he would find a place for himself in America, the Golden Land.

He had been in the United States only a short time when America entered World War I in 1917. He was eager to help his new country and welcomed the chance to don an American uniform, and help make the world safe for democracy. Most of his fellow soldiers in the 77th Division, in training at Camp Upton, were fellow Jewish immigrants. What distinguished them from other American soldiers was their clumsy English.

In the course of time Abe Krotoshinsky was sent overseas, directly to the front lines in France. The battalion in which he served found itself trapped in the vast Argonne Forest, surrounded by Germans, cut off from the main American forces. The troops fought hard, determined to beat the Germans back. Eventually the Americans realized that they had been entrapped, and they dug in, waiting for help. Their supplies of ammunition, food, and medicines were running low.

When the Germans determined that the Lost Battalion, as they came to be known, would not surrender, they increased the barrage of fire against the weary Americans. The officer in command of the force realized that unless help arrived soon, they might all die of hunger, thirst, shelling, or exposure. Word had to be gotten out to the division's headquarters. He asked for volunteers to crawl through the encircling German lines, and Abe Krotoshinsky stepped forward. He was short and thin, did not stand erect, and did not inspire confidence that he would be able to get help.

When he saw his captain hesitate, he said, "Captain, I stole across the Russian border to get to America—I can make it, you'll see." He delivered his brief statement with conviction and with a decided accent. "It's better that I should die than we all should die," he added.

Two other men were chosen to go along, and they set out early in the day, believing that the Germans would be less watchful then since they would expect the Americans to try a breakthrough under cover of darkness. Within a few hours, the two others returned to their unit, both wounded. They had lost contact with Abe, they said.

Like his fellow soldiers, Abe had not eaten a decent meal in days, and as he crawled through the forest, he could feel his head swimming from dizziness and hunger. Cautiously, as bullets and shells flew all around him, he continued to snake his way through the dense foliage. At one point, he heard a German unit approach and hid behind a tree stump, afraid to breathe. What kept him going, he said later, was the knowledge that six hundred soldiers of the Lost Battalion were depending on him.

He continued to inch his way forward for days, resting at night, sipping the small amount of water he carried in his canteen. He remembered that as a youngster in Russia he had skipped meals more than once, and he kept going. Finally, off in the distance he saw what he thought were American units. Suddenly he grew petrified. What if the Americans thought he was a German wearing an American uniform? It had happened before. His English was foreign to American ears. He thought of a word that he could use that would identify him as an American, accent and all, and came up with "Hello." He thought this was one word the Germans were not likely to use.

When he was within hailing distance, he called out, weakly since his strength had almost given out, "Hello!" He was quickly surrounded by suspicious American troops. He tried to explain the situation of his battalion, but he could see that he was regarded with suspicion. It was only when a fellow trainee from Camp Upton was summoned and identified Abe that the soldiers accepted him for what he was. They quickly brought him into a medical tent, fed him, and when plans were developed to break through the enemy lines and rescue the Lost Battalion, Abe was allowed to join them, to help show the way.

Only 250 men survived, but had it not been for Abe Krotoshinsky, they would have died in battle like their comrades. The commander in chief of all American forces, General Pershing, pinned the Croix de Guerre on him, saying that he was certain Abe would be as good a citizen as he had been a soldier. For a while Abe Krotoshinsky was a household word in America.

Earning a living, however, turned out to be difficult for Abe after the war was over. The famous philanthropist Nathan Straus paid his way to Palestine and provided him with a farm, but Abe found pioneering life in Palestine in the early 1920s too tough and came back to New York. He tried for a job with the Post Office but was told he had failed the Civil Service exam. A New York newspaper ran a big story about him, shaming the authorities for the way a hero was being treated. Subsequently, President Coolidge, by special presidential order, appointed him to the Post Office.

Nothing was ever again heard from Abe, who had saved the lives of his 250 fellow soldiers.

LILLIAN WALD

Angel of Henry Street

SHE CAME FROM A WELL-TO-DO HOME and could easily have chosen the life of a rich young lady with nothing more important on her mind than the schedule of parties for next month—but Lillian Wald was a serious, sensitive person, who became aware of the fact that all around her there were large numbers of people whose lives were one long procession of problems and hardships, and she was drawn to the job of helping those less fortunate than she.

She was born soon after the end of the Civil War, grew up in Rochester, New York, studied at Vassar, and decided to become a nurse, even though most parents in those days frowned on nursing, which was then far from the skilled profession it is today.

She began work in an orphan home, caring for children who she felt needed her support more than anyone else. The work was heartbreaking for her, but she persisted and gradually came to realize that the problems she saw all about her were really no more than the tip of the iceberg. As she came to know the children in her care better, and then gradually also the impoverished parents who had been forced to send their partly orphaned children to the home, she realized that the work she was doing was curative and very important, but the thought occurred to her that it would be far better to prevent the problems from developing in the first place. The children she saw every day came from homes where elementary hygiene was unknown, where the idea of nutritious meals was utterly foreign, and where the basic principles of personal cleanliness and good health were never taught.

Lillian Wald was a woman of great compassion, and although she could go home every day to her comfortable residence, she found herself spending more and more time in the slums, seeing for herself how the poor—many of them recent immigrants—were forced to live in overcrowded, unsanitary apartments, with mounds of garbage stored in hallways and on sidewalks. She realized that if she were to make a real contribution to these unfortunate people, she would have to become one of them—she would have to live among them and set an example of how they should guard against disease and make cleanliness second nature.

The Lower East Side in the second half of the nineteenth century was teeming with tens of thousands of newcomers from various European countries, many of them Jewish arrivals who had lived in primitive villages and who knew little about how to cope in a large city like New York. An idea tugged at her—instead of waiting for people to come to her in a health clinic or orphanage or any other institution, she would arrange to pay visits to them in their homes and bring with her the knowledge and experience that modern medicine and modern hygiene had accumulated. She persuaded a friend, Mary Brewster, to join her, and they moved from the comfortable, clean uptown part of New York to the heart of the Lower East Side, to an apartment on Henry Street, right in the middle of the slums.

Without benefit of any government support, the two of them began to go out into the nearby tenements, the first visiting nurses ever, determined to cure the sick, to teach the newcomers the elementary steps they should take for their own and their families' health, and to assure them that their own small apartment was always open for consultation and help.

Lillian Wald's idea caught on immediately. The slum dwellers appreciated the help they were getting, and they began to crowd into the Henry Street apartment, seeking medicines, advice, guidance. The determined young nurse turned to some of her wealthy uptown friends and appealed for funds to enlarge her growing medical center, and soon there was created on Henry Street a center—known as the Henry Street Settlement—which over a period of many years, right down to our own time, has helped scores of thousands of people.

The concept of visiting nurses that Lillian Wald pioneered was shown at once to be one of those simple yet wonderful and effective ideas that someone just had to come up with. Soon, at her insistence, the New York City Health Department launched its own visiting-nurse service, and the program has been adopted by many communities around the world, stressing the importance of teaching good health habits and preventing illness rather than waiting for people to become sick and have to come to a hospital as patients.

One of the first things Lillian Wald learned from her work on the Lower East Side was that children in school could very easily come down with a child's disease from ordinary exposure to classmates in school, and so she launched a program, which later became standard not only in America but throughout the world, whereby every student was given regular medical tests as a first step to prevent the spread of illness. This was in the days long before modern antibiotics, when whooping cough, measles, diphtheria, scarlet fever, and other diseases were a potential disaster for any family. The regular visits of qualified doctors to schools to check the students was something that Lillian Wald pioneered, and there is no doubt that this helped prevent many youngsters from falling victim to diseases that were prevalent in those days.

But Lillian Wald was not one to be satisfied with even these important accomplishments. As she looked about her in the slums that were now her home, she came to realize that the fresh air that she enjoyed as a child would do wonders for the boys and girls forced to live in the tenements. She found a vacant lot in the area, converted it into a tiny oasis with some trees and grass, installed some swings and play areas, and thus started another concept that has caught hold—the neighborhood playground, where children can play safely, away from the busy and dangerous streets, and where sunshine and reasonably clean air can do their best.

Many of the slum children at the time were being brought up without enough milk, either because their parents could not afford to buy milk for them or because they did not realize how important it was for youngsters to consume the healthful food in their growing years. The next step she took to care for her young neighbors was to establish milk stations where children could come and drink fresh milk and where mothers could be taught how to sterilize bottles and feed their babies the milk that would help give them a sound foundation in later life.

Over the years, the Henry Street Settlement grew and expanded its facilities in many directions. The children who had been taught good health habits and who had been prevented from falling victim to the common diseases of childhood of the time were now struggling to rise out of their environment and find better places for themselves in America. It was only natural, therefore, for Lillian Wald to respond to this new need, and soon enough she set up at the Settlement classes in music and art, to encourage the youngsters in their own budding careers. She invited leading Americans to come to the center, to speak to the children about their respective work—in education, in various occupations, in the arts—and help the children of the slums develop confidence and hope that by hard work and proper training they could attain their personal ambitions.

Many outstanding figures in America came to support Lillian Wald's work, including President Theodore Roosevelt, who encouraged her idea of establishing a national Children's Bureau to protect the rights of the young, who were at the time still being exploited in horrible child-labor sweat shops. Poets, prime ministers, and visitors from overseas came to see for themselves the miracle that Lillian Wald, who was known by rich and poor as the Angel of Henry Street, had created. When she died in 1940, she explained to a visitor that everything she had achieved had been possible because "I really love people."

URIAH P. LEVY

The Courageous Commodore

URIAH LEVY WAS BORN IN THE UNITED STATES in 1792, only a few years after the new nation had proclaimed its independence. He grew up in a traditional Jewish household, proud of his heritage and at the same fiercely devoted to helping the new country that was emerging in the Western Hemisphere.

There were at the time only 3,500 Jews in a population of six million Americans. Although Jews had fought in the Revolutionary War and a number of them were engaged in the merchant vessel trade, practically no one in those days thought of a young Jew making the sea a life's career. But even as a small child Uriah Levy was drawn to the sea; he would spend long hours watching boats come and go, comparing the hulls and sails, watching cargoes being loaded and taken off, and dreaming of the day when he too could go to sea, preferably as the master of a vessel that would transport him to distant ports.

When he was ten years old, despite the objections of his parents, he signed on as a cabin boy for a ship named the *New Jerusalem*, but only on condition that he would be permitted to return home after two years so that he could begin to study for his bar mitzvah, which would be held on his thirteenth birthday. It was the beginning of a lifetime career that would take young Uriah from the merchant vessel where he cleaned up to the com-

mand of a whole fleet of U.S. navy vessels, when he would be honored by the title Commodore, at the time the highest rank in the fledgling American navy.

After two years at sea, Uriah returned home and studied for his bar mitzvah. His parents must have hoped that the experience had made him change his mind about a life at sea, but, on the contrary, the excitement of seafaring was now more firmly rooted in the young man's blood than ever. He returned to the sea as an apprentice sailor, learning every craft of maritime life that he could, and attending navigation school in his native Philadelphia. At the age of seventeen he had achieved the rank of second mate.

Once, while he was on shore leave in the British West Indies, he was forcibly seized by British officers, who wanted to impress him into the British navy, a common practice in those days. When he was ordered to remove his cap and swear allegiance on a Christian Bible, he refused, explaining that he was a Jew and that, if he were to take an oath, it would be only on a Jewish Bible and while his head was covered. He was allowed to serve without taking the oath, and worked as a deck hand for a time, until a British admiral permitted him to leave and return to the United States.

He made his way back to America, and became part-owner of a merchant vessel, but his new venture did not last very long, for two of his crew members stole the schooner and later sank it. Levy pursued the two, and while they were being tried, the War of 1812 broke out between the United States and England—and Levy immediately volunteered his services to the navy.

He served with the *Argus*, a heavily armed ship that attacked British coastal stations and became the primary target of the British navy. Levy and other officers were captured after a particularly bloody battle, and he was imprisoned in Dartmoor, known as "a tomb for the living." For more than a year he remained in that cold prison, learning French from French prisoners and trying to maintain the morale of the Americans. An exchange of prisoners brought his release, and he returned to Philadelphia in 1814.

His father had died, and the family pressure on him to give up the sea and take over his father's business was great. His mother and younger brothers and sisters looked to him for leadership. His friends also warned him that becoming a professional navy officer would be very difficult, since there was considerable anti-Semitism in the navy, the most conservative branch of the American armed forces.

But Uriah was determined to achieve his goal, for himself and for future generations of Jews in the United States. He wrote to a friend, "What will be the future of the Navy if others such as I refuse to serve because of the prejudices of a few? There will be other Hebrews, in times to come, of whom America will have need."

For the rest of his life, he served in the U.S. navy, rising eventually to the rank of Commodore, but it was a career filled with many setbacks. Several times he was court-martialed for what the navy brass considered his radical ideas, but in all cases the trial verdicts were reversed. Among the ideas that he fought for, and pushed through, was the abolition of the age-old custom of flogging, a battle he won when Congress outlawed corporal punishment by the lash.

He was also among the first to urge the navy to study the feasibility of converting to steam power, and he wrote a manual of the exact duties and guidelines for young naval officers. He believed that American seamen would do their best by example and encouragement rather than by harsh treatment and punishment.

He was a loyal Jew throughout his lifetime, retaining membership in two synagogues, and on the doorpost of his cabin he affixed a mezuzah. The first permanent Jewish chapel, located in Norfolk, Virginia, was named for him, as was a World War II sub-chaser.

INDEX